Flagstaff
+
Imogene

To Imogene,
a Flagstaff
Love Letter

"Heartwarming, inspiring, and carbo-loaded with breathtaking photography and artwork, To Imogene, a Flagstaff Love Letter *will leave you with a runner's high, even if you've never stood on the precipice of the race's 13,114-foot apex."*

– **NEIL WEINTRAUB,** CO-FOUNDER AND DIRECTOR OF NORTHERN ARIZONA TRAIL RUNNERS ASSOCIATION, RACE DIRECTOR OF SOULSTICE MOUNTAIN TRAIL RUN

"The Flagstaff running community is unique for many reasons, not the least of which is its seemingly collective thirst for adventure. These folks do not just get together for speed workouts and pub runs, they get together and travel to the ends of the earth to find some of the hardest races the world has to offer. And once a year, they embrace one of those that's not too far away—just around the edge of the Colorado Plateau."

– **BEN ROSARIO,** HEAD COACH/EXECUTIVE DIRECTOR, HOKA NORTHERN ARIZONA ELITE

"Many of us are impressed when we read about elite runners. But all of us regular runners, joggers, and walkers can relate to the stories—some funny, some sad, but all inspirational—of meeting the challenge of the famous Imogene Pass Run. These authors have captured the essence of our Flagstaff running community."

– **NAT WHITE,** THREE-TIME IMOGENE AGE-GROUP RECORD HOLDER, EMERITUS ASTRONOMER AT LOWELL OBSERVATORY, FLAGSTAFF, ARIZONA

To Imogene, a Flagstaff Love Letter

One town's long-distance romance with an iconic trail run

...

EDITED BY MYLES SCHRAG AND JULIE HAMMONDS

FOREWORD BY IAN TORRENCE AND EMILY (HARRISON) TORRENCE

Soulstice PUBLISHING

ISBN: 978-1-7331887-0-8

Library of Congress Control Number 2019908456

Designed by Mary Ross
Cover illustration: "Uphill," by Linda Sherman
Watercolors by Linda Sherman
Illustrations by Krista Nicole
Proofreading by Catherine Bell, Carrie Butler, Rory Faust, Nancy Schrag, Claudine Taillac
Printing by Versa Press, East Peoria, Illinois
Composed in InDesign
Text font: Sabon Roman
Display fonts: Neutraface 2 Text, Demi and Bold
Various handwritten fonts throughout

First Edition
Printed in the United States of America 10 9 8 7 6 5 4 3 2 1

Soulstice Publishing
PO Box 791
Flagstaff, AZ 86002
(928) 814-8943
connect@soulsticepublishing.com
www.soulsticepublishing.com

To Flagstaff, "the Running Nation," with love.
You're beautiful when you reach for the heights.

•••

This book was created to celebrate the Flagstaff running community through the lens of our town's unique relationship with the Imogene Pass Run. In accordance with that spirit of community celebration, we're dedicating a portion of net sales to BLE Flagstaff.

This nonprofit organization performs random acts of kindness with the intent to make a positive difference in the community. These acts can take many unexpected forms and include anyone. BLE Flagstaff believes that through kindness, everyone can "pay it forward" and help create a culture of giving that benefits all of us.

Best Life Ever
BLE
Flagstaff • Arizona

Table of Contents

The Flagstaff contingent, 2013.

foreword

EMILY (HARRISON) TORRENCE, *a two-time Olympic Marathon Trials finisher, moved to Flagstaff from northern Virginia to train with an elite development team.* **IAN TORRENCE** *grew up in Maryland but was always drawn to the West, especially Flagstaff—one of the best locales to train for his 208 (and counting) ultramarathon finishes. Though they grew up less than two hours apart, their paths crossed in Flag—where they fell in love and eventually married.*

IAN: In 2001, my dad, Paul Torrence, coaxed me into running the Imogene Pass Run. He was teaching chemistry at Northern Arizona University and had heard hair-raising tales from fellow faculty members about the event. As an avid runner and climber of Colorado's fourteeners, he knew the course's beauty and challenge would be right up his alley—hauling his son along would further sweeten the experience.

His invitation was an easy sell. I, too, had heard stories and read articles about this remote, oxygen-stealing mountain race whose course traverses the mighty, jagged San Juans at one of the range's highest passes. Committing to my father's summons would be my best chance at seeing this race unfold for myself.

We both had good days on the course. I managed to squeeze into the top 10, and my dad finished well in his over-55 age division. Sitting on a bench in a small Telluride park postrace, we recaptured our day. We commiserated, laughed, and shook our heads as we shared similar stories about the lightheaded nausea encountered as we crested the 13,114-foot highpoint and slipped and fumbled our way down the other side.

Turns out, the finish line was our favorite part of the race—done, completely spent, safely back with family, and satisfied with a race well run.

Now, more than 18 years later, my dad doesn't run anymore and I do my best. Imogene 2001 won't happen again, but special moments aren't meant for duplication. When I visit my father and the conversation lulls, I recall our trip to that race in the corner of southwestern Colorado. The conversation begins like this: "Remember that time when you asked me to run with you from Ouray to Telluride?"

EMILY: Because, for much of my running career, my training and racing was road- and track- focused, I've never been an Imogene Pass Run participant. However, Ian and I have passed through "The American Alps" numerous times. Each time, Ian points out the different features of the course and suggests that one day we will enter the race. For me, it's easy to understand how Colorado's mountains grip you and call you back year after year. A trip to Telluride is always welcome, but it's got to be way more exciting shared with friends and family and with a daunting race, like Imogene, staring you in the face.

It's a well-known fact that Flagstaff runners flock to this event, commit their summers to preparation, and invite everyone they know along for the journey. Flagstaffians make up a big part of the Imogene participant list each September. Outsiders might view our town's participation as being a bit obsessive, but it's not such an oddity once you've heard Flagstaff's Imogene stories. This book is your chance to read dozens of those tales and understand the obsession for yourself.

Ian Torrence and Emily (Harrison) Torrence, June 2019
Flagstaff, Arizona

preface

YOU ARE HOLDING AN ENTIRELY UNIQUE running book—which is not an easy bar to clear, or more fittingly, not an easy mountain to climb, for a genre so rich in quality and packed in quantity.

Many running books appeal to the emotional highs and lows that come with distance running, eliciting themes that connect the sport with other challenges and elements of our lives. This wide-ranging collection of essays, quips, tips, poems, illustrations, photos, selfies, and email exchanges is all of that. But you won't find another running book that embraces a place the way *To Imogene, a Flagstaff Love Letter* does, in a heartfelt love letter.

Hokey? Maybe. But this beautiful book will surprise in how eloquently its contributors express themselves, their joys and hardships, their resilience and humor. Flagstaff (we are proud to report) has a romantic side. It comes through in our perspective on Imogene, of course, but in these pages you'll find a wide variety of relationships and partnerships—entirely fitting for a love letter.

To Imogene is not intended to be comprehensive. You won't learn Colorado mining history, receive travel suggestions, or scour pages of records. Rather, you will read diverse stories from Flagstaffians who fell in love with some aspect of the Imogene Pass Run. There will be stories we missed. Many more will be told in the future. We hope yours will be among them, building on the legacy of devotion between our town and that iconic run.

The book was truly a community effort. Every person involved in its development is Arizonan, and most either live or have lived in Flagstaff. In that spirit, our decision to give some proceeds from the book to BLE Flagstaff (**bleflagstaff.org**) was probably the easiest of several thousand that we at Soulstice Publishing have made over the past 18 months. Reaching out to help others through random acts of kindness—yes, their core mission is that refreshingly simple—and consciously choosing to live one's Best Life Ever reflect what we believe Flagstaff, and the Flagstaff running community, are all about.

While *To Imogene* is unabashedly about our town and our favorite race, you don't have to be a Flagstaffian, Imogene veteran, or a runner of any kind to be moved by the stories told in these pages. We hope the book serves as an inspiration to anybody anywhere who seeks to pursue something uncomfortable or difficult, and of course, to anybody who has ever fallen in love.

PARENTAL ADVISORY
Although we like to think we've developed a family-friendly book, despite a smattering of blood and some juicy romantic talk, we want to alert readers to three instances of the F-bomb. As editors, we consciously chose to include profanity only when it was warranted as the best way to express an idea. We're confident you will agree we chose well in these three instances (pages 20, 149, and 184). As one contributor says on page 20, "They won't all be love letters."

introduction

NO AMERICAN FOOTRACE HAS A MORE INTIMATE relationship with one town than the Imogene Pass Run does with Flagstaff, Arizona. I'd welcome a debate with other contenders' advocates about this assertion. I'm looking at you, Boston, New York, Boulder… you too, Duluth, San Francisco, Atlanta. And Leadville or Seward, I admire your underdog status, but I still will win the argument.

I mean no disrespect to these or any of the other thousands of sites that host events each year. Their histories are rich, and in very real ways some of these are the nation's races, or even the world's races. But Imogene belongs to our region—it's the Colorado Plateau's race—and no city embodies the Colorado Plateau's diverse beauty and energy like Flagstaff.

Flagstaff runners are obsessed with Imogene, a 17.1-mile run on old mining trails that starts in Ouray, Colorado (elevation 7,810 feet), climbs 10 miles to Imogene Pass (elevation 13,114 feet), then descends 7.1 miles down into Telluride (elevation 8,750 feet). The mystery of that obsession is that Flagstaff isn't home to the event. It's not even in the same state or, at that season of the year, in the same time zone. The starting line is more than seven hours and almost 400 miles away, with the southwestern flank of the Colorado Rockies to drive over.

Imogene and Flagstaff inhabit together a Goldilocks sweet spot that makes their relationship work. Imogene is neither too exclusive to enter (though you do have to be fast to your computer when registration opens at 6:00 a.m. Mountain Daylight Time—that's 5:00 a.m. Mountain Standard Time, in Arizona—every June 1), nor too large to be personal. Flagstaff is not so small that it can't move the needle on the number of registrants, nor so large that other priorities distract. It also doesn't hurt that by living at 7,000 feet, Flagstaffians aren't intimidated into thinking their lungs will cower when asked to climb to the sky. It should be noted that such assuredness is not always rewarded.

I'm attempting to persuade you with reasonable facts and context, but there's another side to Flagstaff's mad love affair with Imogene. It's not a dating algorithm that makes Flagstaff a good match for her. The feelings don't stem from a Goldilocks moment, some sort of analytical voodoo I'm trying to play with a fairy tale trope. They come from the process, from being vulnerable enough to risk entering the relationship, to experiencing the subsequent euphoria and pains, and eventually to making a deep commitment that pours the foundation for a shared history to reflect and build on from year to year.

Simply put, it's about the stories.

Flagstaffians aren't intimidated into thinking their lungs will cower when asked to climb to the sky.

A Call for Stories

This book was conceived in the days after the 2016 Imogene Pass Run. Later in these pages, you'll hear more about Fon Cordasco, a woman I never met, and Chris Gomez, a man I have thankfully gotten to know better in the development of *To Imogene.* They are the reason a vision for the book you now hold took shape. That's a fact. I am forever indebted to Fon and Chris for making it possible.

I had first run the race four years earlier. My Imogene experiences have been wonderful, and I knew Flagstaff runners were serious and proud about their participation in it. But I had not yet begun to imagine Imogene. It took the story behind the 2016 race results to see clearly how unique the Flagstaff-Imogene relationship is. Inspired by Fon and Chris, I began to talk in more depth with local runners about how that relationship came to be.

On January 8, 2017, on what amounted to a self-imposed dare, I wrote a call for book submissions in High Country Running, the weekly column I then edited for the *Arizona Daily Sun,* Flagstaff's newspaper:

> "I have no doubt that Flag's annual pilgrimage to Telluride is in fact the most participants in one race from a single community other than where the race is held. But it's a mouthful to explain, and really, who cares about quantifying something so arcane?
>
> "The way to show the unparalleled Flag-Imogene connection hit me hard in the aftermath of the Imogene run last September, like that 21 percent grade at Mile 9 just before the summit.
>
> "This is where you, and I hope many, many others like you, chime in. Through stories, not stats.
>
> "We have an opportunity to chronicle a legacy that has been built over many years. I realized something as I talked with Chris Gomez...

Imagine Imogene
— Elevation 13,114 ft. —

> "What I realized is that you don't waste your time proving anything to anyone. You tell the stories that resonate with people. Period. That's as authentic as it gets, and what more do any of us want than that?"

More than 70 members of the Flagstaff running community answered the call. Thanks to them, you are holding an authentic community-wide chronicle of Flagstaff's love affair with Imogene.

Ode to the Strength of Vulnerability

I am impressed with those, yes, I'll say it… numbers. But more than that, I am thankful for the willingness of all these people to share their experiences. This is no easy task for most of us.

In a recently released documentary titled "Love Letters," director Tara Fallaux has couples and singles read love letters they wrote. She says most everybody she talked to about the project loved the idea and would tell their stories to her, but few were willing to go on camera. "Too intimate, too painful, too naked," she said. Reading for a documentary and writing for a book are both public gestures. Fallaux's statement that "making this film is my ode to the strength of vulnerability" applies to our publication too.

The director conceived the film after looking through her collection of love letters and other important letters. "I realized what a treasure box it was," she said. "It was a lifetime of stories, shared thoughts, feelings, and events I had forgotten about. While reading them, the letters brought me right back, almost like time-traveling" (http://bit.ly/AtlanticLoveLetters).

One man in the documentary says reading a love letter is like sharing from your diary. Contributors to this collection have been willing to do that. This, then, is a communal diary. Even if you didn't write your story in these pages, surely some of these emotions and experiences represent yours, whether at Imogene or on the trails, or more broadly in love… in life.

Let's begin our time-travel.

Myles Schrag, February 2019
Flagstaff, Arizona

part 1

Love Letters

An actual love letter and other expressions (from swoon-worthy to profane) of Flagstaff's commitment to Imogene

My Dearest Imogene,

As I sit here in the cold, still night, my headlamp glowing on these faded pages, I already miss you. Though I have only just left your side, I have but now that old, familiar ache beginning to creep into me, the one that builds ever so slowly as the hours go by once we've parted ways. But as has been said many a time across this constantly floating planet, "Time heals all wounds." So, I sit here knowing that eventually, my mind will start looking to others. Others who will fill my spring mornings. Others who will seem mere trials and precursors to those predawn September hours when we shall meet again.

As the cold begins to creep into my jacket, I remember, my beautiful Imogene, when our paths first crossed. Being teased by hints of your beauty, I was immediately intrigued. The more I learned about you, the more I began to want you, to need you. So, I sought you out. I began thinking of ways and devising plans to get to you.

At first, it seemed impossible. There were no more chances, no more ways for me to make it happen. I waited patiently for any opportunity that might come, and soon it did! My chance to see you for the first time was granted by someone else's denial. Their heartbreak was now my joy. Such joy, in fact, that I immediately hugged the person; an inappropriate gesture, perhaps, toward another's broken heart.

Now, beginning to shiver under this pine beneath the night stars outside Dolores, I'm thinking of you and our four rendezvous together.

How you've always made me nervous, the hours, nay, days, nay, MONTHS before our meetings.

How just thinking about your grandeur can make my palms sweat.

How the paths we travel together curve so effortlessly and never cease to intrigue my mind as to what is just beyond.

How you constantly push me, push who I am, push what I can achieve, and keep that fire burning inside to just keep trying. That insistence, as amazingly difficult as it can be, I know is good. It is good for my heart. YOU are good for my heart, dear Imogene, both metaphorically and physically.

How you make me stronger, even as it feels like you are igniting my lungs and leaving me gasping for air when we are together. Through that struggle comes the strength.

How being with you makes my pulse race until I can feel my heart pounding against my ribs.

How your presence alone can leave me overwhelmed, my hands on my knees as I try to take in all your beauty.

How we have and will continue to have many rocky times together. We fight, we stumble, we curse in a passionate struggle to react to and learn from each other.

How being with you makes me feel like 13,114 feet is actually the top of the world.

As I prepare to slink inside my sleeping bag for the evening, hoping to dream of your beauty and awe, I think to our future. I await that Christmas-like feeling on the morning of June 1, when I'll know that we will meet again. Until then, I will train my body and my mind to give you my best, as you have always given yours to me.

Yours until my legs no longer carry me along,

—Nick Irvine

Mountain girl

BY JULIE HAMMONDS

WHEN I JOINED TEAM RUN FLAGSTAFF IN 2015, Liz Brauer was one of the first people I met. As we trotted around the track together one Tuesday night (at our Jack Daniels–approved interval pace), she invited me to a run with the Flagstaff Trail Divas. I'd already been thinking about it. Her personal invitation helped me decide to get in on the fun.

The next year, Liz was training for her second Imogene, under the guidance of coach Emily (Harrison) Torrence. When she told the Divas about it one Thursday night, I was too proud to admit I'd never heard of Imogene, but honestly, I didn't know what she was talking about. Once she described it, I knew two things: Liz was Wonder Woman, and Imogene was something I could never do. It turns out only one of those things is true.

That year, I started reading the weekly High Country Running column in the *Arizona Daily Sun*. After the 2016 Imogene, I read Myles Schrag's column called "Of Fon, Nate and Flag… BLE." Chris Gomez had carried Fon Cordasco's race bib to honor the life of a remarkable woman. Reading it, I began to realize there was more going on at Imogene than a "simple" run up and over some crazy-high Colorado mountain pass.

Becoming a Flagstaff Runner

By 2018, I'd been a trail runner for seven years. My racing career had included three half marathons. I was ready for a tougher challenge—a challenge that could cement my identity as not just a runner, but a Flagstaff runner.

A Flagstaff runner was something I dearly wanted to be. I love to run now, but I came to the party late. When I began running in my 40s, it was partly because in my job, I always answered to someone else; running filled a gut-level need to be accountable only to myself. It was something I could earn and own. A lot of this, for me, is defiance.

But that's not why I wanted to be a FLAGSTAFF runner. This tribe is inclusive of everyone, first-timers and nationally ranked athletes alike. It's both welcoming and impressive; to be a Flagstaff runner is to be something special (because really, how many people regularly choose to run at 7,000 feet?) and to belong to something that is (in my mind) wholly positive, a force for good.

This community spirit inspires its members to be healthy, spend time outdoors, and compete at whatever level we choose. Anyone can earn a place in the Flagstaff running community, and I like that; I'm all about effort and reward.

The one long hill is where Imogene runners earn their wings.

This town has rewarded my effort from my first day at Step Into Running in 2011 with coach Mike Smith. I didn't do my first Imogene because I loved the idea of Imogene. I did my first Imogene because I love the Flagstaff running community.

With My Flagstaff Running Tribe

When I decided to train for Imogene, the Flagstaff running community was there for me again. I signed up with coach Emily, as Liz had. A.J. Gregg at HYPO2 challenged me to do the strength training that keeps you going when the ascent is hands on knees and one foot in front of the other. Massage therapists Carolyn Yazzie and Brandie Tremper beat me back into shape after tough workouts. I was a pampered athlete with a crew! And if my spirits flagged, there were the Flagstaff Trail Divas to encourage me.

I needed it. Before training for Imogene, I had never run more than 13.1 miles. It had been decades since I'd ventured to 13,000 feet, and I'd certainly never run there. I pored over the race website and YouTube, trying to prepare. And as I trained, I asked the hard questions. Will I be ready? Am I strong enough? Who do I think I am, anyway?

I did a crazy thing during training: I went to sea level for nearly four weeks. In August. While my friends were posting pictures of themselves summiting various Flagstaff-area peaks, I was trying to do hill training on the coast of Maine.

Don't feel sorry for me; I was in Maine. Still, the one thing we Flagstaff runners have going for us when it comes to Imogene is that we sleep and train at altitude. Well, that AND the fact that hundreds of Flagstaffians have run this thing before us.

Once I got back to town in late August, the lore and mystique of Imogene infused every conversation. I was back with my Flagstaff running tribe, and though most of my final training runs were solos, it was comforting to know that friends and strangers alike were running the same trails I was, feeling the same nerves and excitement I felt.

And then it was September. I drove to Colorado alone, stopping often, awed by those mountains. I was even more daunted by the idea of running from Ouray to Telluride once I had driven from Telluride to Ouray. I barely slept that night. But in the morning, as I walked to the starting line at the dawn of a gorgeous fall day, the first person I ran into was Emily Hunt—a Flagstaff Trail Diva. No Flagstaff runner is ever alone at the Imogene starting line.

A Quiet Mind

Thinking back on that run now, it's the feelings I remember: frustration, elation, defiance, and acceptance; fierce joy in my body's willful endurance; compassion for my body's pain as the one (monster) hill took its toll. Gratitude for all of it: the people who helped me train, the race organizers and volunteers, the mountain and its sublime soul.

My Imogene Mantra:
"You are a mountain girl."

One thing I recall is how quiet my mind was. There was some frustration in the first mile, as the tightly packed river of humanity forced its way up the mountain at a walking pace. I could have run parts of that, under other circumstances. Once we got going, I concentrated on reaching Upper Camp Bird before the 2½-hour cutoff, but I was also looking up at blue sky framed by vertical gray rock walls, and around at the singing forest and my fellow runners, and ahead toward the western horizon, where impossibly high cliffs proclaimed how much more climbing there was to do. I was paying attention to my body and breathing and fueling, but in a relaxed way. Neither was I bored or in need of entertainment or distraction; I don't race with music, but as I climbed that one long hill, I didn't miss it.

When we emerged from forest shade into sunlight for the first time, the line of runners in their bright shirts created a shimmering burst of color like the bejeweled tail of a dragon. Farther up, as we left the tree line behind, I could see the trail yet to go, scrawled across the rock face like the signature of some mountain-loving god. Shadows and sunlight chased each other across the rock. It looked long and steep. It was long and steep. I kept thinking of a message I'd received from a close friend the day before. "You are a mountain girl. You're in your element." That became my mantra as I moved up toward Imogene Pass.

When we reached the top of the steep track, a young Colorado search-and-rescue volunteer was offering runners a hand up onto the flatter dirt road that would take us to the Pass. I could have kissed him.

At the Pass, I was not hungry for sugar, so I grabbed pretzels and drank water. There was a huge bowl of Ibuprofen; I laughed, and then I took one, because why not? I looked at the aid station clock without registering the time. At the wooden Imogene Pass sign, someone (was he wearing a chicken suit? My memories are hazy) was taking people's pictures. I wasn't carrying my phone. I made eye contact with a guy who was standing back, watching all the runners who came through. I think he was another search-and-rescue guy, looking for signs of distress. I decided I was not in distress.

Then I started thinking, not about the 10 miles I'd already done, but about the seven miles yet to go; the worst miles of the run, I had long ago decided. The downhill.

I, Too, Can Fly

Now I felt distressed. If I stopped much longer, could I get going again? With that thought ringing through my oxygen-deprived brain, I grabbed a few more pretzels and headed down.

Was it the right decision?

I'm not sure. My legs tightened up so much in the miles that followed that I lost agility, which increased the prospect of falling and slowed me down. If I'd stayed longer at the Pass, fueled more, maybe even stretched, would my feet still have cramped every time I tried to stop? I don't know.

Liz said later, "You were at high elevation. It's not easy to think straight up there, and you did what you did. It wasn't a bad decision. It's a hard effort no matter what you do." She's an engineer: I don't think she would let me off the hook without data to back it up.

On the way down, I was scared, and sad about my legs, cowed by the pain and a tad irked by all the runners who passed me. Along that rough trail there were times when I didn't feel like ceding the easiest footing so they could get by; let them run in the rock-filled ruts! But most of the time, I scooted aside. My mantra became, "Feet are not expendable." It was a reminder not to be cavalier about the important things.

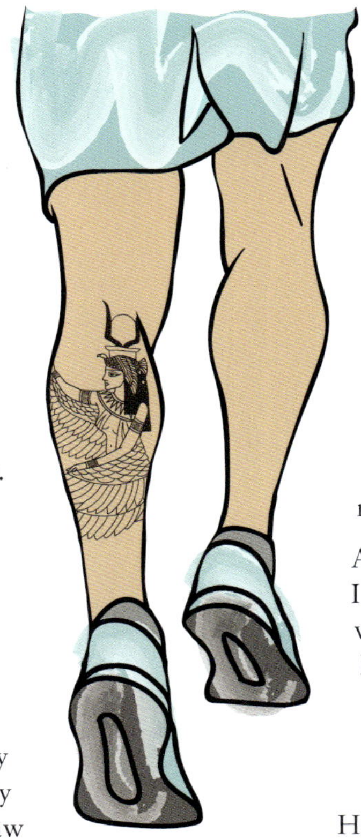

I was also encouraged whenever another runner commented on the temporary tattoo on my calf, an Egyptian symbol, winged Isis. Their words reminded me that even here, I too can fly.

Support and Solitude

When you get close to Telluride, onlookers start saying, "You're almost there," which, when you still have two miles to go that may as well be 20, is inaccurate and unhelpful. By the time I made the turn onto asphalt and saw the crowd and, not too far off, the finish line, I was spent and just looking forward to not running in pain anymore.

Then I heard people cheering my name!

It was Joen Troxel, Marsha Jensen, and Mary Mohr, Flagstaff Trail Divas who've run the race in years past but this time were there to support all the Flagstaff runners. Most of the Divas were sharing a house in Telluride, runners and crew; I was the only one who'd opted for the quieter Ouray, so I hadn't seen them before the run. But now here they were, yelling for me! Mary took my (red-faced) picture and gave me a high five as I trotted by. Then I was at the finish line and could finally stop.

Later, back in Ouray alone, I had a shower and a blissful session in the indoor hot spring at my hotel, which by some gift of the mountain gods I had all to myself. I knelt in the pool and let the 103-degree water take hold of my body and felt oh, so glad I had finally done the Imogene Pass Run—cementing my coveted membership in the Flagstaff running tribe—and that it was truly, mercifully, finally over.

About two seconds later, I started to ponder what I could have done differently along the route. Maybe with more food and a few minutes of stretching, my legs wouldn't have tightened like guitar strings on that hellacious downhill. But would stopping longer at the Pass really have helped? I may have to go run it again and see, I mused.

Had I just made a decision? Yes.

That's Imogene for you. She gets inside your soul, and once she does, you have to return.

Imogene – Transcending Limits

BY CARRIE BUTLER

A treasured one-hill race over four decades strong,
hosting countless stories for all who run it.
Seventeen-point-one miners' miles disguised as road,
swelling with colors, voices, vigor—true grit.

Deep behind one's wonder of her grandeur
lies the stark lucidity of impending stress.
As the mind centers on the quest ahead
internal mountains will present no less.

A metaphor of life in its simplest form,
to physically claim the daunting Pass is to see
that climbing to the very fringes of set dreams
is yours to have, if you only will it to be.

Then the bald and breathing peaks come alive
with encouraging whispers heard in the wind.
Ethereal energy to fuel the advancing finish
and chasing joyous rapture, we transcend.

Best race ever

BY DAWN BEGLEY

THE BELOVED FON CORDASCO AND HER MOM, Sandy Vanlandingham, introduced the Imogene Pass Run to my mom, Pat Taylor, and me in 1996. Pretty sure you won't find us in the race results that year, though, because we didn't actually register. Back then, Imogene was a small walk with a few runners, and we heard about it after it was full. So we just showed up and walked it without race numbers.

Many years and official race numbers later, Mom had back surgery in 2011. As she left the hospital, she asked her surgeon, Nate Avery, if she could compete in Imogene in the coming year to celebrate her 70th birthday. "As long as you don't pass me!" was his jovial answer.

So in 2012—16 years after our first Imogene race—we set out to complete Mom's fifth IPR and my eighth.

•••

Mom would typically train and do Imogene at her own pace while I ran, walked, or crawled on ahead. That year, however, Mom got lost on the San Francisco Peaks during a training run.

At 113 pounds and 69 years young, Mom was no stranger to epic adventures. She had done countless hikes on the Peaks and around Flagstaff with me or her best friend, Sandy. She had hiked the Grand Canyon rim to rim twice, gone on a couple river trips, and run many races. She even coached a kids' cross country team in her little community near Roosevelt Lake.

Cory and Gene Roberdeau, aka "the tiger shirt couple," with Mom and me at Imogene Pass.

The "tiger lady" tells her story on page 91.

But when Mom got lost on the Peaks that day, something hit me about her fragility. This was a difficult realization, as she was not only one of my best friends but also someone I considered to be mentally and physically my equal. We talked on the phone at least once a day and often met on the trail for countless runs, hikes, skis, and snowshoes.

We were constantly on the move together, but my relationship with Mom went beyond exercise. During the 10 years my parents lived in Flagstaff, my husband and I would go to Mom and Dad's house downtown during our lunch hour. The four of us spent weekends exploring northern Arizona and working on house projects, and we went on countless vacations together.

After Mom got lost on the Peaks that day, I decided it would be a good year for the two of us to do Imogene together.

That year, we were excited to introduce Imogene to my niece, Tara Taylor, putting three generations of our family on the Pass. Julie Harpt, my best friend from fourth grade, joined us. This was gonna be fun!

It wasn't far into the race when I told everyone to go on ahead… Mom was having a hard time.

As we approached Upper Camp Bird aid station, Mom began struggling and doubting her ability to finish the race. This was unlike my mother, as she finished everything she started and Imogene, while a huge challenge, was not going to be different. I needed to motivate her.

"Hurry!" the man running the cutoff ahead yelled. "She has three minutes!"

Mom and I.

"I'm trying!" I yelled back. "You come get her!"

And sure enough, he ran down the trail, grabbed her by the hand, and pulled Mom across the mat with little time to spare before the cutoff.

Whew! We could relax a bit after making that cutoff… NOT!

As we approached the difficult miles between the first cutoff and Imogene Pass, I could tell that along with her confidence, Mom had completely lost her footing. I kept trying verbal reassurance and motivation, while people nearby helped with encouragement, but she was fading.

One of the best things about Imogene for someone from Flagstaff is that someone else from Flagstaff is usually nearby. A couple—dressed in tiger shirts—who kept encouraging Mom and me turned out to be from KNAU, the Flagstaff NPR station. A longtime friend from Flagstaff, Sean Hickey, just showed up and helped us as well.

Out of the blue, Mom even whispered to me that Nate (Avery, her back surgeon, who had passed away unexpectedly just weeks before the race) was encouraging her.

By the time we got to the final climb to the Pass, Mom had stopped talking and was holding onto the top of my CamelBak with both hands, head bobbing between her arms, one foot moving at a time. It took every ounce of mental and physical strength I had to pull her step by step to the Pass. Turning around was not an option because I knew that this year—more than other years Mom had done Imogene—she was determined to do this race. She would not have let me quit in the same situation, so there was no way I was letting her quit.

When we reached Imogene Pass, we were met by the tiger couple and Sean, who had waited to make sure we made it. They enveloped us in big hugs. Making it to Imogene Pass that year was by far the most difficult thing I had ever done—and yes, I have given birth.

That year, Mom and I finished Imogene second-to-last. We came in so late that we had to run to the buses to Ouray.

We found Annette Avery and Maureen Meyer, the wife and sister of Nate Avery, standing in front of the buses. Mom hugged them and told them that Nate was there with her.

In return, they informed us that Mom had won a medal! Second in her age group!

Two weeks later, Mom was diagnosed with glioblastoma, a terminal brain cancer. She died the following July. The next year, 2013, Sean Hickey (the friend who had helped Mom and me) and Michelle Wesson (another dear friend) ran Mom's ashes up to Imogene Pass.

The 2012 Imogene Pass Run was emotional for many people in many ways, but I will always consider it my "best race ever"—and Mom's, too.

The gang! Back row (from left): Julie Harpt, me, Jennie Alderidge, Mom, Tara Taylor. Front row (from left): Annalea Evans, Clayton Evans.

Sean Hickey and Mom.

Rhythm of the run: NAU prof heads to Imogene Pass Run

BY RORY FAUST

This article originally appeared in the Arizona Daily Sun *on September 3, 2008.*

AS AN ACCOMPLISHED MUSICIAN, TOM SHEELEY is accustomed to hearing harmonious tunes dance through his head.

When he competes in the Imogene Pass Run, however, those sweet sounds are replaced by a rugged rhythm that matches the terrain.

Sheeley, a professional guitarist and music professor at Northern Arizona University, has traversed the unkempt but stunningly beautiful 17.1-mile Colorado mountain course in each of the last 11 years.

He'll return for the annual event this weekend and, undoubtedly, so will the repulsive music that fills his mind while he runs.

"Unfortunately, the repetitive motion will quite often kick in probably one of the worst songs you can remember," Sheeley said. "One of the most beautiful places on Earth and you just can't get 'Johnny Get Angry' out of your head."

Sheeley is one of a growing contingent of Flagstaff runners who make the annual trek to Colorado for the wildly popular event, which filled its registration capacity of 1,500 runners in less than two days.

Tom Sheeley
Imogene Pass Run, 1997

The course boasts a 5,310-foot climb in elevation, winding from Ouray (7,810 feet) to Telluride (8,820 feet) by way of 13,120-foot Imogene Pass. Runners can encounter all kinds of weather, including snow.

"You have to be kind of a knucklehead like me to enjoy that sort of thing," Sheeley quipped.

"Imogene is extremely strenuous, but I like the challenge," he added. "Part of being a musician is you can play a piece of music that could just make a fool out of you in front of everybody right on stage, but you like the challenge of figuring out a way to make it happen."

You have to be kind of a knucklehead like me to enjoy that sort of thing.

– TOM SHEELEY

A recreational runner and avid hiker, Sheeley said his daughter Cory, then a track athlete at Flagstaff High, talked him into running Imogene 12 years ago. They ran as a pair for about a decade, with daughter usually beating father to the finish line, until she moved to Tucson a couple years ago.

"She'd blow me into the weeds," he said with a laugh. "She would usually get in a half hour or 45 minutes before me. She got a medal a couple of times."

Now he goes solo, with only the music in his head and the breathtaking scenery to keep him company.

Cory Sheeley
mogene Pass Run, 1997

The 58-year-old Flagstaff resident has performed as a musician on the global stage, winning the international M. Ponce guitar competition, and said running events like Imogene have helped balance him as a musician.

"For me, because I'm a professional musician, I need to have some sort of a goal to work with physically," said Sheeley, who has been teaching at NAU since 1974. "It's like a performance. You can plan, but when it comes for the time to do it, you only get one chance.

"I'm a much better musician than I am an athlete, but I think the two play off each other quite well," he added. "I become a better musician by trying to be an athlete."

Sheeley insists he's not a competitor, however, at least not in the athletic realm. He says he participates in local events like the Soulstice Mountain Trail Run and the Big Brothers Big Sisters Half Marathon purely for fun and fitness.

But the challenge and sheer beauty of the Imogene run form a unique combination that Sheeley finds almost therapeutic. He looks forward to the annual event, despite the toll it takes on his body, and typically makes a weekend out of the trip.

Tom and Cory at 2012 IPR.

"It's such a beautiful drive, I hate to turn right around and come back," he said. "I like to spend an extra day up there if I can. You run that race and you're pretty much paralyzed, so it's kind of nice to sit in the hot tub the next day."

It also gives him a chance to clear his mind—something he can often accomplish while playing guitar but rarely achieves during a rugged running event like Imogene.

"When I'm performing, I try not to think of anything," Sheeley said. "Blank mind... if you can do that, it's quite a zone you can get yourself in."

But when he's running?

"I try to," he said with a laugh, "but I usually can't get a cigarette commercial from 1962 out of my head."

The wind whispers its name

BY STACI WHITMAN

Imogene... this name... If you're part of the running community in Flagstaff, this name is everywhere. It's whispered in the wind and heard in the cry of birds above as you run the trails.

"Imogene... Imogene."

"I signed up!" I told my friend. I got up at 4:30 a.m. and went into my closet so the light of my phone wouldn't wake my sleeping husband. I waited, with internet ready and credit card in hand, to get my place in this legendary challenge I'd heard about for so many years from so many people.

"I got my spot! Now, how do we train for this?"

Well, I found out, you meet your running group at 5:00 a.m. all summer long and you run uphill, and when you're tired, you run uphill some more. Then you repeat the pattern. BUT don't forget, you have to train for the downhill, too! So, when you're exhausted from the uphill, with legs shaking and heart pounding, you turn around and pound it downhill.

"Do you think I'm ready?" I asked my friend the morning of the race, as we lined up to run in Ouray. She said, "However hard you think it's going to be, IT'S SO MUCH HARDER!"

My friend was right, but I survived. When I crossed the finish line and heard my name announced, it was a triumphant victory over this diabolically beautiful Pass that continues to whisper its name in the wind and through the cries of birds overhead with every trail run I take.

"Imogene, let's do it again..."

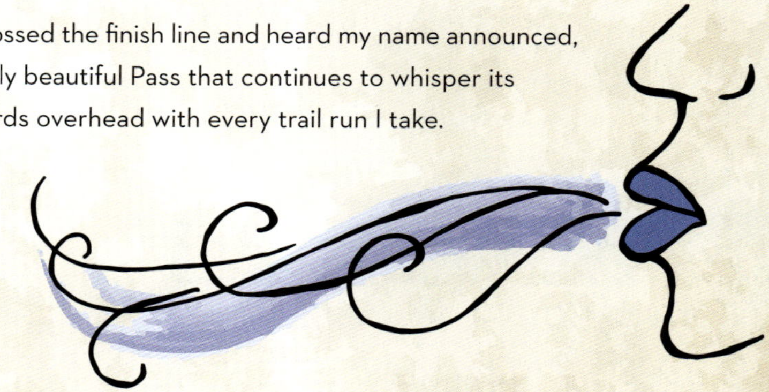

I

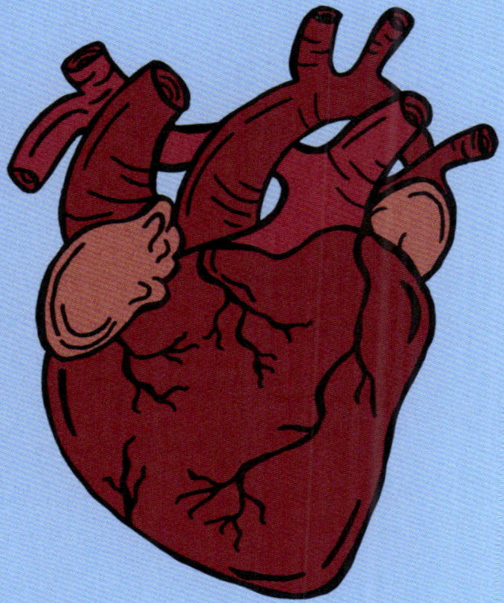

IMOGENE

Right up there with labor

BY BEVERLY TEW

I DEVELOPED A LOVE AFFAIR WITH TELLURIDE in the summer of 1993. We were a group of seven college students exploring the West, venturing to live in the small town of Telluride for a few short months. The San Juan Mountains offered miles of outdoor entertainment—dense, winding forest trails, beautiful waterfalls, snow in July—all fascinating to this wide-eyed, adventurous southern girl.

Breathlessness was new to me as I climbed the steps in our condo at 8,750 feet elevation, but by the end of the summer, the norm was long bike rides up the winding road to what is now Mountain Village, 10-mile hikes (or longer) in the woods followed by indulgence in cheesy pizza slices at One World Cafe, late nights under the starry sky, and morning brunches at Floradora Saloon. I was 19 and working two jobs to live in Telluride, and I was in heaven! Yet somehow, I never heard of the Imogene Pass Run.

My beautiful twins were born on Valentine's Day, and not even four months later, I committed to doing this race.

Fast-forward 20 years to 2013, and I'm now living and working in Flagstaff. My 2½ months out West made such an impression on me as a young student that when I finished my education and training in 2012, that great, wild place became my destination. I landed in Flagstaff due to a wonderful job opportunity, which gave me a chance to experience all the natural splendor that surrounds our community. I knew Telluride was somewhere out there, but I had no idea how closely connected Flagstaff and Telluride were.

Soon after moving to Flagstaff, I was lucky enough to become friends with a great group of gals who valued the outdoors fun that I did, and we spent many hours on trails learning about each other. That's when I heard of the famous Imogene Pass Run. When my friends prepped for Imogene in 2013, I had a burning desire to join—but I was intimidated.

First, I was not fit enough yet, and second, I had to prove to myself that it was "doable." So I signed up to volunteer at the race. Off to the well-beaten path we went—my friends with their trail shoes on, and me in a Jeep with a couple from

Texas. We met again at the top, where I helped maintain the aid station. I was more interested in watching every face that came across that Pass and experiencing the joy they felt. I had to do it too. One day.

Well, the next logical time would be the following year, but by that time I was pregnant with twins, so Imogene was moved aside. As I gained more weight and my thighs swelled like tree trunks, making me waddle in my third trimester and find a new joy in the motorized cart at Target, all I could think about was how I would be so happy to have these babies in my arms and feel normal in my own skin again.

My beautiful twins were born on Valentine's Day, and not even four months later, I committed to doing this race. On June 1, 2015, I was camping with my gal pals and little ones in Moab. We set alarms, snuck out of the campsite in the dark, used Wi-Fi at the McDonald's in Moab, and tried to register for the race. My heart was beating fast as my two friends received their acceptance notices while my computer was still working… and working… I was going to be crushed if I didn't get in.

A few minutes later, I'm in. Game on. Here we go!

From then on, it was my job to train for this race. My littles slept a lot as they were growing fast, so while they slept away, I would rise early, pump breast milk, hit the trails, come home, breastfeed, go to work while they went to day care, come home, repeat.

We hiked the Weatherford Trail and Humphreys Peak. Our final prerace preparation was the Grand Canyon in August—South Rim to North Rim (breast pump in backpack), meet my family at the top, enjoy a layover day, then North Rim to South Rim. We covered a lot of miles and had fun doing it.

I was doing it! I wasn't the fastest, and that wasn't my goal, but I was finishing the hikes we set out to finish, and I was proud. I was going to do this race, so I started raising money for our intended charity, Every Mother Counts, a nonprofit that works to make pregnancy and childbirth safe for every mother, everywhere.

We descended on Telluride the day before the race. All I hoped for was sunshine at the top—no beating rain or hail. I was ready. I managed to sleep some that night, even with two seven-month-olds in the room. The next morning, we rose early, ate, and made our way to the starting line.

One of my dear friends, longtime Imogene runner Darcy Sawdy, had decided to tag along with me. She had been injured some and wanted to take it a bit slower, she said, but she was also invested in helping me finish.

What a feeling of joy! I wanted to enjoy the beautiful scenery, but I also wanted to finish the race.

My Imogene Mantra:
"You birthed two babies in less than an hour.
You can do this."

She is a beautiful soul. If it weren't for her, I honestly don't know if I would have been able to pace myself for the cutoffs. My goal was to meet them, even if I was the last one. I remember being within sight of Upper Camp Bird when they called "Five minutes to cutoff." About three minutes later, I passed through. I had made it.

What a feeling of joy! I wanted to enjoy the beautiful scenery, but I also wanted to finish the race. Whew! A breather, but no, keep going…

Next, I remember long stretches of incline, and the sheer determination in my heart and soul. I tried to look up and take it all in, but I mostly remember it was hard. Very hard. The last mile brought thin air and sore muscles, and I remember thinking that this was right up there in terms of difficulty with labor, fresh on my mind. I think I was in disbelief when I took that final step to the top, but I was there, with Darcy, our other friends well on their way down by then…

With Darcy (left) in 2015.

I enjoyed the downhill somewhat because the pressure was off. I had made it to the top, met the cutoffs, and reached my goal. My friends ran circles around me, but I didn't care. I did it. Mission accomplished. I reached the bottom six hours after starting out. The finish line was deserted but for a few stragglers and the big clock showing the digital red numbers, but all that mattered was that my little babies and their father, Chris, were there, waiting on me, proud of me. I was so happy.

Our celebratory lunch was at The Cornerstone Grille, where coincidentally we had spent many a summer night playing pool in 1993 and where Chris and I enjoyed a meal in 2013, long before kids and training for Imogene. I soaked in the beauty of the environment, the years, the memories, and the tasty burger. Twenty years had passed since I first fell in love with mountain towns. Now I was living a fruitful life in Flagstaff practicing a career I love, and I had completed the Imogene Pass Run. Life had come full circle.

Imogene, You Motherfucker

BY SHERI YOUNG

They said it was long—they were right.
They said it was hard—they were right.
They said it was beautiful—boy, were they right.
They said I would crush it—eh, not quite right, but I kept moving.

Through the initial ascent out of Ouray, I kept moving.
Through the rolling climb to Lower Camp Bird, I kept moving.
Through the streams and on the rocky path to Upper Camp Bird, I kept moving.
Through the long slog to the summit, I kept moving.

With my mind rebelling and shouting, "Fuck, this is hard," I kept moving.
With the words "incessant forward motion" on my lips, I kept moving.
With my pace so slow that at times my Strava thought I had stopped, I kept moving.
With tired legs and achy joints, I kept moving.

Through the final push to the Pass, I kept moving.
Through the thrill of making the cutoff at the top, I kept moving.
Through the joy of seeing the descent, I kept moving.
Through the miles of wondering when it would end, I kept moving.

With the encouraging words of the volunteers, I kept moving.
With a glimpse of Telluride waiting below, I kept moving.
With my friends cheering me on to the finish, I kept moving.
With my love by my side, I kept moving.

They said it was long—they were right.
They said it was hard—fuck, were they right.
They said it was beautiful—oh man, were they right.
They said I would crush it—not quite, but it did not crush me.
I kept moving.

"They won't all be love letters."
- MARSHA JENSEN

SHERI YOUNG + GREG SZYMANSKI
9/8/18

part 2

You Had Me at Hello

Days gone by—how Flagstaff fell in love

What a trip it was! 26 years at the IPR

BY RICH HAAG

MY IMOGENE PASS RUN MEMORIES BEGAN IN 1982, the ninth year of the race. A running friend of mine heard about it and called me to suggest we attempt it. I had never run that distance, that elevation, or, as it turned out, in those weather conditions, but we went up to Ouray anyway. That Saturday morning, it was misting, cold, and the cloud ceiling was at the level where the highway meets the dirt road; from that point on, you were invisible.

There were approximately 150 of us that year. Seconds after the starting gun sounded, I found myself in 149th place, followed closely by a lovely, middle-aged woman who tried valiantly to keep me from backing out. She failed. So I returned to Ouray, hitched a ride to Telluride, and met my wife and the friend's wife. They thought I'd finished first since no one else had come in.

Walking with my wife, Jennie, in 1999.

I left with a not-so-good feeling about the run. To put it bluntly, I was terrified and vowed never to attempt it again. Well, as things usually happen, that abject terror subsided, and in a paltry eight years, some friends from Flagstaff and I decided to attempt it—me for the second time, them for the first. That year, 1990, the weather was beautiful, and the four of us completed the run. Needless to say, I was ecstatic. My time was all right; nothing extraordinary, but for a 50-year-old I was as happy as the proverbial pig. And that began my addiction.

I ran—I use the term loosely—most of the races for the next 18 years. Back in the 1990s, they had a walker's division. One of my friends and I signed up for the running division, and we talked our wives into signing up for the walker's division. At the last minute, Tom Grabarek and I thought it would be nice and husbandly to walk with our wives and have some "quality time" with them. We did, and had a great time—until the results came out.

We finished last in the runner's division by several hours. Mortified, we debated on returning the next year and even considered wearing disguises.

In retrospect, however, most of the years the weather was terrific, and once I became familiar with the course, even the bad weather didn't deter me. The race became the event of the year for the Flagstaff running population. I honestly believe non-runners became runners just so they could participate at Imogene. That may be a slight exaggeration, but I believe it. I've heard it said, and it does seem a little far-fetched, that the only place with more runners at Imogene than Flagstaff was the entire state of Colorado.

Age and its resultant infirmities finally caught up with me. After the 2008 run, I decided to throw in the towel. What a trip it was! The beauty of the area is almost indescribable. The friendships formed were true, strong, and everlasting. And I have all these T-shirts to boot.

I honestly believe non-runners became runners just so they could participate at Imogene.

Above (from left): Tom Grabarek, Dave Klensin, and me with the end in sight, 2002.

Below (from left): Some early Flagstaff Imogene devotees in 1995: Walt Taylor, Roberta Motter, me, Nancy Taylor, and Dave Klensin.

Imogene defined our summers

BY WALT TAYLOR

OUR FAMILY WAS IN TELLURIDE ON MEMORIAL DAY weekend in 1988. While there, I saw posters announcing the Imogene Pass Run. It piqued my interest, as I'd been a hiker, backcountry explorer, and trail runner all my life, going back to my boyhood days growing up in a wooded area in southern Michigan.

Third place, 2003 (wearing 347).

I ran track in high school but never placed in a race. My wife, Nancy, was very fit and enjoyed similar adventures. That weekend in Telluride, I hiked up to Tomboy to explore the area, then ran down to avoid a thunderstorm.

With that background, Nancy and I entered the 1989 IPR and prepared for it with several runs on the San Francisco Peaks trails. We stayed in Telluride, bused over to Ouray, and gave it a go. There were 351 runners and 10 more in the separate walking division. It was hard, but the scenery and camaraderie of the participants were inspiring and I clocked 3:53; Nancy had a 4:10. I was 51 and Nancy 48—my first race since high school and her first ever. We came home tired but enthused. It became an annual event for us and many friends… people who thought, "If the Taylors can do it, then so can we."

We usually stayed in Ouray and shared a condo and meals with Al and Sarah Hendricks and other friends. We loved the summer training runs on the Peaks, including Kendrick, Sunset Trail, Schultz Pass, Inner Basin, Doyle Saddle, and Elden Lookout Road. We did the IPR 20 times through 2011, missing only a few times due to illness or a friend's wedding.

Looking back on our IPR runs, we had weather conditions ranging from perfect to very windy to rain and snow. No matter the weather, it was always rewarding to share the experience with hundreds of healthy people testing themselves against the course, the altitude, the weather, and others. To me it wasn't so much a race as a test of will and training, and a chance to share beautiful mountain country with others.

Nancy discovered that she was a talented runner and won her age group six times: 1992–1995, 2002, and 2009. She was also second in 2000 and 2010, and third in 1999 and 2008. I never achieved my goal of winning my age group, but I had three second places and a third—thanks in part to there being very few in my age group.

We have so many great memories of race weekends and all the friendships we made. The IPR and the runs to prepare for it defined our summers. In 1994, our whole family participated with us, and we were recognized at the awards ceremony. During the 22 years described, we saw a steady increase in Flagstaff participants, and that was rewarding to be part of. There were scores of folks with whom we would share the summer trails and the experience of the event itself.

We were blessed with our whole Imogene adventure.

Gratitude... to my pard and many pals

BY NANCY TAYLOR

A LOVE LETTER MUST INCLUDE GRATITUDE. Mine is to all the aid-station volunteers over the years who cheered my husband Walt and me and zippered my parka when my fingers were too frozen to move. To the cowbell ringers on the high catwalk, a welcoming sound echoing in the wind, and the helpers at Imogene Pass, nourishing us and sharing the euphoria of being on top of the world. To the Tomboy and Society Arch folks urging us on for the big downhill sprint, and the neighbors with kegs on the finish sidelines to whet our spirits and quench our thirst. And what a high to celebrate race finishes in Telluride town square with high-altitude runners from all over the Four Corners, and now and then some brave souls from sea level. Thanks, too, for the bus rides back to Ouray. The Imogene team never missed a beat!

My love extends to all our Flagstaff Imogene pals with whom we trained over the summers, our drivers to Telluride with ever-hydrating passengers needing to stop along the way to pee as we crossed the Rez. Of course, I have to give a shout-out to my pard, Walt, for putting up with my pre-race jitters, which prompted me to say practically every single year, "I'm not up for this." But with storm clouds over Ouray moments before the race, we always decided with our peeps to go to the starting line anyway.

"Yikes, we could always turn back," we said. But we never did!

Smiling down the home stretch, 2003.

Not so lovely was the collective grunt up the first embankment, everyone about to hurl with no one there who would care, and runners dashing way ahead of me in the first three miles. Only then, settling in, did I find the steady pace of enjoying every moment of the time and place, the beauty of the mountains and canyons, the silence, and being alone with myself (well, not entirely alone. Gotta admit, I was also trying to pass the next runner!).

Some years were warm, with golden aspens and falling leaves paving our way; other times, the fury of wind and storm spit at us.

I'll never know the runner who caught me as I fell back in a powerful gust close to the Pass. I met a young Phoenix woman years later on Flagstaff's Sunset Trail who said, "I chased your butt for a long time at Imogene!" All of this is to say we're a varied group of outdoor enthusiasts who have the Imogene Pass Run to thank for many years of fun, camaraderie, and accomplishment.

Last but not least, my most poignant Imogene memory—a true love letter—is to honor my pard and our three Taylor kids, Mary, Annie, and John. In 1994, when Mary was 28 years old, Annie 25, and John 23, our family ran Imogene together along with other dear friends. And now Flagstaff boasts the most participants. We are a proud, healthy mountain town.

Maybe someday I'll have the guts to enter again. As our friend Nathan Avery said, "How can I be late if I'm already here?" Or better yet, "Slow down and taper." I'll be slower in my old age and ever more respectful (this race is tough!) and appreciative of what Imogene has brought to me personally, my family, and my town.

With love, I thank you, Imogene.

THE FLAGSTAFF CONTINGENT PHOTO has become a postrace tradition in Telluride's town park. This photo from 1994 includes Walt and Nancy Taylor and their three children, when the family was acknowledged during the closing ceremony for doing the run together. Front row (from left): Jim Marzolf, Elena Kirschner, Christine Maher. Second row (from left): Walt Taylor, Annie Taylor, Nancy Taylor, Gerri Gunn. Third row (from left): Paul Brinkmann, Janet Dubrava, Alan Motter, John Taylor, Steve Weishapl, Mary Taylor, John Gunn.

From left: John Gates, Walt, Roberta Motter, Christine Maher, and Nancy, 2003.

THAT'S RUNNERS FOR YOU!

BY AL AND SARAH HENDRICKS

Al Hendricks first ran the Imogene Pass Run in 1995 and has had an unbroken streak ever since. Sarah Hendricks would have completed 22 in a row in 2018. Despite being scheduled for knee surgery the next week, she started the run, making the Upper Camp Bird cutoff before she decided to call it. Al has been on the podium in his age group several times, and Sarah took third in her age group in 2016.

HOW IT ALL BEGAN

AL: Rich Haag invited me to go in 1995, along with his wife, Jennie, and Dave Klensin and his wife, Linda. We joined Walt and Nancy Taylor, Wyatt Woodard, and others. Later, Tom and Ellen Grabarek joined the group. We rented six-person condos. We chose to stay in Ouray because of the early start and the time difference between Arizona and Colorado.

The last few years, most of those people have dropped out, so now we just go by ourselves. We like to stay in a cabin at the KOA campground between Ouray and Ridgeway.

SARAH: There's no other race that is part of our tradition like this one.

AL: What makes it special now is the streak. There was a time when I was getting bored of doing the same thing, and I thought of running a different race. Nothing else had the appeal of Imogene. It's not just a race; it's an opportunity to travel. And it's ironic: You travel 300 miles, and when you get there, you see all these people from Flagstaff. Every year, it's a reunion of sorts.

SARAH: Now our added bonus is that our grandkids are in Farmington, so we go up Thursday and visit them on the way to Ouray.

A FUNNY THING HAPPENED

AL: One time, the transmission went out on Sarah's truck in Teec Nos Pos, Arizona, on the Navajo Reservation. We went out to the highway and stuck our thumbs out, and the first car that came along was Rich Haag's. At the maximum, about 250 people from Flagstaff would register for Imogene. Given that, I guess it's not too surprising that the next person who drove by was going from Flagstaff to the race. They had four people in that Saab already, but they added two of us, plus our bags. It was pretty tight.

The two of us, 2008.

And then there was the time I forgot my chip in the condo. I ran without it and came in third in my age group. Bruce Higgins was right behind me, so I told him, "You remembered your chip, I didn't, so you deserve it." He got the award. I found out later that Caleb Schiff had forgotten his chip, too, but he had told the race organizers, and other runners vouched for him. If I had done the same thing, I would've gotten an award… but I didn't. I did make sure John Jett counted me as having completed the race, to keep my streak going.

One year, I left my running shoes in Flagstaff. Todd Landrum, a ranger at Sunset Crater who was part of our group for a while, just happened to have an extra pair. He let me borrow them.

SARAH: And they fit!

AL: Well, they were the right size, but they felt large. After the race, we realized they didn't have insoles, and that's why they'd felt so big.

That year, I ran the fastest Imogene I've ever run: 3:07. It was the year a very good friend of mine, Joe Wegener, got lung cancer. He had been in the hospital for a long while, and I got word the night before the race that he had yanked out all of his IVs and passed away. I probably ran as fast as I did because I dedicated my race to him.

TRADITIONS

AL: One time, the group rented a 15-person van. Everything was fine going up. Going back, Dave Klensin was driving the van. We heard the same Fleetwood Mac tape what seemed like over and over and over. He's speeding down the Million-Dollar Highway (between Ouray and Silverton) around those corners, and the people in back are swaying back and forth, all scared to death because alongside the highway, it just goes straight down. I think someone else drove after we got to Durango.

Rich Haag started the tradition of going to the Durango Diner the morning after the run. We don't go to restaurants like that as a rule because it's not very healthy, but every year, the group would stop at the Durango Diner on the way home, to have breakfast. We still do that. Sarah gets "The Cure," and I get the "Kitchen Sink" omelet.

YOU CAN'T RUN THAT

AL: There used to be bad weather every year at Imogene; it's only recently that it's been nice. I think it's climate change. Anyway, in 2006, it was snowing when we woke up. I think they had between one and two feet of snow at Imogene Pass. John Jett, the race director, shortened the race because of the liability of having people run and volunteer in those conditions. We went to Upper Camp Bird and then took the road to the right up to Yankee Boy Basin, where we turned around and came back. So that year, the race started and finished in Ouray, the only year that's ever happened.

But Rick Trujillo, one of the founders of the race, was standing at the turnaround saying, "It's not Imogene if you don't go all the way to Telluride." He was taking people's chips; maybe he worked a deal with John Jett to take the chips away, so John was no longer liable. I don't know. A lot of people went over the top, but we didn't. We went back to Ouray, because it was very understandable why John made that decision. It also might have ended our streak if we'd continued because if they took your chip away, your name wouldn't be on the finishers list.

One year, we started the run in the rain, which turned to snow. I was wearing a singlet and shorts and carrying a long-sleeve shirt. I had to wrap the shirt around my head, it was so cold, but that was enough to keep my body heat in so I could make it. That was pretty ugly. And there have been years when there would be black ice on the downhill. You can't run that: You have to just walk it or tiptoe really slow and gingerly.

YOU HAVE TO BOUNCE

SARAH: I went to Flagstaff High School with Fon Cordasco (her maiden name was Hartman). We took classes together and ran cross country and track together. We never went up to Imogene together. I would just see her around town. At the run, she would be behind me at the start, but then when it came to the steep part, there she would go right past me. She just had this bounce to her step.

Two or three years before she passed away, we were talking about Imogene and she told me a secret, kind of a strategy. She told me, "You have to bounce with every step when you're walking up. If you bounce, you pass so many people." In my head, I'm thinking, "Bouncing sounds like a waste of energy." But I tried it at Imogene that fall, and I've been doing it ever since. It works!

AL: Fon was a good runner. The year she passed away would have been her 21st consecutive Imogene Pass Run.

SOUNDS LIKE FUN

Al, 2012.

SARAH: I saw Imogene from the back this year, and it was really different. My best time was 3:49. I've finished a little bit over four hours some years and under four hours some years. To be at the back this year was pretty strange. I talked and walked with a lot of walkers. I made the cutoff at Upper Camp Bird just by walking, and I didn't have any muscle issues or cramping or anything. When I decided to call it and go back, there were already walkers struggling to make the cutoff. They were just sitting beside the trail. The website says to prepare, but they must not have trained.

AL: To get ready, I train up on the San Francisco Peaks, up Weatherford or Waterline Road or Kachina Trail. We also like to go up Kendrick Mountain, or Elden Lookout Road from the place four miles below where the road splits at the top.

SARAH: I try to work on just building time on my feet. If I can do three hours on my feet at lower elevation rather than up high, I can do Imogene. But I do go up with Al sometimes, and sometimes we just do long runs together.

AL: Until you do it, you have no idea what you're getting into. Reaching the famous false summit is hard, but when you get past it, then comes the worst part. It's as steep as 22 percent going uphill. When you're in Flagstaff, you think, "I'll be able to run it," but when you get there, you're running and pretty soon, you're power walking. There isn't a noticeable transition; it just happens. I've never been able to run to Upper Camp Bird without power walking partway.

The footing has gotten way worse on the Telluride side over the years. It's such a grind going up to the top, 10 miles with over one mile of vertical elevation gain, so the downhill is welcome. But your muscles are so worn out from climbing to Imogene Pass. I've had muscle cramping many years going down.

SARAH: I've had so many years where that has been the worst cramping I've ever experienced, especially going downhill. Every step, your legs tighten. One year, we ran with my daughter Melissa Schossow, her husband Kurt, and Kurt's brother, Erik. Erik was behind me to start, but he's faster than I am, so he caught up with me going downhill. He was cramping, and he said, "I don't know what to do!" I just told him, "Keep moving, keep moving, that's all you can do right now." At the finish line, he thanked me for telling him that. He said, "I would still have been up there in pain, without you."

AL: I've fallen a few times, and it's always on the way down. When I fell, I would cramp from head to foot. It was really painful; my muscles were just worn out. You know, the longer you run, the stiffer you get. I would fall and just lie there for a few seconds until the cramping subsided, and then I would get up. Falling really interrupts your rhythm.

Why do people do Imogene? That's like asking why people run. Runners like to do things such as running a 50K. You say, "That sounds like pain and suffering," and they say, "It sounds like fun." That's runners for you!

Flagstaff should be first!

BY SUSIE GARRETSON

I TAUGHT SCHOOL IN CORTEZ, COLORADO, in the mid-1970s, spending many of my weekends and holidays in Telluride with friends, exploring, hiking, biking, playing cards, and just a little partying.

I met my future husband, Jim Garretson, there. He owned the Bushwacker Inn and built spec houses. Once we got together, I taught school in Nucla and Naturita (small Colorado towns northwest of Telluride), but beautiful Telluride was always our center.

I remember when the Imogene Pass Run started in 1974, but I didn't pay too much attention to it. I wasn't a dedicated runner, as the participants I knew seemed to be.

Jim and I had been trying to think of a business we could do together, and we came up with the idea of a racquetball/athletic club. We decided that the Telluride area wasn't the right place to start one, so we traveled all over the Southwest looking for the best spot. For a variety of different reasons, we settled on Flagstaff. One of the reasons that made it seem right was the runners we saw all over the place. We decided athletics and fitness were important to Flagstaff residents. That was all we needed to know, despite many who advised that we needed to do a study of the area first.

We moved here in August 1978 and broke ground in October. The Flagstaff Athletic Club (FAC) opened on the west side in February 1979 and then FAC East came in 1984. The clubs continue to be a successful operation today.

•••

Sometime in the late 1980s, I started running just for fitness. One of our more charismatic FAC members, Dennis Connell, a local policeman, knew my Telluride background and kept urging me to do Imogene. My consistent response: "I don't run to race."

Finally, he wore me down, as I'm sure he did many others. So, in 1995 I gathered together a group of eight girlfriends, and off to Telluride we went.

When we picked up our race bibs, I saw an acquaintance, Jack Pera, who turned out to be one of the organizers. He was the owner of Telluride Hardware. He told me I should be so proud because Flagstaff came in third in number of entries, behind Denver and Boulder.

My first thought was "Yeah!"

My second thought was, "Wait a minute; Flagstaff should be first!"

Flagstaff is as close as or closer in distance than those two towns, and it is filled with amazing athletes who run. So over the course of the run the next day, I mulled over how I could influence that goal. After the award ceremonies, I asked Jack if he could send me 200 race applications next year that I could put out at FAC. This of course was before the days of signing up online. He seemed thrilled to be asked. I called him in early April the next year to remind him to send them, and he did.

I displayed the applications at the club, pointed them out to members whom I thought might be interested, and wrote an article in the club newsletter encouraging people to enter.

In 1996, according to Jack, Flagstaff came in second for number of entrants, and then in 1997 we made it. We came in first at last. I continued the same routine yearly, and Flagstaff remained in first place for all the succeeding years that I did the race. Despite

From left: Camille Paulin, me, Liz Gumerman, Julie Pastrick, Cissy Olsen, and Suzanne Berman, 1997.

being much smaller than Denver and Boulder, Flagstaff has never ceded that title—that includes my last adventure with IPR in 2007 and every year since. The official records don't show that Flagstaff came in first as I report here, but I have learned that the record only shows the number of people who completed the race, not number of entrants.

I participated nine times. Two more years I went with friends and hiked up to meet them. I was never one of the winners. In fact, I came in close to the end most years, and got turned away from the top one year when they shut down the race because of the number of people becoming hypothermic. But I loved it and still have most of my t-shirts.

Also, for the record, I consider Dennis Connell primarily responsible for getting so many people from Flagstaff to participate. He definitely was one of the first Flagstaffians to fall in love with the race in the early years, the 1980s. I know for certain that Dennis ran the race in 1990, because he stayed at the condo I own in Telluride and left a note in our guestbook. Sadly, Dennis passed away from a heart condition on April 18, 2003. At FAC, I loved all of our members, but there were some who were so wonderful and he was one of them. He was always so kind to our staff, and encouraging to members working out, giving helpful and correct advice. When he talked about the Imogene race, he gave you the feeling that you could do it. That's what got me! I know he will be mentioned by others in this book, and if there is a heaven, I think he'll be there smiling when this book gets published.

I hope this book will inspire more Flagstaffians to take up the challenge.

•••

I have lots of good memories of the race, as well as a few that are not so good. Mostly, I just loved being there with my friends and the thrill of being able to physically do it, making it to the cutoff points in time and to the finish line before they shut down the course. In the early days, walkers got to start the race at 7:00 a.m. and runners at 8:00. It was so much fun to cheer the runners as they went by us. But I guess the runners didn't like it, possibly because the walkers got in their way, so it was later changed to have everyone start at the same time.

I so appreciated all the people working the race, most especially those angels at the top who constantly yelled encouragement as we plodded up the last ascent. The unpleasant memories are petty complaints: having to train all summer when I really wanted to be doing other things, or needing a restroom in the most inopportune places (above the tree line) during the race. For the last few years I participated, I offered to pay for additional portable toilets. No one took me up on my offer. During the first few years I participated, the published race materials said the route was more than 18 miles long and topped 14,000 feet, but then I guess better measuring devices came along, corrections were made, and so the race actually was only a little over 17 miles, and the elevation was under 14,000 feet. That was a little disheartening.

All in all, though, I cherish all of the memories from the races, the fun with my friends, the beauty of the run, all the workers and volunteers, and the knowledge that I met the challenge. Even though Jim and I are no longer together and I am not with FAC, I am proud of the role FAC played in helping to make Flagstaff first. I hope this book will inspire more Flagstaffians to take up the challenge.

As this collection from Nancy Taylor shows, Imogene has had wildly colorful race T-shirts through the years.

Susie Garretson sports the 1995 version at Buffalo Park 24 years later.

FLAGSTAFF FINISHES FIRST!

These data are from imogenerun.com as of February 2019 and only represent finishers (not entrants).

YEAR	FLAGSTAFF	DURANGO	DENVER	TELLURIDE	BOULDER
1992	27	35	28	67	53
1993	22	47	26	76	52
1994	30	60	25	81	59
1995	36	56	37	88	52
1996	51	37	20	104	65
1997	57	38	27	114	69
1998	44	36	21	82	68
1999	42	26	21	75	72
2000	62	25	24	61	65
2001	132	59	32	63	75
2002	133	66	38	81	85
2003	148	47	51	83	100
2004	177	40	57	77	92
2005	169	63	75	53	85
2006	153	68	67	42	71
2007	157	56	72	40	103
2008	154	76	44	52	98
2009	133	81	59	74	73
2010	121	65	71	79	107
2011	157	91	70	64	122
2012	156	127	93	72	90
2013	165	81	93	82	75
2014	166	84	80	77	109
2015	170	90	89	102	85
2016	122	98	102	82	58
2017	151	103	123	87	58

DATA COMPILED BY JULIE HAMMONDS

When I heard that Flagstaff regularly sends more runners across the IPR finish line than any town in Colorado, I wanted to see for myself. Here's what I found. Flagstaff rocks!

– **JULIE HAMMONDS**

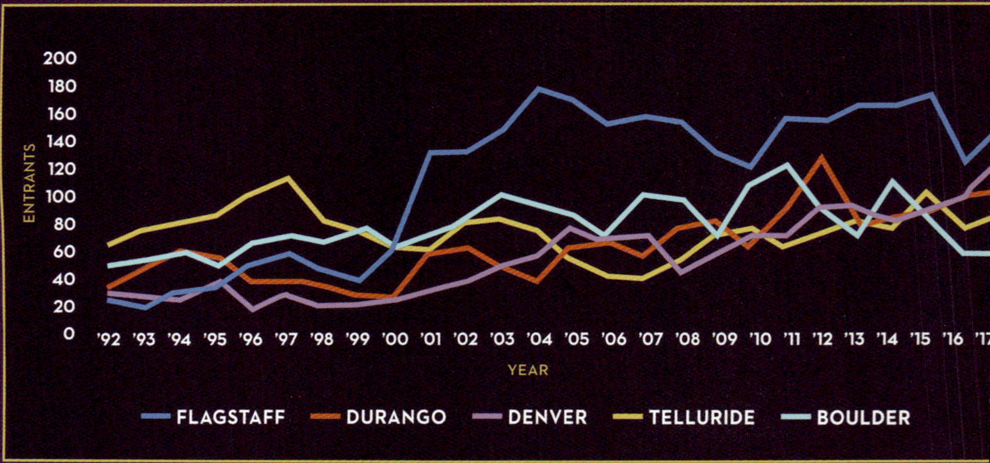

Head them off at the Pass

BY CAMILLE PAULIN

I RAN (AND COMPLETED) THE IMOGENE PASS RUN 9 times in 11 years. My first race was in 1995. I went to Colorado with a group of Flagstaff women, some of whom are well known in town. That first group included Susie Garretson (Museum of Northern Arizona), Julie Pastrick (president of the Flagstaff Chamber of Commerce), Karen Butterfield (founder of Flagstaff Arts and Leadership Academy), Susan Golightly, and several others.

It was a memorable experience for all of us, and we enjoyed it so much that a majority of us ran in multiple years.

The race in 1998 stands out in my memory as being exceptionally challenging. It was very cold and windy, with blowing snow showers. Many of the racers were woefully underdressed for the conditions. A large portion of the racers were either turned back at Upper Camp Bird or taken down to Telluride in Jeeps. I had just purchased a high-quality rain shell that allowed me to complete the race. I tightened the hood around my face so just my nose and eyes were exposed. I pulled my hands inside the shell's sleeves. When I got down to an aid station below the Pass where it had warmed up a bit, I had to have a station worker untie my hood—my hands were too cold to work the ties. It was after this year that the race organizers required racers to bring gloves and warmer clothing.

In 1999, I ran with my husband, Greg Paulin, and our daughter, Daina. That was the only year the three of us ran it. They were both well ahead of my finish time. I ran with my daughter four times. The year she was 16, she won the 15–19 age group. That was 1999, and her time was 4:28. Her medal still hangs in her bedroom with her other trophies. My best time was just over five hours, in 2000.

When we first ran the race, the Flagstaff contingent was a very small group. A photo of all the Flagstaff runners appeared in the *Arizona Daily Sun*. The photo caption was "Head them off at the Pass." These days, the number of Flagstaff runners is huge. Our little city should be proud to be so well represented in Telluride.

The Flagstaff contingent in 1995: Front row (from left): Suzanne Berman, Susan Golightly, Colleen Pouquette, Karen Butterfield, (unknown), Kim Kasic, Kathy Oliver. Back row: Camille Paulin, John Hildebrand, Susie Garretson, Julie Pastrick, Nat White, Theresa Sotomayor, Jim Kasic, Robin Burris, Walt Taylor, Beth Bermingham, Richard Boston, (unknown), Nancy Taylor.

Because Dennis Connell said I could

BY MONICA J. BAKER

I FIRST MET DENNIS CONNELL IN 1996. HE CAME TO Coconino Community College to teach for me in the Administration of Justice area and eventually built a full program.

Dennis knew I was a runner, and sometimes we would bump into each other at Flagstaff Athletic Club. One day, I was in the cardio room, where I had been on the treadmill for quite some time.

Dennis walked over with his usual saunter.

"You're a very strong runner," he said.

I smiled a sweaty, whatever-but-thanks smile.

At this point, he took over the controls of the treadmill to test my running strength. With his famous Dennis Connell grin, he changed the speed from 7 to 9 and confidently said, "Hold that for a minute."

"No problem," I blurted out, feeling the need to show him up.

After returning the speed to 7, he decided 10 was next. I survived and once again got back to 7. He then went to 11 for one minute.

"Are you trying to kill me?" I said.

"Nope, just checking," he replied.

Of course, he had to go to 12. My short, weightlifter-type legs were moving fast—faster than I had intended when I hopped on the treadmill before this lunatic ever showed up.

"You are fired!" I yelled out for the whole cardio room to hear over the pounding of my feet.

Dennis just laughed and returned the machine to 7—but only after I held 12 for the one-minute interval. Then he wandered off.

After a bit, I shut the treadmill down and went on the hunt to find him.

"What are you up to?" I asked.

"You're a strong runner," he said again.

"Thank you."

"You need to run Imogene. I'll train you."

"Imo-what?"

•••

Dennis first ran the Imogene Pass Run in the mid-1980s and is known by many as the initiation point of Flagstaff's presence at the run. He certainly was for me. After our FAC exchange, I started researching the race. Hmmm, 17.1 miles and an elevation of 13,114 feet. I put it aside. I figured a run like that was beyond my skills and finding time to train while doing my job would be impossible.

Dennis persisted. Over the next couple of years, he added different elements to my running routine and eventually

"IMO-what?" A new runner's response, the first time someone invites them to run Imogene.

convinced me to join him on weekend runs in the San Francisco Peaks. I was quite nervous for our first outdoor workout.

"I'll pick something easy," Dennis said.

"Not a lot of climb," I insisted.

"Ya, I got it," he assured me.

That first run was up Lost Burrito Trail on Mount Elden! Lost Burrito Trail rises steeply up the side of Elden. The mountain rises 2,400 feet to an elevation of 9,300. This is not what a reasonable person would call a run with "not a lot of climb."

But that was Dennis as a trainer. He knew what someone was capable of, even if she did not know it herself. That was also Dennis as a friend. He supported a person wholeheartedly. He not only encouraged my running but also my pursuit of a doctoral degree.

Our weekend runs continued whether sunny skies, rain, or snow. We ran all over the mountain, and it was beautiful and inspiring. Finally, I agreed to attempt to run Imogene. Dennis adjusted my training routine to include Rocky Ridge, then up Brookbank, through the Dry Lakes and down Lost Burrito.

He also added Kachina Trail so that I would be running at 9,000 feet. He emphasized that it wasn't as much about distance as it was about time spent running. I remember one run on the big Dry Lakes Loop. Dennis was the ever-present and observing trainer. As I ran up Brookbank, he ran behind me, critiquing my form. He noticed that my poor use of muscles led to an inefficient uphill run. This form wasted energy, he said, and I needed to modify it if I was going to run Imogene.

One time on the top of Dry Lakes, Dennis suddenly stopped. He reached into his running pack and produced a small package of peanut-butter-and-chocolate somethings.

"Here, you need to eat," he said.

"No thanks, I'm good."

He was more than a bit insistent, and we actually stood there arguing, loudly, for about five minutes. Realizing I was attempting to win an argument with Dennis Connell and how ridiculous that was, I gave in and ate the stuff. We finally took off running again.

"There, isn't that better," he said in his smug, confident tone.

"No," I said, "and I'm going to throw up on you now."

He laughed the whole way down the mountain.

•••

The 2001 Imogene was approaching quickly. I was being trained by the best and would be at peak form, but I waited too long to sign up. Although Dennis was an amazing trainer, he lacked a bit in timeliness of paperwork! The race was full and closed. There were supposedly 160 people entered from Flagstaff! I was bummed. I didn't realize the race filled so quickly. Two of my friends had signed up, and I planned on going with them. Dennis provided me with directions to another run in the area that went to a beautiful waterfall and said I should go with my friends and enjoy the atmosphere of Imogene. So, I did.

Once in Ouray, the three of us checked into our hotel and walked to the spaghetti dinner. I listened to the presentation about running the mountain and watched the slideshow. The speaker went on about the dangers of running the mountain, including exposure to the elements and how quickly conditions can change. He stated that once you are on the mountain, it is your own responsibility to get yourself down. Over and over again, he uttered those three words any Imogene participant who has attended the prerace meal in Ouray knows full well: "incessant forward motion."

I got the message and figured I would remember it for next year when I returned to actually race Imogene. After dinner, the three of us sat in the jacuzzi at the hotel with another lady. She asked if we were doing Imogene the next morning. I explained that my friends were but I tried to register too late. I just came to cheer on my friends.

A cheerleader is important, she said, but the trail is a public road and I could be on that road too, on race day or any other day, for that matter. Even though I wasn't registered, I should run the mountain, she suggested.

"Oh, and I am on the race board," she said.

So, at 8:00 p.m. the night before the Imogene Pass Run, I decided to run it in the morning. No waiting until next year!

I have found the words "incessant forward motion" to be applicable in many other areas of my life.

I should note that non-racers are no longer allowed to be on the course on race day. The event has gotten too big, and rogue running is strongly discouraged. Still, back when it was allowed, I'm grateful that this race board member encouraged me on that night to jump in.

The run went great. I felt strong, and it was an exhilarating and beautiful experience. I bought a postcard of Imogene Pass before returning to Flagstaff. I wrote my run time on the card and left it on Dennis's desk at work. When he got the card, he came dancing into my office grinning and full of pride, asking a million questions about how I did.

•••

We continued our running for the next couple years. I ran Imogene officially in 2002, when it rained the whole morning. Oh, except above tree line. Then Mother Nature threw ice chips at us. I still loved the run and enjoyed the feeling of knowing I ran over a mountain in a rain and ice storm.

One year as I was running up the Pass near the tree line, I saw a man in the distance running back down. As he got closer, I recognized him. It was Nat White, a fellow Flagstaff runner.

"Nat, what are you doing?" I yelled. "Telluride is the other way! You are going the wrong direction!"

"Yes, I know," he said. "I pulled a muscle. I'm going back to Ouray."

"But Nat..." It was too late. We were too far apart for him to hear me.

Later, in Telluride, I saw Nat. He walked up and looked at me sheepishly.

"Yes, I know, it would have been quicker to run to Telluride," he said.

He added that he had left his van in Telluride so then he had to figure out how to get from Ouray to Telluride to retrieve it. Even 15 years later, we still laugh about this.

Another year as I was running above the tree line, I felt the air getting quite thin. As I was working on the mental challenge, telling myself, "I am from the high country; I can take this," and repeating the mantra, "incessant forward motion," a motorcycle pulled up next to me. The motorcycle confirmed how thin the air was when it stalled out because of the altitude.

"That really isn't helpful," I mumbled to the man attempting to start it.

I have found the words "incessant forward motion" to be applicable in many other areas of my life. Those words carried me up and over the Pass, but they also carried me when I was off the trails—not just for other physical fitness challenges but also for career, mental, and emotional challenges throughout my life, including a daughter diagnosed with cancer, the journey through chemotherapy, and the completion of a doctoral program.

My last Imogene was in 2003. Dennis died suddenly on April 18 of that same year. We had planned a run after Easter, but it never happened. Imogene that year was more difficult to complete than usual, and I knew my time with that special place was done. I continued to tackle other running events with confidence, though. I knew if I had completed Imogene, I could conquer any other course presented to me.

Amazing (G)race

BY NAT WHITE

I WAS BORN RUNNING, BUT THAT'S A DIFFERENT STORY. My first Imogene Pass Run was in 1995 at the age of 54, and it was my first experience in competitive mountain running. I've spent four decades of running around Flagstaff and the San Francisco Peaks. However, Imogene introduced me to a new adventure.

IPR and Me: A Good Fit

Running IPR fit my trail-running personality. Despite the hundreds of participants strung along the trail, it was always just me against the mountain. If there were a competitor in my age division, I would have never recognized him. For me, it was a solo run with the simplest of challenges: how hard could I go… and for how long?

For competitive 800-meter and 1,500-meter runs, which I also enjoy, strategy is as important as training. However, in my mind, IPR is 90 percent training and 10 percent strategy. Unlike the short races where jockeying for position, when to coast, and when to dig deep are racing through your mind, the Imogene strategy is simply to drive each step at a time.

Folks had encouraged me to run IPR for several years. Dennis Connell, with whom I had led a Cub Scout pack decades before, was the primary encourager. I was a resistant audience. Having the Peaks in my backyard and some of the best open-land running in the country, why would I want to interrupt a busy life to travel to Colorado for the weekend to run? Besides, despite the relatively small running community then, I wasn't familiar with Dennis as a runner and was unsure of what the heck he was promoting.

Sometime during the summer of 1995, I became aware that Susie Garretson, co-owner of Flagstaff Athletic Club, was encouraging local runners to do Imogene, expanding Flagstaff's reputation as a running community. It worked. Years later, race director John Jett referred to Flagstaff as the "Running Nation" because of the quantity and quality of our participants.

Me in 2011.

Without any special preparation, I drove up on my own, exploring places that caught my interest as I traveled across the Navajo Nation and into the San Juan Mountains. This first excursion, with the exception of two significant changes, set my IPR MO to the present. The race was just part of an exploring expedition—a break in a busy life.

Planning My Unplanned Adventure

For several years, I followed the same routine. Drive up to Lizard Head Pass on Thursday, sleep in my car at 10,000 feet, go for a mountain run Friday morning again at 10,000 feet and above, and then drive into Telluride and car camp in the town campground. Saturday morning, I'd take the 5:30 a.m. bus ride to Ouray for the 7:30 a.m. start. (I wish the early morning bus trip would routinely stop for a potty break along the way.)

The Lizard Head Pass overnighter was not smart. Instead of camping at 10,000 feet, I should have been stoking up on oxygen at as low an elevation as possible. Instead of going for a brisk mountain run at altitude the day before, I should have been resting and relaxing.

Someone interested in my IPR times asked why my times got better relative to my age-group competition after some five IPR runs. The real answer, which I didn't share, was no more 10,000-foot camping and running before the race. In fact, spending the night before in Ouray or Ridgway at the most convenient lowest elevation is a much better idea. Telluride, on the other hand, is such an inviting place, with the pre-race anticipation and chance meetings of Flagstaff runners.

My first IPR was an unplanned adventure, including the trip to and from Telluride. The run itself was exhilarating. I loved the steady strain climbing the hill and the leg speed and agility needed to get down the other side without falling. Seeing the mountain scenery, the streams and snow, and being surrounded by healthy folks, most much younger than myself, made me smile. Tempered by age, the experience is still the same after 21 years.

Always Expect the Unusual

Each year features at least one experience outside the normal. Sometimes it's the weather, sometimes it's how I feel, and sometimes it's some bizarre happening before or after the race. The unpredictable makes for special memories and lessons learned. All IPR runners are familiar with that short, steep gravely dip around Mile 9 and close to 12,000 feet. I think it was my second IPR where I took advantage of that short downhill and kicked up my speed. Big mistake. Immediate oxygen debt commenced as I climbed out of the dip. The next thing I remember was a very strong African-American man holding me upright.

"Are you OK?"

"Yeah, I'm OK."

"Thanks."

And on we went. The lesson learned is to maintain a steady pace on the way to the Pass, because precarious oxygen debt is only a short kick away.

Another time, I was nursing a strained muscle. Again at about Mile 9 I decided it might be too much of a strain to run down the other side. I turned around and ran back very fast to Ouray. It must have been the altitude affecting my thinking. I ended up running farther than if I had completed the race! Afterward, I found out that Monica Baker (page 38) had tried to stop me before I made that error, but I didn't hear her.

Consistency Through the Years

A running log can be very beneficial in improving one's training by documenting trends, planning workouts, and analyzing a race. The question we runners consistently ask ourselves: What could I have done to improve the result?

The following is a quote from my running log after the 2004 IPR:

> *"Age 63 Imogene pass, Warm, Sunny, blue wind breaker, knit hat, cotton long sleeve shirt, racing shorts. 2 mi, 20:42, 5 mi 34:56 (55:38), 8 mi 46:31 (1:42:10), 10 mi 43:00 (2:25:10), 17.1 52:28 (3:17:39) About 7 minute miles downhill. Won Open Senior and age group, second place runner 17 minutes behind. Felt fine but just did not run the first 5 to 10 mile stretch very fast. Could use more 50 mile weeks in July and faster downhill training. Weight was great. More strength. Need to start training distance in early May. (2003 times, 2 mile 20:12, 5 mile 54:24, 8 mile 1:41, 10 mile 2:23, 17.1 mile, 3:15)"*

Although the logged times changed as I moved up in the age groups, there is a lesson in habit. My observations have almost always been the same after each run. That is, I could have run the uphill faster and used more strength training and mileage. And never—never—ease up on the downhill training. Even when I was 75, I wrote down similar conclusions: Start hill and distance training early, as in May. Speed training is essential for the downhill. Your greatest effort on race day should come in the first 10 miles. Let leg speed and gravity carry you down the mountain.

I've never planned to break any records or win an age group. My MO has remained consistent: run as hard and as long as I can with little strategy and enjoy the effort. It has been gratifying to make a Flagstaff statement by setting three age-group records and at least win the age division just about every time I have run IPR. In 2016, what I expected to be my last IPR, I managed to set a new record for age 75 and up.

I returned in 2017 and lowered the age-group mark by more than two minutes. The next year, 2018, I finished first at age 77 but several minutes slower. However, it was pleasing in that there were enough competitors that medals for first, second, and third place were awarded. This time, I could not make my regular quip that at my age the race is a dead heat because everyone else in the heat is dead.

Trombone Above Tomboy

I didn't run IPR for a few years in my early 70s, but I made the trip to cheer on those who did. I would start hiking the course backward from Telluride about the time the race started in Ouray. That would get me above Tomboy about the time the first runner ran by. I have this plastic, carbon-fiber trombone that is light enough to carry on my hike, and I'd play tunes as the runners passed. "She'll Be Coming 'Round the Mountain" and "When the Saints Go Marching In" seemed appropriate.

It was fun to hear folks after the race make comments like, "Were you the guy playing the trombone?" Or, "I was really hurting until the music changed my whole focus." Or simply, "That was cool."

I played "Amazing Grace" one time. After the race, one of Flagstaff's elite runners, Michelle Wesson, came up to me and emotionally described starting the downhill and hearing the song wafting up in the mountain air. She was running the race in honor of a friend who had died (see page 136). Hearing "Amazing Grace" high in the mountains, she said it was meant to be.

As are many runners, Nat White is meticulous with his training log notes. This is how he recorded his 2004 IPR weekend, his 10th go at the course, at age 63, from elk sightings and clothing choices to splits and plans for the coming year...

A weekend with Imogene

09-09-04 1 Easy FAC, stretch, light weight, left Flag about 11:15 AM, Thursday, 89 Caravan, 330 miles to Lizard head and about 6 hours driving time, 170lbs, Ray Lobato stopped at same gas station on the way and we talked. Did a 40 min walk west on highway about 6 pm. Bedded down after sun set. Couple of Native Americans carrying on a conversation. Flag car stopped by.

09-10-04 2 Lizard Head Pass, 9:13 am MST DST, Rained during night, fog shrouded Sheep Mountain, 13,000 ft. Good sleep, pulse about 58. Hunters are out. Slight head ache due to altitude? Started for Telluride driving slowly in the mist and rain watching scenes and taking pictures. About 10 AM watched a herd of 50 or so elk from the highway on the hill into Telluride. They came out a fenced aspen grove about 800 yards away. Skittish with bolts occasionally and jumping over the fence. Bulls would stay on the outside of the herd. When they went back into the aspen grove, the last cow wasn't sure she could jump it. She kept circling around and then finally jumped.

Drove into Telluride and registered in the camp site. Watched an old expert equipment operator work a big track hoe and bull dozer move a rock pile with 8ft boulders. He wasted no moves and was smooth as silk.

Rained most of Friday, took some cloudy pictures. Friday night sleep was fitful. Peed about 5 times during the night. Up at 4 am, took a Tylenol, 1 pill, banana, nuts, drink half and half Gatorade.

Shower, poop, sun screen, tape feet, park by bus stop and race end.

09-11-04 17.1 Imogene pass, Warm, Sunny, blue wind breaker, knit hat, cotton long sleeve shirt, racing shorts. 2 mi, 20:42, 5 mi 34:56 (55:38), 8 mi 46:31 (1:42:10), 10 mi 43:00 (2:25:10), 17.1 52:28 (3:17:39).

Won Open Senior and age group. Second place 17 min behind.

Felt fine but just did not run the 5 to 10 mile stretch very fast. Could use more 50 mile weeks in July and more fast downhill training. Weight was great. More strength. Need to start training distance in early May.

09-12-04 0 Walked some and drove to Flag.

"Flagstaff, the Running Nation"

Our IPR experiences are many and varied. This book is evidence of that. For many of us, walkers and runners, the race is just the hook. The entire process, from planning and training for the run to the pre- and post-run camaraderie, is what elevates IPR to a uniquely special happening. It is an annual opportunity for Flagstaff to confirm once again that we are, as John Jett proclaimed, "Flagstaff, the Running Nation."

The Godmother of Soulstice and NATRA

BY NEIL WEINTRAUB

IN 1995, I REGISTERED FOR MY FIRST IMOGENE Pass Run to understand why hundreds of Flagstaff runners made the great migration to race the 17.1 miles from Ouray to Telluride. Due to its high altitude, I figured it would be a tough final long run for my first St. George Marathon, where I hoped to qualify for the Boston Marathon.

Flagstaff folks seemed to divide into two camps; those who chilled in Ouray, and those who partied in Telluride. The majority seemed to stay in Telluride, with its great restaurants and hotels; however, I was in the Ouray camp, as I knew that after the run, all I would dream of was soaking in the hot springs to recover. Another benefit would be waking up and walking to the start rather than taking the shuttle.

It was a picture-perfect weekend. The race proved grueling, but the scenery and sense of elation from topping out at 13,114 feet won me over. The thrill of taking a deep breath and bombing downhill for seven miles was more exciting than the scariest of rollercoasters. With legs burning and wobbly, I crossed the finish line in 3:32:51. Half of Flagstaff was there, it seemed, so I drank a quick beer in Telluride before returning to Ouray to unwind in the hot springs. I remember thinking, That was a fun accomplishment.

Meanwhile, every muscle in my body ached.

•••

It would take another 10 years before I was ready to make a go of it again. The memory of all those Flagstaff runners and the camaraderie of the participants at the finish line lingered in the back of my head. Imogene was something special, but I couldn't put my finger on exactly what it meant.

In 1997, I heard rumors that a group of runners were putting on one of Flagstaff's first trail races in many years. The Soulstice Mountain Trail Run was conceived when William Ring, Wiley Addis, and Paul Brinkmann returned home from Imogene believing Flagstaff could have its own version of the famous run from Ouray to Telluride. Soulstice was first directed by Bill Ring's Soulstice Racing Company, with a $500 sponsorship from Pay-N-Take.

> In 1997, I heard rumors that a group of runners were putting on one of Flagstaff's first trail races in many years.

I was already registered for the St. George Marathon and couldn't take part that year, but several friends raved about the grueling race. Much to my disappointment, it was not held the next year due to low registration.

In 2001, Shelly Welch and Bill Ring revived Soulstice.

The horror of 9/11 was still etched on everyone's minds, so reviving the race was an idea to bring the Flagstaff running community together. Again, only about three dozen runners competed. After the race, several of us sat around the keg and wondered how IPR could attract 150 Flagstaff runners, yet locals showed little interest in Soulstice. To attract trail runners and make them believe in our home-grown race, we started an email list and began picking different Flagstaff trails to run together each Saturday. Thus, Northern Arizona Trail Runners Association was born. NATRA began organizing Soulstice with help from Bill Ring in 2002.

Perhaps the biggest decision that made Soulstice a local institution was adding a "short course" of six miles as an alternative to the grueling original 12.25-mile course. This opened the door for beginner trail runners, and Soulstice participation jumped from 35 to 160 runners in 2002.

As stories of Soulstice and its legendary postrace party spread, we achieved our goal of selling out the race when 200 runners registered in 2003. It's been a sellout ever since. Soulstice entry is now capped at 225 runners, or roughly the number of Flagstaffians who participate at Imogene.

At the 2005 Imogene, to increase the lore of Soulstice outside of Flagstaff, about a dozen runners from here (including me) wore T-shirts designed with the NATRA logo on the front and on the back a bold statement: "Imogene is great training for SOULSTICE 2005." The following year, Soulstice became so popular we began the lottery entry system that is still in place.

We were all surprised when, in 2012, *Runner's World* magazine named Soulstice among the top 32 trail races in North America. It was an honor to be listed among the many giants, the foremost being Soulstice's godmother: Imogene.

GENE PASS RUN
HOOK

part 3

Virgins

You never forget the first time

Four days, two volcanoes

BY M. ELISE RUMPF

FOUR DAYS UNTIL MY FIRST IMOGENE. FOUR DAYS until we all see how months of training, planning, and hoping for good weather play out. Four days until we all get an extra-heavy dose of that beautiful, soul-awakening, life-affirming suffering each of us craves. Or maybe four days until we get snowed out and spend some unanticipated time day-drinking in Telluride.

Four days until Imogene means it's Tuesday; track practice. Afternoon thunderstorms threatened cancellation. That would be almost welcome today, even though we always feel better after a few laps alongside friendly faces moving at all speeds. Tonight, there's a chill in the air, which means the coming of fall. Tonight, the track is wet, my lungs are tired, motivation is fleeting.

Luckily, it's four days before Imogene—an excuse to taper and eat and sleep. Our workout is 12 x 1 minute at sprint pace. Fighting the balance between needing to hold back and wanting a good workout, we're treated to a beautiful post-storm sky: full, heavy clouds punctuating the blue. And that skyline, our ever-present backdrop: the San Francisco Peaks.

•••

My training for Imogene was defined by two volcanic fields: The San Francisco, the ancient peaks and hills that are the training ground for Flagstaff's trail and ultrarunners, and the Lower East Rift Zone of Kīlauea, whose abrupt change in activity in 2018 amazed the world, displaced thousands of residents, and took over the lives of volcanologists everywhere.

I study lava flows for a living. It's the type of job you dream of having as a kid. I didn't hesitate for a moment when the eruption started and I was needed on the Big Island. I took two trips, spending nearly a month in Hawai'i between May and July. I worked the night geology shift. I collected data. I led the drone team. I wrote flight plans. I coordinated activity

Researching the lava flows at Kilauea, Hawai'i, in summer 2018.

A bird's eye view.

with the Federal Emergency Management Agency and the National Park Service. I talked story with locals and tourists, scientists and emergency responders. I worked hard because the work mattered. This eruption made me a volcanologist in ways that over a decade of training couldn't. This eruption taught me why I do what I do.

There was the afternoon when a family stopped to talk as we prepared drones for flight. They had driven as close as they could, then hiked an hour to get one last load of belongings before the lava consumed their house, their farm. I promised, whether or not I had permission, to send them pictures when we saw it happen.

Nature repeats herself. The patterns of fury and creation are the same wherever we travel, if we keep our eyes open.

Then there was the night we visited Lanipuna Subdivision, as we had the previous nights; except this night, the subdivision was gone, overrun by lava flows from a 500-meter-long fissure that had opened above it. We flew drones over the area first, to be sure our escape routes wouldn't be cut, then drove into the apocalyptic landscape. No hyperbole: artist renditions of an early magmatic Earth have captured this scene well.

The orange glow of lava flows and fountains lit the night sky for miles. Everything was gone, covered or burning. The smells, the smoke, the heat, the banging and hissing fissures… at the end of my shift, I got a seat on the routine 6:00 a.m. helicopter overflight. By then, the flows were halfway to the ocean, moving so quickly they were visibly destroying property in the 10 minutes between passes over an area. The flows appeared to sparkle with the fires of individual burning trees they picked up as they progressed. Their main channels moved as fast as rivers. It was stunning—quite literally breathtaking, and absolutely heartbreaking.

Needless to say, there wasn't time to train in Hawai'i. Eruption response is physically and mentally exhausting. The concept of "free time" seems frivolous, and there is always more work to do. It felt strange to leave, but I was happy to head home. I missed my long runs in Flagstaff, the normalcy of training for a race.

Training in Flagstaff, I'd wake up at 4:30 a.m. to hug some cold coffee and force down an apple, a granola bar, a cookie; anything to get some calories in. Then I'd head for the trailhead. The early bird misses the crowd, the heat, the monsoons. In May and June, the forests were closed. If I was in town, I'd usually headed to Kendrick Mountain. At first, I'd go up to the tower, then straight back down. In subsequent visits, I'd repeat the top mile, then the top two miles, trying to increase endurance and time at altitude, usually pausing at the top to snap a picture, get a quick bite in, or chat with Ken or one of the other dutiful lookout volunteers.

I missed most of July and returned to a fully opened forest. I started tackling Humphreys and Weatherford; took the Bear Jaw or Inner Basin trails to get to the top of Waterline Road, where moss grows and one can

quickly forget we live in a desert. I pushed my lungs through the smoky days. I rolled my trick ankle again and again on the cobbles.

Between Fremont and Agassiz peaks, I found fulgurite—petrified lightning—formed when sand weathered from the lava rock that makes up the peaks is struck. From the top of the Inner Basin, I looked into the gaping valley left when the volcano blew its top five million years ago, revealing old, sloping lava flows. Surrounding the peaks, the landscape is lumpy with of hundreds of small volcanic vents and lava flows, not unlike the one that built itself in Hawaiʻi this summer. Nature repeats herself. The patterns of fury and creation are the same wherever we travel, if we keep our eyes open.

After watching the eruption in Hawaiʻi, I can now see how A1 Mountain must have spewed lava into the air, and how Observatory Mesa emerged as a broad, thick lava flow from its base. After weeks of 12- to 16-hour days, my alarm going off before the sun, I no longer complain about meeting in the dark before the crowds and the lightning for a long, steep run up the side of a volcano. This summer has been tough. Even though I missed a month of training, I'm feeling strong, confident. Imogene's got nothing on volcanoes.

•••

And so, tonight I'll finish my laps, then grab dinner with my running friends, who are the best part of running in Flagstaff. Then four sleeps and four wake-ups until Imogene. ◈

Elated to have reached the Pass, 2018.

SO YOU'VE DONE IMOGENE?

BY ANDREW BENFORD

MY MEMORY OF THE IMOGENE PASS RUN IS SIMILAR to the memories I have of going to Myrtle Beach, South Carolina, as a kid. The joke where I'm from goes something like, "You're not truly a West Virginian unless you've been to Myrtle."

I can remember piling into the van with my family and taking the eight-hour trip south to "get away," only to get there and realize that all my buddies from West Virginia had come too. Bonus!

If you're connected to Flagstaff running circles in any way, you have inevitably heard about, and very likely been a part of, the magic that is the Imogene Pass Run. Here's a typical conversation:

ME: "I like to run."

FLAGSTAFF LOCAL: "So you've done Imogene?"

A noticeable energy shift happened once Imogene entered the conversation. A description of Imogene starts with wide-eyed excitement, transitions to a knowing smile, and always ends with, "Ya gotta do it."

I joined the mass exodus out of Flagstaff in the fall of 2015 to see what this Imogene character was all about. Looking back now, I can't recall much about the race itself. Difficult? Supremely. Blisters the size of a half-dollar on my feet? Absolutely.

Racing downhill, 2015.

What really sticks out in my mind, however, is the sense of belonging and connection I felt throughout the weekend. I remember rolling into Telluride for packet pickup and being welcomed by dozens of friendly Flagstaff faces. I remember a jam-packed school bus ride to Ouray at the crack of dawn, all of us anxiously yet eagerly awaiting the daunting ascent. I remember riding the gondola from Telluride to Mountain Village, taking in the indescribable beauty of the San Juans with A.J. Sobrilsky, Chris Gomez, and Ryan Stevens, fellow Flagstaff runners and my lifelong friends.

Thanks to that unforgettable weekend, I now understand where the magic comes from—Imogene is a place in Colorado where a Flagstaff runner goes to feel right at home.

The contradictions are real

BY CHRISTOPHER McQUIVEY

WHAT HAPPENS WHEN YOU MOVE TO FLAGSTAFF having never run a race in your life?

Well, you sign up for the Imogene Pass Run, of course.

Is this a good idea? It depends who you ask. Flagstaffians talk about Imogene in vastly different ways.

On the positive side, you'll get responses that are hyperbolic ("It's the best race in the world!"), humorous ("It's easy... just run up a hill and down the other side"), deflecting ("It's so pretty"), or comforting ("You'll be fine").

From the naysayers, answers are, well... more alarming:

"That race almost killed me!"
"It's super hard."
"Are you sure that's a good idea?"

Or the inevitable,

"Be careful."

I was perplexed when I heard these responses. I didn't have the slightest idea why those people would have such different reactions to the same race.

I came to Flagstaff in 2010 ready to start my career. Before moving, I was a pretty good rock climber, but when I got to Flag I had no money, and other than my family I didn't know a soul. Without cash, the climbing gym was out. There was no gas in the car and my bike had been stolen months earlier. I figured the best way to explore was to run around a bit. I laced my shoes and started to discover the trails.

I still remember how badly my side ached and my lungs burned when I ran four miles, the most I had ever continuously run in my life. Four miles turned to eight, and before long I was able to run to the climbing crag instead of driving. Funny thing is, I enjoyed running there more than climbing; soon, climbing took a back seat.

Still, I never thought about racing until a friend suggested it. I didn't like the idea. I was afraid racing would take away from the freedom and joy of a morning run and degrade it to a simple competition. That all changed one winter when I saw Imogene Pass from the gondola. My friend pointed. "You see that pass? There's a race over that pass every year. You should try it."

I had no idea a race could be in such an amazing place. I figured that if I was going to enter a race, it should be on a pass like the one I saw from the gondola. A race like that wouldn't just be a competition; it would be an adventure.

So, never having run a race in my life—not a 5K or a one-mile fun run—I signed up for the Imogene Pass Run.

A few months later I was toeing the line, not having a clue what I'd gotten myself into. With a pop of the gun and a flurry of feet propelling people forward, my first race was underway.

The IPR is not forgiving. It starts high and gets higher fast. I did my best to run but found myself power-hiking more than I wanted and being winded the entire time. I started having all sorts of crazy contradicting thoughts and feelings, just like the comments you get from Imogene veterans: some positive (focusing on the beauty surrounding me), some negative (wanting to give up right there).

At one particularly hard section, I remember looking up and seeing a waterfall. It totally changed my attitude. All of a sudden I was whole again. The competition was not why I'd come. I was there for the scenery, the sounds, the effort. I was there to test myself. So I smiled, dug deeper, and continued. One minute I felt great; the next I worried I would pass out. But I kept going.

"A race like that wouldn't just be a competition; it would be an adventure.... I was there to test myself. So I smiled, dug deeper, and continued."

I remember reaching the Pass and plunging down the steep section with more than a little apprehension. My legs were heavy and my whole body was tired. I was thirsty and hungry despite the handfuls of aid station food I had grabbed along the way, and I knew that if I was going to finish, I would have to run farther than I ever had. (My longest training run had been just 16 miles.)

I ran as fast as I could. The lower I got, the better I felt. I knew it was almost over. As I rounded one of the last switchbacks, I could hear the crowd cheering. I was ecstatic but on the verge of cramping. Two seconds later, my calves were in knots. My running form must have looked a bit strange to the spectators lining Oak Street, but I'm sure they've seen worse. I crossed that finish line and heard my name called out. It was exhilarating. I immediately sat down, smiled, and wondered when I would do it again. So many feelings and thoughts ran through my mind that it's hard to explain them all.

That's Imogene though. Let's just say that the contradictions are real. All those comments about the race are completely accurate. It's all of that wrapped into one great adventure. It hurts, it's gorgeous, it's hard, it's amazing, it's painful, it's wonderful. No wonder Flagstaffians love it. I love it! It was literally the first race I ever entered and the first time I felt all those conflicting things in myself. The majesty, the beauty, the crowd, the smells of pine and waterfalls, the summit, the steep descent on shaking legs, the loose rocks, the pain, the cramps, the thin air... I love it all.

Imogene shaped me into who I am today. I have gone on to run many other races. Every time I enter one, I hope the race will be a grand adventure like my first race. That is still usually my baseline for deciding whether to enter. Imogene preserved the purity of running for me even as I got more into racing.

When people ask me about Imogene, I tell them I don't think there is a better race. For me, it's not just another race or another mountain pass. It's Imogene. It's a rite of passage for Flagstaff runners.

So whether Imogene is your first race or your 50th, it will probably give you what you're looking for and perhaps a bit of unexpected more. Imogene, thanks for teaching me that adventure comes in all sorts of terrible and wonderful ways.

With love,

Chris

Imo do WHAT?

BY CRISTY ZELLER

This essay originally appeared in the High Country Running column of the Arizona Daily Sun *on September 1, 2013.*

MY GOAL WHEN I TURNED 40 IN 2012 WAS TO run a 5K.

I fell in love with the soul-cleanse of trail running, the finish-line high, and the Flagstaff running community. When an Imogene Pass Run transfer fell into my lap that July, I couldn't say no.

A week before Imogene, I went for a run up Elden Lookout Road. Suddenly, I felt a sharp pain in my left leg, and I knew something was terribly wrong. A visit to the doctor confirmed a severe strain to the iliotibial band. I submitted to all sorts of traditional and alternative therapies. The pain was not improving. I was crushed.

We drove to Telluride anyway. At dinner the night before the race, I put on a cheerful face with my training group, but I felt deflated. At bedtime, I still didn't know if I would even get up. My husband calmed me and told me to at least go check out the bus in the morning. That was the moment when I knew no one was letting me off the hook.

•••

Alarm goes off; I limp to the bus stop. There is a nervous, quiet buzz aboard. Maybe the bus will crash. This seems like a good outcome.

There are so many familiar faces from Flagstaff at the start. I begin to feel something like determination and think that maybe I will try to make the first checkpoint. Seems futile, but I'm here, so I should try.

Shotgun start. Don't think, just go.

It's beautiful, invigorating, and I can't take it all in. I just ran two miles? That can't be right. I see a sign that says, "RUN FLAGSTAFF RUN." I snap a picture because that is awesome.

It's now time to go down, and I feel almost crippled with pain as I face the seven miles ahead. Even if I am in last place, and frankly I don't care at this point, I will cross that finish line.

I make the checkpoint only 20 minutes behind my original goal, pre-injury. I want to weep but I will hyperventilate.

The miles pass, and we are above tree line. I can see the summit. It's far. The air is so thin. I am taking three steps and pausing. Over and over. I think about moving one foot in front of the other. Just make it to that rock. Then that one. I'm inching closer. Don't look up. It's too discouraging.

I see the aid workers jumping up and down like tiny little ant people. They are cheering us on and clanking cowbells. We have to climb up footholds carved in the steep mountainside. There's a man holding his hand out, and he literally pulls me up. I cross the checkpoint and we are all hugging and crying. I cannot believe I did this! We take a few pictures and enjoy the majestic view.

It's now time to go down, and I feel almost crippled with pain as I face the seven miles ahead. Even if I am in last place, and frankly I don't care at this point, I will cross that finish line.

Dozens of people run past me, however as Telluride comes into view I start to jog and am able to catch up with some of them. I'll probably be crippled for life, but who cares. I come into town and I'm determined to run across the finish. My son comes out to run with me and we hold hands as I collapse across the line in smiles and tears. I look around at these faces and I am so moved and proud to be a part of them.

I did it, and I can't wait to do it again. Who's in?

When I did the Imogene Pass Run in 2002, it rained 14 out of the 17.1 miles. When I did the Mountain to Desert Ride from Telluride to Gateway in 2017, it rained 52 out of the 104 miles. I'm afraid of ever registering for another race in Telluride because if I do, it will rain.

– PAULA PLUTA

RUN FLAGSTAFF RUN!

We made the "Run Flagstaff Run" sign as a family the night before the Imogene Pass Run on an old banner I had left over from sponsoring Flagstaff Little League. After using it once, we didn't want it to go to waste, so we kept bringing it back up the hill. Some people said really nice things about the sign. People would stop to take photos when they saw the banner. I even saw one guy run up and kiss it.

– MATT BRYDENTHAL

Part of the Tradition

BY MARY MOHR

From left: Me, Marsha, and Patti in Telluride, 2014.

IMOGENE PASS RUN, 2014: PATTI QUIGLEY, Marsha Jensen, and I decided to run it that year. We trained together, rented a condo together, and did the race.

It remains one of the most memorable vacations I've ever had. This was a vacation for us, not a visit to family. We also had our partners with us.

It was very special to be with great friends and share the event with our special people. On our way to Telluride, my husband and I visited Monument Valley Tribal Park and Mesa Verde National Park. After the race, we went to visit longtime friends in Paonia, Colorado.

I was 59 years old. I wasn't sure I would make the time cutoffs; however, I did manage to. I was so happy to be in the "run, not the race," as race director John Jett says. I wanted to be part of the tradition of Flagstaff having the most registered entrants, and I was. Every time I look at the photo of me standing at the Imogene Pass sign, it makes me feel good.

Flag first-timers sweep Imogene titles

BY MYLES SCHRAG

This article originally appeared in the Arizona Daily Sun *on September 11, 2017.*

FOR THE THIRD TIME IN SEVEN YEARS, Flagstaff runners swept the men's and women's overall titles at the Imogene Pass Run on Saturday.

It didn't come easy for Katie McGee and David Sinclair, both competing in their first Imogene race.

McGee overcame a hard fall a mile from the finish line in Telluride to hold off the wonderfully named Imogen Ainsworth of Durango, Colorado, by 2 minutes, 20 seconds, and take the women's crown.

Sinclair kept Timmy Parr of Leadville, Colorado, from a third consecutive victory by crossing the finish line just under four minutes faster in a time of 2:13:23. Sinclair's hometown is Burlington, Vermont, but he is a graduate student at Northern Arizona University who has lived in Flagstaff for the past year.

"I never had (run Imogene), and I was terrified," said McGee, a coach with McMillan Running. "It was this bucket list thing, but I'd heard so many horror stories from people like me who do more roads. The backside was really steep and technical."

Her fears were not unfounded. Despite this assessment—"It was hard the first mile. It was hard at 17.1 miles. It never relented."—McGee led on the ascent out of Ouray, and when she reached the Pass still in the lead, the competitive juices kicked in.

"My only goal at the start of the race, once I got a feel for the race and who was in it, was to be the first woman to the top," McGee said. "I got to the top, and I was saying, 'I'm not losing my lead!'"

She attacked the ultra-steep and slippery first mile down to Telluride, but quickly reeled herself back in.

"I just couldn't," McGee said. "I could feel the tears welling up in my eyes."

Regaining control, she retained the lead all the way down the mountain but fell near the finish, hitting her head and quad.

Speaking about the victory on Monday, McGee still felt banged up but was grateful to represent Flagstaff.

"I feel like somebody pushed me off a cliff," she quipped. "I did every section of that race as hard as I could for my ability.

"I knew a lot of Flagstaff people did it. It was really special because it was important to the community. (Flagstaff) is so connected to that race. It's more fun when the whole community is excited and supportive of you."

Sinclair, a geology student who said several professors recommended Imogene, was also enthused about representing his new residence in the 44th edition of the fabled run.

It's more fun when the whole community is excited and supportive of you. – KATE McGEE, p. 64

"I'm definitely proud to represent Flagstaff, and it was awesome to have a large contingent of Flagstaff runners at the race. It seemed like half the racers were from Flagstaff. I've been living here for just over a near now, so Flagstaff is starting to feel like home."

McGee and Sinclair equaled the feat of Michael Smith and Jenny McCarthy (2011) and Sara Wagner and Jason Wolfe (2013) as king and queen double winners from Flagstaff in the same year.

•••

An estimated 149 Flagstaff runners were included in the 1,214 total finishers, an impressive 12 percent of the field. Three took first place in their age division, including Catie Guinan (15–19 women), Austin Horn (20–24 men), and Nat White, who lowered his men's 75-older age group record by more than two minutes.

Two more Flagstaffians placed second in their age group—Zach Bednar (15–19 men) and Annette Adams (60–64 women).

Five other Flagstaff runners placed third in their age group—Tess Siemens (15–19 women), Seth Watkins (35–39 men), Kristi Borling (40–44 women), Margaret Montfort (55–59 women), and Mark Thurston (55–59 men).

Chris McQuivey was one of eight Flagstaff runners in the top 50. He placed 19th overall in 2:49:02 in his fourth Imogene appearance despite dealing with an injury.

"I was there just to have a good time in the mountains," McQuivey said. "I feel like Imogene is Flagstaff's new year. I love the fact that our little town has so many people willing to take a huge leap of faith and run a difficult trail run. Imogene is one beautiful and hard run that brings amazing people to an amazing place. I haven't figured out if it's the place that makes the people amazing or the people that make the race amazing."

Running wild

BY KATE MCGEE

REVERIES ON THE ROAD TO TELLURIDE

AS I STAND IN OURAY AT THE START OF THE 2017 Imogene Pass Run, it seems to me that the race, long mythologized over beers at Pay-N-Take or while trotting along on the Bagel Run, has not been exaggerated. Gasping for breath simply jogging around during my warm-up gave me a small taste of what was to come. The story "Thinking Like A Mountain," from Aldo Leopold's book *A Sand County Almanac,* is on my mind. I'm not sure why. Perhaps I am searching for a way to externalize the fear I'm feeling about the daunting task I am about to undertake. The San Juan Mountains between Telluride and Ouray have a godlike visage about them. Soaring to 14,000 feet, these eternal beings appear to be in deep meditation. I wonder, how will they reward or punish the scourge of humanity about to invade their inner circle of contemplation?

In the story, Leopold fires his rifle into a pack of wolves, fatally wounding the alpha female and hitting an adolescent pup in the leg. Gleeful he has hit the mark, he runs to his kill, arriving at the side of the wounded wolf just in time to see the green light fade from her eyes. In this moment, he deeply regrets his actions, admitting, "I was young and full of trigger itch; I thought fewer wolves meant more deer, that no wolves would be a hunter's paradise." He understands he has committed a terrible act of brutality, all for a bit of fun and excitement with his buddies. Extinguishing the life of the old wolf, he has altered every other life inhabiting the mountain. He cites Thoreau's dictum, "In wildness is the salvation of the world," attempting to capture the magnitude of the wolf's loss to the ecosystem. If in wildness is the salvation, it stands to reason, then the end of wildness will signal our damnation.

What wisdom will the mountain impart upon me? I hope it won't be too painful.

Before I have more time to ruminate, the pistol cracks and we're on our way. The start is a scramble for position. At the top of the first set of switchbacks, I am already hypoxic. Two more hours? I stuff the thought before it even has time to materialize. I settle in behind a young'un, aptly named Imogen. She seems relaxed and stronger than me. She has a steady rhythm going, effortlessly chuffing her way up the steep gravel road. Her footfalls are practically mocking me: "I think I can, I think I can, I think I can…".

When the real suffering commences, endurance athletes like to talk about "digging deep," about "going into the pain cave." I would argue that these metaphors aren't going to help you in a race like Imogene.

"I'm a badass! I'm slaying this mountain!" Such mantras are punishable acts of hubris. To survive the mountain, you need to prostrate yourself before the Old Ones. Be grateful when you're not sloughed off in a rockslide.

On one of the few flat sections of the ascent, something urges me to surge and try to break the blonde locomotive. To my surprise, she doesn't react, letting me go without a fight. She probably thinks I'm foolish to be sprinting at this point in the race. Hypothesizing different race scenarios is a strategic error when running the mountain. Does a wolf consider the opportune time to take down a weakening deer?

TO SURVIVE THE MOUNTAIN, YOU NEED TO PROSTRATE YOURSELF BEFORE THE OLD ONES.

Once I am confident I have a good lead, I take the irresistible glance back, wondering if I will be turned into a pillar of salt. I've established a hard-won gap over Imogen and the rest of the women on the mountain. I can relax the pace momentarily. I lift my gaze to the trail ahead. The men look like a ribbon of ants dutifully marching to the bidding of their queen. Possessed to get to her first, I set my sights on catching each one in turn. Most people above Upper Camp Bird are hiking more than running. Passing on the trail near the top practically entails crawling over the man in front of you if he won't yield the path, which few are willing to do.

An anxiety dream I have sometimes before races revisits me now. In the dream, I am running a cross country race in college. I'm feeling strong, about to shift gears and unleash a wicked finishing kick. Suddenly my legs won't move. I fall to my hands and knees. The finish is right in front of me, but I have to claw the grass to make my way forward. The thundering herd is coming for me. Then I wake up.

As in the nightmare, I find myself again resorting to crawling, except this time the technique is enabling me to pass other runners. They are too proud to clamber over the rocks on their hands and knees. I have no shame. I'm determined to get up the mountain however I can.

When I finally hear the cowbell urging me on at the top of the Pass, euphoria grips me. I pump my arms and high-five the people at the aid station. The harpies' perpetual taunting, "You can't breathe. You're going to have an asthma attack and die!" is momentarily silenced. But as I head down the other side, fatigue and exaltation are quickly replaced by terror. Instead of bear-crawling, I am crab-walking. My feet suddenly feel like they're five sizes too big. They're skis, sliding out from under me on the scree. The ants I had worked so hard to pass have metamorphosed, sprouted wings, and are flying by me. I try to stand up and run.

Tears pour from my eyes. I hear myself crying, "Oh god, Oh god, Help me! Help me!" I'm not sure how I make it down the first two miles of the descent; my gloves and the butt of my shorts are shredded. The trail becomes less steep, and I can run. I am a woman with nothing to lose. I go into a kind of trance. My feet are small and light again, skittering over the rocks. I come upon Chris Gomez, an accomplished mountain racer from Flagstaff. Fear grips me again.

I shouldn't be anywhere near Chris. He urges me on: "I'm fine. Stomach issues from early on. Go! You're killing it!" Ahead is the sign proclaiming, "One mile to go," and for a split-second, I lose focus. I have a lethal thought, "I've got this!"

My toe clips a rock, and before I can put my hands out, I hit the ground. I lie there crumpled, my face in the rock. We've all had that feeling of anticipation in an accident before the pain rushes to the injured areas. "How bad is it? Can I move?" I lie there motionless, waiting. "What tithe did the mountain take from me?" I try my legs first and then my arms. I sit up. My limbs work! Adrenaline floods my body. I can finish! I hit the pavement, running full tilt. I am a bloody mess coming down the finishing stretch. I choke back tears of relief. I've vanquished the demons of self-pity and fear. I'm not unscathed, but I am victorious.

In my running circles, I'm known as a roadie. People ask me why I decided to run Imogene. Until I raced it, I didn't have a good answer. Because it's a bucket list race if you live in Flagstaff? Because all my friends were going for a 50th birthday party?

In hindsight, I understand why this race has such a cult following. Running that mountain took everything I had. It occurs to me that "thinking like a mountain" means understanding something dangerous, something palpable about wildness, that isn't possible without encountering a force of nature that will push you to the point where you're no longer in control. In such moments you're ruled by your instincts. Your sole purpose becomes survival. Human beings seek out these experiences as a means of understanding something elemental about themselves. People ask me whether I will run the IPR again. The truth is, that race scared the shit out of me. I learned my lesson.

Banged up by the race (above) but happy to be on the podium (below) in 2017.

Man, that was so tough

BY JIM STRAIGHT

I HAD SAID MY ENTIRE ADULT LIFE THAT I DIDN'T LIKE running. Then one winter, I decided I wasn't going to accept that statement anymore since I hadn't run in so long, and I started running for the first time in about 20 years.

By the beginning of my second year, I was being told by a number of friends that if I am a runner in Flagstaff, I have to do the Imogene Pass Run. At coffee on May 31, 2018, my training partners and I (we call ourselves "Team Tortuga") decided to register the next morning.

The idea of trying to run up and over a mountain pass in the San Juans had always been, in my opinion, "dumb" or "idiotic" or any number of opinions that I would spout off like an angry old man. Then I signed up. At just after 5:00 a.m., I sent my confirmation email to the team. I soon found out I was the only one who had registered. One teammate "forgot about the time difference," even though he had signed up for the run many times. One said he was already kind of injured. One just decided not to. Tortugas! How do you say "I guess I'm on my own" in Spanish?

Later, I did talk to a couple non-Tortuga friends who had signed up, making me feel a little more comfortable with my decision. As Imogene got closer, though, for a number of reasons some of those people also bowed out.

With my wife and some friends along to provide pre- and postrace "hydration," I had a nice support crew, but it still felt like I was rolling into Telluride all by myself. I was admittedly nervous. But my nerves disappeared almost immediately when I started seeing Flagstaff friends all over town. I'd been told that Telluride feels like a mini-Flagstaff during Imogene weekend, but I was blown away by how that felt. Maybe you don't have regular contact with all these people throughout the year, but when you see them in Telluride and Ouray, it's something special. The love affair is real, and Flagstaff represents itself well.

I enjoy the Flagstaff Summer Series because even after only two years of competing, I have a familiarity with the people, courses, and even packet pickups. But with its distance, elevation gain, altitude, number of participants, bus ride to Ouray, etc., Imogene was a completely new experience.

Although it's called a "run," I knew how competitive the IPR is. Finishing was my No. 1 goal, but I wanted to honor that spirit and go as fast as possible. As I toed the line, my competitive juices kicked in. All of a sudden, I wanted to pass the person in front of me and not let anyone go around me.

The race went mostly as expected. My finishing time was right around where I thought it would be. I knew it would be a big "suffer-fest," which it was. I went as fast as I could for as long as possible. The views were over-the-top beautiful. I had a difficult time getting up and over the Pass. It seemed like dozens of people passed me in the last two miles before I got to the Pass, which was difficult to process. I totally forgot to have soup at the top, partly because my brain had a third of the oxygen it normally has, and partly because my competitive juices were flowing. I wanted to get back ahead of all the runners who had just gone past me. I don't remember going around anyone on the way down, which was frustrating at the time. In my experience, the Imogene Pass "Run" was definitely a race.

When I got close to Telluride, my emotions overflowed. I was raised to think men don't cry, but I'm not ashamed to say my emotions brought me to tears about two miles from the finish. I was overwhelmed to complete something I had previously thought impossible. I was grateful for my friends and especially my beautiful wife, JoLena, waiting for me on Oak Street.

Also, it is so beautiful coming down into Telluride. The views themselves can bring you to tears if you focus on them enough.

There was a cold beer in my hand by the time I crossed the finish line… support crew for the win! Over the next couple hours, I probably ate half a dozen Palisades peaches. I am convinced they have healing powers. I sat down for a couple hours just watching participants finish. If you need motivation for anything, sit on Oak Street the second Saturday in September and just watch.

I ended up with many other racers soaking in the creek postrace for a while, drinking and talking about how difficult the morning was. JoLena had to tell me to quit saying, "Man, that was so tough." I guess when you push yourself up to the limit and over a mountain pass, it is tough to get the thoughts out of your head.

I used to think the only times you should cry are if a dog dies or if the Cleveland Indians win the World Series. I guess you can add finishing the Imogene Pass Run to the list. There really is no other love affair like this one, in which so many people in my town push themselves to the limit. They run and race up and over a towering mountain pass and down into a breathtaking valley and love (almost) every minute of it.

I dream of Imogene

BY CLAUDINE TAILLAC

BECAUSE PEOPLE DON'T KNOW MUCH ABOUT RUNNING, I am often mistaken for a runner. It's possible I resemble a runner in some ways—at least to people who do not know any real runners. Outwardly, things must add up. On the spectrum of fitness, I am nowhere near the low end, but neither am I at the level of a dedicated endurance runner. When this mistake happens, I get asked the question that stumps me more than any other: "Are you a runner?"

I pause. It's an uncomfortable pause. Images of myself running come to mind. Yes, I run. I have countless memories now of putting on my trail shoes and hitting the trail, just like runners do. That pause is me trying to not bust out with the truth, which is that while I am lacing my shoes, I am overcome by the competing emotions of dread and fear. Questions run swiftly through my mind.

"Will this hurt?"

"When will this be over?" (It hasn't started yet.)

"What is the minimum I have to run today to reach my future goals?"

"I wonder if I will ever enjoy this?"

I dream, "If only I could run that fast…".

So, am I a runner? Somehow, I doubt it.

This won't come as a surprise to my boyfriend: I have a love/anti-love relationship with running… and with runners.

A Thwarted Running Life

Here's a memory: I am six, seven, eight, nine, ten years old. I am in the back seat of the green Impala, a cavernous well that carries me unbidden on a day I should be at school. Past the car window, the golden rolling hills of suburbia at some point give way to the gray blur of urban Oakland. The day is spent at Oakland Children's Hospital, with friendly nurses dabbing cold goop on my bare chest and then attaching nodes of some sort that are also attached to a machine. Then the judgment begins. Said machine records just how defective my heart is compared to last year.

It turns out that the defect—mild mitral valve prolapse—is epic and dangerous only in my mother's mind. But I am given an excuse anyway, a written one, from my chain-smoking cardiologist to skip all activities involving running during P.E. class at school.

So that's what I do: I don't run. During any running that happens in P.E., I stay clad in my heather-blue P.E. shirt with the dark-blue trim and the dark-blue shorts. The best thing is finding a walnut tree where the ground is littered with suitable halved walnuts that, when dragged on the ground using the bottom of my non-running running shoe, are worn down and can be turned into buttons. I'm a gymnast, so this time is also spent on cartwheels and back walkovers, as I watch my classmates huff up the steep hill next to the schoolyard.

At some point later in life, I turn 40. And I start to run.

Imogene Is for Amazing People

Setting the stage in this way, one might ask how I ended up on the long, steep trail that leads to Imogene Pass. Well, ignorance is ~~bliss~~ ignorance, and when my boyfriend, Gunter Ziwey, and I signed up online at 5:00 a.m. one morning in June 2017, I really had no idea what I was signing up to do. Signing up was easy! I had this. Lots of people totally bonked and missed the signup. Real runners, in fact, missed the signup. I had already cleared the first obstacle.

Flagstaff's almost cult-like obsession with Imogene is well documented. My inaugural experience with it was in 2013. Tagging along on a trip to Telluride was one of the first things I did after moving back to Flagstaff after a three-year absence. I had friends who had done Imogene many times, and they were going, and I had recently begun dating a runner. A real runner. So I went. And afterward, I was left with the overriding impression that Imogene was for amazing people. I was totally impressed and knew without a doubt I would never, could never, do it. And that was fine with me. I was happy challenging myself with the little bit of running I had started to do. It would help me hike the Grand Canyon better, and I liked the feeling of being freed from that handwritten excuse from long ago.

The high of clearing the signup hurdle was soon dispatched by Gunter's insistence that training should begin now. Now? The race was three months away! Sheesh. Of course I knew I would have to spend time and effort training. But in the future... Thankfully, I listened to him, and training commenced.

I can't remember exactly when I fully understood that this race was going to be hard, really hard, and that training—no, excuse me—the specific way I trained would make all the difference. So I started to be more strategic with my training. I even started telling people *I was training for Imogene.* Another huge hurdle: saying it out loud. Then all the advice began pouring in. Veteran Imogeners were everywhere, at the Athlete's Flow yoga class on Mondays, in line for iced tea at Macy's, and of course on Friday nights at Pay-N-Take. All of them had a different take on what mattered in training. TFR: Train For Recovery. Train for the downhill. Run 30 miles a week, minimum. Run up and down Schultz Pass Road once a week, plus other runs, and a week before the race, run up and down Schultz Pass Road twice in a row. Do as many high-elevation, steep peaks near Flagstaff as I could between signup and the race. Start drinking beet juice a week before the race (this one seemed like some sort of secret weapon).

So I did these things, and I did them early in the morning when I would rather be in bed, and I did them when it was hot, and when it was windy, and even when I was getting pelted with monsoon rain and hail. Hardest of all, sometimes I did them with people who were also training—people I didn't know—and the only thing harder for me than running is running with other runners *whom I do not know.* I was added to a mass text about when and where to meet up to train. I had entered a foreign land.

I trained alone a lot, and I began to love the rhythm of my own rhythm, of planning my route on the mountain and being so absorbed by my legs and lungs working, my feet churning, that I got lost on trails I knew well, several times, and ended up running more miles than planned.

Anxieties

The eating I was doing was astonishing, and it was exhilarating to gorge on lox and bagels with my Gunter after workouts and talk about the training. I was beginning to not recognize myself, and I still had no idea what TFR meant. This worried me a bit, but clearly I had bigger things to concern myself with, like how exactly I was going to get up and down that mountain even with all the training. I had never run more than 10 miles at one time before. I started reading about the race over and over.

Contradictions such as "incessant forward motion" and "stop to smell the roses" were plentiful.

And then I learned about the cutoff, this cruel, Zeus-like twist that was surely designed to ferret out the fake runners such as myself. And then I knew it; I would not make the cutoff. From all the training, I knew my pace, and my panicked calculations seemed to belie the idea that I could make it to the cutoff, which loomed at the 7½-mile mark after a grueling uphill climb at an insane grade, at a crushing altitude. This is the point at which my training regimen started to include losing sleep.

People everywhere wanted to talk about Imogene: the lady who cut my hair downtown assured me that I would run three minutes per mile faster during the race than I did while training. I especially liked this random information, even though she had no facts to back it up, as it helped me believe I could make the cutoff.

One person told me how distractingly annoying her arms were to her on the uphill (a new thing to worry about). Another told me about the deep snow the year she did it and the ice she slipped and fell on at the top (holy @#*!) only to hit her head, look up, and see her husband looming over her, telling her to get up if she wanted to make her time (these two runners, I actually like a lot).

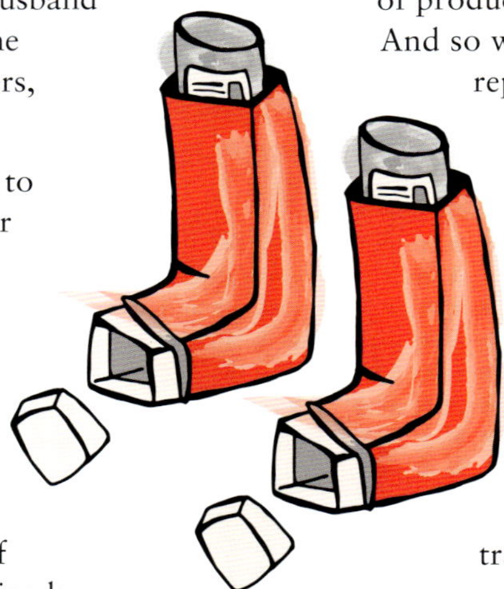

Other people told me what to bring, what to wear. Long discussions ensued with Gunter about what we should bring, what we should wear. Overnight, I had become a menace to pedicurists throughout Flagstaff for how trashed and calloused my feet were. Soon, pedicures ceased altogether. I started texting my BFF in Texas (a veteran Imogener) about my training runs, which was kind of a way of keeping myself honest with my training. Friends were starting to predict my time. I was starting to figure out exactly the kind of insanity I had signed up for on that innocuous June morning.

I was officially, categorically nervous.

And then my BFF from Texas said she was coming, not to race but to be my bandit pacer. I had no idea what this was, but I said yes, yes, yes to the bandit pacer!

Things were going well; I couldn't believe it. I was training and enjoying it. Yes, all my other favorite summer activities were going by the wayside, but I had a goal. My runner boyfriend and I were doing a real running event together. It was going to be great.

Disaster Strikes

As with any good suspense story, be most afraid when things are going smoothly. I suppose I should have been glancing behind for the ensuing disaster, but the excitement of producing visible progress made me forget to glance back. And so when the library where I work started the carpet-replacement project, I thought nothing of it.

To clarify: all of the carpet was torn out, which is specifically the layer of carpet that had been installed over the first layer of carpet from 30 years prior. The air was filled with ancient dust and debris floating into our nostrils and lungs. And then came the noxious glue, which was applied before the off-gassing new carpet could be laid. Many felt the effects; dormant asthma flared up right and left. To my astonishment, this included me: the not-real-runner who was training for the run of her life.

Two inhalers later, I could barely train. The race was five weeks away, and I was sick.

Anger has never been a go-to emotion for me, but I have heard how motivating it can be. As I was morphing in unexpected ways due to Imogene training, I had also

My Imogene Mantra:
"Comparison is the thief of joy."

changed emotionally. I got angry. I had trained hard, and I felt almost ready when this disaster struck. Instead of worrying now about what to wear and the cutoff, I was worrying about getting to the starting line. And the anger worked; I was determined.

I felt like hell, but the race hadn't yet begun, which meant it wasn't over yet, either.

A week before the race, Gunter and I left for Colorado, our bags packed with energy goo and blocks and the specially ordered beet juice. The plan was to hole up in a remote, high-elevation cabin that had no electricity and soaring views. I would escape the carpet-installation project at work; we would acclimate to the higher altitude; we would hike; we would run just a little; we would soak in some hot springs. And it worked. I started to feel a lot better, although the inhalers were still necessary.

Two days before the race, we drove to Ouray to check out the start of the course. We set out together up the first hill and then he quickly left me behind. I looked around and got a feel for the ground, a sense of the uphill stretches and how they eventually leveled. It was good to get acquainted with what awaited me, but the race had also become real, and I was unsure how I felt about that.

Race Day

There is a unique atmosphere created by the invasion of Imogene runners upon Telluride. Even to those on the periphery, the energy is electric. For me, a person living in the space between, of being kind of a runner but kind of a non-runner, it was a fun fall down the rabbit hole. Gunter and our condo-mates were all real runners, people who had competed their whole lives and had the wins and record times to validate their participation. I refrained from comparing our experiences, reminding myself of the summer's mantra given to me by a dear friend: comparison is the thief of joy. Because, dammit, I was going to enjoy this.

The mantra paid off, because the drive to the race early that Saturday morning revealed everyone's nerves, even Gunter's, although he had once competed in the Olympic Trials. Kate McGee, who would be the first female finisher (see page 64), was especially nervous and doubtful. It was the 50th birthday of another companion, Rob Fleet, which counted as two milestones in one day for him. I sat in the backseat next to a blessedly unruly five-year-old (there is no better distraction from fear) and was just thrilled to be feeling better, and happy for Gunter, so often sidelined by injury, who was feeling strong and who would go on to place second in his age group.

All of my companions' impressive feats were yet to come. We all still had to face the starting line, and although there were more than 1,600 other people gathered, ultimately we were each alone.

A Face for Every Mile

It took forever for the race to begin, and then it began before I was ready. The first mile was rough, not physically but mentally. The mass of people was a new and uncomfortable experience for me. I wanted to quit, to run back to the car, that entire mile. Who was this person, me, who was doing this race? I had an acute and sharp memory of being there years before with complete certainty that I *would never have such an experience*—a contradiction larger than the mountain I was running up.

And then suddenly, I was just back training, knowing I was doing this thing, just this thing, for a handful of hours. That's when the race began.

I was supported by my BFF, who fed me energy blocks at exactly the right time, each time. I was moved to tears by the volunteers and awed by the sight of the route snaking up, up, and ahead of me, and the coursing of human forms in the distance, every one of those foreign bodies reaching out collectively for individual achievement. I thought of everyone I loved. That's how I clocked the miles—a face for each one.

The higher I climbed and the less oxygen available to my muscles, the more intense became the gratitude for my life, for the people in it. I could feel Fon Cordasco there, and I looked at the other runners, some of whom wore BLE (Best Life Ever) socks and T-shirts, and pictured them with the same thought bubble over their heads as I had: Fon's love for this race and her infectious enthusiasm that had brought so many others to also love it.

Annie Dillard wrote that "how we spend our days is, of course, how we spend our lives," and I was spending this day.

Free to Fly

Upper Camp Bird, the dreaded cutoff, came and went. There were a couple of comforting, familiar Flagstaff faces there, and although I still had more than half of the race to complete, I was solid because the prospect of quitting had faded away long ago. I was free to fly because I had made the cutoff with a lot of time to spare. I allowed myself a glance back instead of always forward, and with pleasure realized I was not in last place.

The race itself is spectacular and not. The route climbs high to the point of light-headedness, which I experienced after Upper Camp Bird to an extent that I could not focus on anything but the feet in front of mine for fear of falling off the trail. The Pass was nothing overly momentous—a pause, a selfie with the BFF, a breath taken, a look around. A chance for an eyes-to-the-sky moment of quiet gratitude.

I hadn't planned on experiencing any of it the way I did, and it was superb. I had become part of it, whatever "it" was. I don't think "it" was the race at all.

The treacherous downhill running was overshadowed by the song in my head: I had done it! There were still seven miles to go, but I had taken the advice and trained for the downhill, people! There were plenty of fallen soldiers on the downhill, bloody messes that required more attention than my good heart could have provided. I just kept going. I wasn't myself. Something else had taken over, and I was happy to be the passenger, flinging this foreign body down a mine-filled trail with total abandon. At least, that's how it felt. I still wasn't running as fast as most, but I did make some successful passes.

The Roar of the Crowd

And then there were two miles to go. Because I don't like public attention, the fog that contained the dread of the finish line started to appear. It slowly edged its way higher and higher, until I was wishing for a way to escape. And then it happened: the roar of the crowd! Never in my life would I have thought I would experience the roar of the crowd. I was still lucid enough to understand that the roar was not for me specifically but, rather, for me collectively. Regardless, it worked. The last two miles were a wonder of cowbells and cheers flowing from the finish line; all of those strangers wishing us well. Beauty, beauty, beauty.

The rest is the rest. In the end, I ran it 50 minutes faster than I thought I would. My friends got awards, and I reveled in their successes. Celebration after great effort with others who have also efforted and those who have cheered, filled with love for those who are there, those who are not, and those who are gone from us forever, is a mixture so complex yet crystal clear that it reflects the gods.

I did all of the requisite things: crossed the finish line, lost toenails, and came to understand what TFR means. I think that, for at least a while, I will measure my challenges by Imogene, and hopefully—hopefully—I will continue to remember those miles filled with gratitude for this life, whatever it is, and for those I love. Without them, it would have been just a thing.

Mad-Lib

MY FIRST IMOGENE: A FLAGSTAFF VIRGIN'S STORY

1. Flagstaff runner ______
2. adjective ______
3. number ______
4. number ______
5. large animal ______
6. body part ______
7. verb ______
8. time ______
9. number ______
10. adjective ______
11. name of Flagstaff trail ______
12. a food ______
13. a drink ______
14. famous athlete ______
15. song lyric ______
16. a Flagstaff restaurant ______
17. adjective ______
18. plural noun ______
19. plural noun ______
20. brand of car ______
21. international landmark ______
22. plural magical animal ______
23. name of your first pet ______
24. favorite comfort food ______
25. adverb ______
26. running cliché ______
27. noun ______
28. noun ______
29. number ______
30. adjective ______
31. adjective ______
32. plural smelly objects ______
33. adverb ______
34. number ______
35. larger number ______
36. verb ending in -s ______
37. past-tense verb ending in -ed ______
38. dead celebrity ______
39. past-tense verb ending in -ed ______
40. adverb or expletive ______
41. job title ______
42. past-tense verb ending in -ed ______
43. cartoon character ______
44. food item ______
45. item found in a doctor's office ______
46. a superhero ______
47. body part ______
48. gerund/-ing verb ______
49. verb ______
50. verb ending in -ing ______
51. verb ending in -ing ______
52. adjective ______
53. favorite drink ______
54. past-tense verb ending in -ed ______
55. your name ______
56. bucket-list item ______
57. dream date ______
58. past-tense verb ending in -ed ______
59. emotion ______

Mad-Lib

MY FIRST IMOGENE: A FLAGSTAFF VIRGIN'S STORY

My friend ______________ (FLAGSTAFF RUNNER) was the first person to tell me about the Imogene Pass Run. Apparently I had to do it if I wanted to call myself a ______________ (ADJECTIVE) Flagstaff runner. I said, "Imo-WHAT?"

Then my friend told me this race is ________ (NUMBER) miles long, up and over a Colorado mountain pass that's ________ (NUMBER) feet high. It feels like you're carrying a ______________ (LARGE ANIMAL) on your ______________ (BODY PART) at the really steep parts.

It sounded absolutely crazy. But inside me a voice started whispering, "You can ______________ (VERB) this."

I set my alarm for ________ (TIME) on June 1 and after ________ (NUMBER) tries, I got in… I was registered for this ______________ (ADJECTIVE) race.

I was reasonably fit, but now it was time to train for Imogene! So I ran on the ______________ (NAME OF FLAGSTAFF TRAIL), ate lots of ______________ (A FOOD), and drank plenty of ______________ (A DRINK). My training partner ______________ (FAMOUS ATHLETE) was always there with me, telling me "______________ (SONG LYRIC)" during our post-workout talks at ______________ (A FLAGSTAFF RESTAURANT).

It turns out that one of the biggest decisions to make before Imogene is whether to stay in Ouray or Telluride. Ouray is more ______________ (ADJECTIVE), while Telluride has all the ______________ (PLURAL NOUN). It was a tough choice.

Finally, race weekend was here. I drove to Colorado with a few extra ______________ (PLURAL NOUN) packed into my ______________ (BRAND OF CAR). Along the way, we saw the ______________ (INTERNATIONAL LANDMARK) and a few ______________ (PLURAL MAGICAL ANIMAL).

After settling in at the ______________ (NAME OF YOUR FIRST PET) Hot Springs, I carbo-loaded on ______________ (FAVORITE COMFORT FOOD) and then went to packet pickup. Since this was my first Imogene, I stayed for race orientation. There was a slideshow with scary pictures of the steep trail. This is when I first heard the phrase, "______________ (ADVERB) forward motion." I heard it in my dreams all night long.

Getting dressed in the dark the next morning, I reminded myself, "______________ (RUNNING CLICHÉ)." As I packed, I realized I had remembered to bring ______________ (NOUN) but forgotten ____________ (NOUN). What would I do without it?

At the starting line, I saw ________ (NUMBER) other ____________ (ADJECTIVE) Flagstaffians all feeling as ________________ (ADJECTIVE) as I did. No Flagstaff runner is ever alone at the Imogene starting line.

We listened to the race director reminding us all to enjoy the day and stop to smell the ________________ (PLURAL SMELLY OBJECTS) along the way. We laughed ________________ (ADVERB) as we pondered what we were getting ready to do.

In those first two miles, there was a huge crowd. At Lower Camp Bird, when you're _______ (NUMBER) miles in but it feels like __________ (LARGER NUMBER), I remembered what they said at orientation; "This is where the race __________ (VERB ENDING IN -S)." I ________________ (PAST-TENSE VERB ENDING IN -ED) hard toward the Upper Camp Bird cutoff, and I made it. Phew!

In the next few miles, I got above treeline and saw what I thought was the top of Imogene Pass. Wrong! It was the infamous false summit, tricking me into thinking I was almost there. As the air thinned, I began having hallucinations; I think I saw ________________________ (DEAD CELEBRITY).

I know I saw a marmot wearing a puffy yellow jacket. As I ____________ (PAST-TENSE VERB ENDING IN -ED) toward the real Pass, I felt more and more ______________ (ADVERB OR EXPLETIVE). But at the top of the steepest part, a ______________ (JOB TITLE) from Colorado search-and-rescue gave me a hand up onto the final road. I could have ______________ (PAST-TENSE VERB ENDING IN -ED) him.

Finally, I made it to Imogene Pass! Someone dressed as ______________ (CARTOON CHARACTER) took my photo at the sign. I grabbed handfuls of ____________________ (FOOD ITEM) and ______________________ (ITEM FOUND IN A DOCTOR'S OFFICE) from the aid station table. Feeling like ____________________ (A SUPERHERO), I took off on the first downhill stretch, my ____________________ (BODY PART) chafing and my heart __________________ (GERUND/-ING VERB). Somewhere on the downhill, I started to ________________ (VERB). The people around me were ________________ (VERB ENDING IN -ING), but I just kept ______________ (VERB ENDING IN -ING). As we got closer to Telluride, it all began to seem very ________________ (ADJECTIVE). Suddenly, there I was, running down Oak Street! Someone put a ________________ (FAVORITE DRINK) in my hand. I think my legs __________________ (PAST-TENSE VERB ENDING IN -ED). And then, as I crossed the finish line, I heard the announcer call out, "____________________ (YOUR NAME), from Flagstaff, Arizona!" All I wanted to do was ______________________ (BUCKET-LIST ITEM) with ______________________ (DREAM DATE) 'til I ________________________ (PAST-TENSE VERB ENDING IN -ED). Finally, I was a full-fledged citizen of Flagstaff, the Running Nation. It felt __________________ (EMOTION).

______________________________________ (YOUR NAME) ______________ (DATE)

part 4

I Just Can't Quit You

Lovers so devoted, they keep coming back for more

That race in Colorado

BY SARA WAGNER

WHEN I THINK OF IMOGENE, ANDRA COMES TO MIND. I moved to the Southwest in 1999. My colleague Andra Battocchio at the Navajo Area Indian Health Service in Chinle was always talking about the Imogene Pass Run. I mean always. Andra developed an injury that precluded her from doing the race for a while; she was devastated—then elated, once she could do it again.

Curious about why this race was so significant, one day I looked it up online. The race website featured a picture of a woman with long, dark hair smiling atop a mountain in shorts and a long-sleeve shirt. I could relate to her. From time to time I'd revisit the website. She was still there, happy and strong. She became my beacon. It wouldn't be till I lived in Flagstaff, many years later, that I would get my first taste of the Imogene Pass Run.

Racing the downhill, 2012.

That year was 2008. A Flagstaff friend, Al Hendricks, and his wife, Sarah, invited me to join them. I rode to and from the race with Bob Steele, who was staying really close to us in Ouray. The Hendricks were one of those couples who had done Imogene an inconceivable number of times. Their tradition was to stay in Ouray and rent a place with Dr. Richard Haag (my former dentist, before he retired) and his wife, as well as Dr. Walt and Nancy Taylor.

The Haags couldn't make it that year, so it was me and everyone else, plus Flagstaff newbie Paul Saladino.

At the prerace meeting, I learned that the race's origins involved Rick Trujillo chasing deer up the mountain and that "Imogene" was meant to be pronounced like a woman's name. We enjoyed Nancy's homemade pasta sauce and the rest of a really tasty meal that Friday night, before making our way to Main Street the next morning. The starting line in Ouray on race day morning is in a class of its own.

Me with Caleb Schiff, 2013.

Countless familiar faces surround you, from myriad life chapters. For these moments in time, before the race starts, hundreds spill out into the streets, in this place that becomes timeless. The years swirl together. We become one, as race director John Jett delivers his megaphone address, preparing us for the journey ahead.

That first year, I had the good fortune of starting the race with Keri Nelson (it would be my only chance to do so, since it was the last year she did the race). I can still see her yellow La Sportiva kit, before she disappeared around one of those first bends on the climb. She's a Gunnison legend I will always respect. She was just as kind as she was fast (I met this course record–holder and her mom in that little park where the awards ceremony is held, postrace; in contrast to her racing demeanor, she offered gentle, gracious words, and wore a top adorned with tiny, delicate flowers).

I experienced the joys of Imogene Pass that day. I made it all the way up, the highest I had ever been, thrilled to discover the top wasn't as sketchy as Flagstaff friends had made it out to be. That day I also discovered the delights of Tomboy Road and what it's like to descend into Telluride on foot, the town slowly taking shape. The road relaxed me because its surface reminded me of the road to Sandy Creek—a coveted swimming hole when I was a kid—so to me it's always been the beach road, where a fun reward awaits at its end. Rounding the final corner and seeing the chute, that one-of-a-kind, human-lined, best-downhill-anywhere to that glorious finish line, is a fabulous experience. Oh the cheers!!!! Ohh those juicy Colorado peaches!!! Ohhh that homemade chicken noodle soup!! Ohhhh the elation of having completed this particular race!

Ohh those juicy Colorado peaches!!! Ohhh that homemade chicken noodle soup!! Ohhhh the elation of having completed this particular race!

I placed third overall for women that year and won my age group, as I would the next time I tried, in 2011. In 2012, with Denver's Sarah Pizzo just 23.5 seconds behind me, I earned my first hand-blown glass vase, with "First Place Female" etched in by a local artist. That win was hard-fought. While I had led to Upper Camp Bird, two women went by me shortly thereafter.

At this point in the race, one still has to climb awhile at an average gradient of nearly 15 percent before reaching Imogene Pass. Sarah was just ahead of me in this stretch and was a great motivator; beyond being someone to focus on, she gave me encouraging words when I needed them most. As we approached the Pass, the terrain leveled out and there were a few moments to take in the stunning scenery: incredibly beautiful mountains, clouds, and sky. Then we switched gears, and the race was on to the finish!

There were four of us in contention near the top, so it was a true race down the mountain. I was really fit due to Chicago Marathon training (thanks to my coach, Mike Smith, who had me doing all kinds of crazy workouts that summer) and attempted to fly. I took a nasty spill on the steep downgrade while descending into Tomboy Basin a couple of miles from the top. Upright again, I regained confidence. I went on to have one of my best races ever.

In 2013, during the 40th annual event, I again encountered Sarah. She was the last person I wanted to see as I approached Lower Camp Bird! "Back for more fun?" she said, and we ground it out together once more. That year I earned my second vase, with a new personal best time.

Sarah has one of those runner dads (who had even raced Imogene in the 1970s!). He was right there after we once again crossed the finish line 1-2, both running our fastest times. We became friends.

Above left: With Sarah Pizzo postrace, 2013.
Above right: Racing the downhill, 2012.

In 2016, I cheered her on during the Flagstaff Sky Race, meeting her and Paco (her husband) the night before. A month later, during the USATF Marathon Trail Championships in Moab, Utah, Sarah easily passed me, imploring, "C'mon, buddy."

I was so honored when Sarah asked me to sign the new, pink "Trail Sisters" trucker hat she brought to the awards ceremony. Everyone was sitting around a campfire when she handed me a marker. I sheepishly added my name to the mix of women she looked up to (which included Skyrunner® World Series Champion Emelie Forsberg and ultra/Skyrunning phenom Anna Frost). She invited me to camp with her, her husband, and other friends of theirs that night, not far from where the race took place (already a badass attorney, she went on to earn a spot on the U.S. Trail Team that competed in the 2018 Trail World Championships in Spain).

Sarah Pizzo and me after my 2012 fall.

These cobalt-blue vases are right up there with my most prized possessions. I feel it's our Flagstaff community, bolstering everyone, that helps us beat runners from Colorado (and other locales) who have a plethora of nearby mountains to train in. Every aspect of this event is special, just like the years. Favorite snapshots in time include Nat White playing a colorful plastic trombone from an unexpected perch above Tomboy ghost town (cheering on Flag runners between tunes) and Darlene Ryan and her husband, Peter Rosenthal, offering heartfelt words and hydration from Tomboy aid station, eliciting smiles and a boost of energy.

In 2012, a remarkable number of us were falling—we blamed it on loose surface rocks. We found our way to the medical tent postrace and were comparing notes; that is, until Ray Lobato showed up. We all fell silent. He was covered in blood from head to toe, having made a final dive across the finish line (also known as the Shirtless Wonder, he prefers to race sans shirt, so perhaps he simply had more exposed skin than the rest of us… he had fallen three times during the race!).

A tremendous surprise awaited me there. A pair of 10-year-old girls, Annalea and Mia (daughters of new friends), had followed me in. Without saying a word, each took one of my shoulders and began massaging it while medical staff tended to me. After that, they retrieved my bag from the finish line, helped me get warm clothes out/on, and brought me all kinds of delicious postrace nourishment.

They treated me like a queen. I was blown away by their maturity in knowing this would help me recover and replenish. These are the rewards of being part of a community. Even the young ones are observing us—and wanting to contribute.

I had an unanticipated incentive to try hard in 2012. The friend I was traveling with, David McKee, was at least 90 minutes late arriving to my house, which delayed us getting on the road. I hadn't heard from him and was wishing I'd slept in—or been doing anything other than sitting there waiting for him! Then he pulled up and wheeled a tiny, custom-built bike up to my porch, saying I could keep it if I won the race.

To explain the context: My first-ever mountain race was a snowshoe event at the Tennessee Pass Nordic Center in Leadville in 2006; unaccustomed to altitude, I finished last. I was working for Kahtoola at the time and had traveled to and from that race with David and my coworker friend Brian Cannon. This gift was meaningful because David knew I didn't have a reliable bike and had resurrected a vintage one, painting it "Badger Red" to remind of my home state of Wisconsin, and also because he knew how far I had come since I first arrived in Flagstaff.

•••

Fellow runners (some known to me, others just kindred spirits) say and do the most kind-hearted things because of Imogene. The unique feelings this race elicits are forever emblazoned upon my memory. It's wonderful we have a proud tradition of sending more runners to this race than any Colorado town.

We don't get there alone, and we don't enjoy triumphs in isolation. While the names of stellar Colorado women (aside from those already mentioned, people like Cindy O'Neill and Stacey Chamberlain, who pushed me to train harder) and men will always be esteemed, it's truly amazing to hear "Flagstaff" called for nearly every category at the cozy awards ceremony, from the 15-year-old age division on up. In 2011, John Jett finally just started saying, "And now from the great Running Nation of Flagstaff...". It's awesome to be part of this.

I'm richer for knowing the steep route that connects these distinctive towns, and especially for those I've shared the journey with.

My Imogene scar from 2012 has faded, but these memories I cherish have grown more prominent. I am grateful for having made the trek to Ouray and Telluride. I'm richer for knowing the steep route that connects these distinctive towns, and especially for those I've shared the journey with.

The mass exodus of Flag runners is greeted by extraordinary people like my Flagstaff neighbor Eric Whiteman, who owns a centrally located condo in Telluride. Rather than turning a profit by renting it out on this popular race weekend, he tells me to go up early to relax, adding, "Bring your friends—this is my donation to the Flagstaff running community."

I've had just four doses of Imogene. I can only imagine how this event has impacted those like Al and Sarah, who have done the race 20 times or more. The indelible impression left by the late Fon Cordasco, a phenomenally courageous woman most of us feel we knew—by virtue of sharing the same community and passion—speak to the power of the Imogene Pass Run. Billy Cordasco (Fon's husband) created bracelets that many of us wear. "IMOGENE PASS" is imprinted inside (much like it is always inside us, now). The outside reads, "BREATHE FREE," with an appeal to "TOUCH THE SKY."

We all need a Ctrl Alt Delete on life

BY CARRIE BUTLER

MY ANNUAL PILGRIMAGE TO TELLURIDE FOR THE Imogene Pass Run is a core event planned far in advance. Apparently, my decision is made rather zealously, deep in the heart where life's most meaningful decisions should always be made if I'm doing it right. That's because, if I were deciding to go each year based on logic and practicality alone, I doubt it would happen. Yet there's something about the legendary event which makes it right, despite all the reasons not to do it.

Celebrating at the Pass, 2017.

One must admit, it's a little gut-punch to the pocketbook. Costs for gas, lodging for three nights, pizza at Brown Dog (of course), groceries, drinks, and the random impulse buys can tap you out when you're traveling as a family. I've noticed the town of Telluride relies on our relaxed, indulgent state of mind to feed a very vibrant, tourism-based economy. Sticker shock from the prices tends to mellow after a few days and we happily become stewards of the fiscal health of the community, contributing our fair share to ensure it continues to thrive well into the future.

Then, there's the hit to life's fundamentals: home, work, and school. Imogene is always the first week in September, feverishly busy for most families. Yet for us, we honor this obligatory tradition by devoting four days to it. We travel up on Thursday, two days before the race. This allows time to be leisurely spent settling in, acclimating to the slight boost in altitude, shopping for groceries, meandering around town, sharing beers with friends, perusing the farmers market, and whimsically absorbing the beauty and unique geographical wonders surrounding us. Yet our tariff is missing two whole days of work and school.

Deciding to register for the run can be an agonizing decision in itself. The frenzied scramble to log on and register at 5:00 a.m. (Arizona time) on the first of June is only intensified by knowing that a gajillion other people are frantically trying to secure a bib number along with you, all in the course of about a 25-minute window that shrinks even more every single year. I suppose the whole registration craze is one of the allures—a little taste of the electricity and rush this unforgettable race brings.

Then if you're lucky, you're in! You realize you've willingly chosen to endure a true suffer-fest complete with the rigors of training, which is undeniably an investment. Hucking yourself up and over the Pass as quickly as you can manage takes work in the distance, technical trail, and altitude departments of running. Many days of physically stretching your limits and challenging your mind along the three-month journey lie ahead. Carving out time to train around work and family obligations can easily sour the joys that mountain running brings, if you let it. It's a balancing act that can get tricky.

Here's the deal. Committing to this special race each year takes a bite out of my finances and shakes up any life-work homeostasis I may have struck. Yet, like so many others in Flagstaff, I find myself longing to experience the BLE (Best Life Ever) magic surrounding Imogene. All of the reasons not to do it are simply outshined by the more meaningful motivations as to why I must.

I would guess this is also true for many in the Flagstaff running community who come to participate too. Casually connecting with this matrix, you quickly discover the common denominator that binds us—a communal health and vibrancy gained by living, breathing, and running in Flagstaff. Collectively, we also know we have a cool advantage "representing" Flagstaff, where we often dominate the podium. Flagstaff friends easily open up during post-race beers to share their love of the race and tell personal stories of various glories and plights of races past. The tales tend to float around personal highlights, i.e., running partners, bad weather, falls, food, complications, times, DNFs, and many unexpected adventures. I believe the morning spent crossing over the 13,114-foot Pass is still insatiable fun! And judging by the hoots, hollers, and smiles at the top, it is for most everyone else too.

For so many of us, the run lets us shake out stresses and center ourselves again. It's like my own "control-alt-delete" each year. The rewards of it, coupled with the challenges of it, harmonize perfectly. It ensures I nourish my physical health and well-being all year long, which plays into my positive role modeling for my daughter to also live a balanced life. I'll continue to return as long as the traditions, challenges, and burning motivation to live the Best Life Ever continue to lure me. Imogene Pass Run is so much more than just a race. The relationship one has with the event is personal. For me, it translates as a metaphor of life, akin to the endless, personal mountains we continually climb.

Imogene again? Ha! Absolutely, yes.

My ever-expanding Imogene family

BAKED IN TELLURIDE, CHICKEN SOUP, AND THE HAND OF GOD

BY TESS SIEMENS

FOR JUST ABOUT AS LONG AS I CAN REMEMBER, September has marked one of my favorite family traditions: the Imogene Pass Run. My mom, Margaret Montfort, ran her first in 2005 (see page 181) when I was seven years old, and it became a de facto family holiday the moment she made it up and over the Pass. She fell in love with the race, the people, and Telluride in the fall. She made sure to be up at the crack of dawn the day of registration almost every year to guarantee her reason to go back, and I was always lucky enough to get to tag along.

Until I was old enough to participate myself, my Imogene tradition consisted of sleeping in, then grabbing breakfast at Baked in Telluride on my way to cheer Mom across the finish line. It was always a lively celebration; I was never too far from a familiar face, be it a family member, friend, or Flagstaff local, and I couldn't wait to cross that finish line myself someday.

As soon as I turned 15, I begged my mom to sign me up for Imogene. It didn't take much convincing, and I reached the Pass for the first time September 6, 2014, surrounded by our Flagstaff family. I didn't get to experience the top with my mom that year (she was behind us, encouraging my cousin), but I was helped to the top with kind words of encouragement and more than a push or two from some of her dearest friends. They had dubbed themselves the "Fon-tourage" for Fon Cordasco, a seasoned Imogene veteran who was in the midst of a battle with cancer and still managed to kick my ass the whole way up.

There was a whole lot of hooting and hollering as I was overcome by a feeling of pure bliss at 13,114 feet. I don't know that I've ever felt such overwhelming relief, love, and gratitude as I did in that moment, and I know I have never been more amazed by the strength and determination of the people in my life. I crossed the finish line after almost six hours of laughs, thoughts about what the hell I'd gotten myself into, and a whole lot of hard work.

•••

I've since completed Imogene twice more. Each time, I was reminded why it's one of my favorite yearly traditions.

After telling my friends all about how incredible my experience was (and how life-changing the chicken soup was at the Pass),

Above: In 2018, I followed in Mom's footsteps by bringing home a medal. Here we are, celebrating in Telluride.

we decided we would run it together our freshman year of college. It turns out the advantage of altitude training is not a myth. We found that out the hard way when we all piled into the car and made the trek up from Tucson for the race. But I wouldn't trade the unbelievably long car ride, the early morning, or the pain in my calves for anything. Luckily, they fell in love just as quickly as my mom and I had. The potluck-style dinners before and after the race, spending time together in one of the most beautiful towns in the Southwest, and the ice-cold soak in the creek after realizing just how exhausted our race-battered bodies were sealed the deal.

This was the beginning of our own traditions.

We all told more people the story of the soup, and the man at the top who literally pulls you that last step onto the final stretch to the Pass. I don't know who he is, but he is the only reason I actually make it to my soup every year, and for him we are all eternally grateful. Our Imogene family grew one more, and we brought more old Flagstaff and new Tucson friends to participate in 2018 so they could experience our traditions for themselves—the struggle of Mile 10 and the relief that comes with the "Hand of God" pulling you up and saving you that last bit of energy for the long way down, fresh peaches at the finish, and the Baked in Telluride breakfast before heading home. They were amazed at how many familiar faces they saw around Telluride. As we all shuffled our sore bodies around various gas stations on our way back, it was impossible to miss their excitement about returning to do it again next year.

With my friends on the trail, 2018.

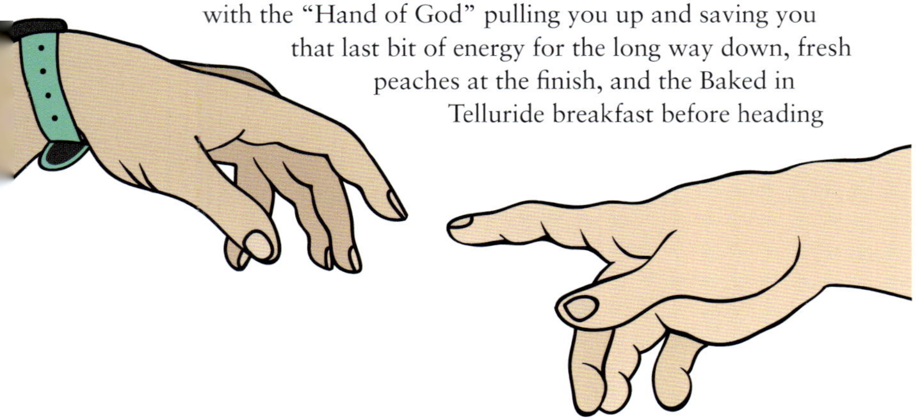

... the relief that comes with the Hand of God pulling you up and saving you that last bit of energy for the long way down ...

I still haven't reached the Pass or finished with my mom because she's kind of unbelievably fast, but I've had some truly memorable times sharing this experience with my Flagstaff family. I have a good feeling about this upcoming year, though. My older sister, Hannah, will be traveling from Portland, Oregon, to run her first Imogene (only because we accidentally forgot to register her for last year's race—sorry again, Hannah Banana), and my mom has promised us she won't be racing it so that she can stick with us (stay tuned). I cannot wait to share one of my dearest traditions with her, and I hope that we'll be able to spend it together for many years to come with the rest of my Imogene family, which just seems to keep growing and growing.

Our traveling trophy

BY TONY MANGINE

I RAN THE IMOGENE PASS RUN ALMOST EVERY YEAR from 1984 until about 2009. My knees no longer get so excited about taking me on long runs, so after that I ran it sporadically, and in recent years not at all.

The early years were more special to me. It wasn't nearly as big an event then; I could probably have counted the Flagstaff crowd on my fingers. The only Flagstaffians I remember seeing were Nancy and Walt Taylor. Many parts of the run actually got a bit lonely, with no one in sight either ahead or behind. More recent runs have seen a steady stream of runners up and down the mountain.

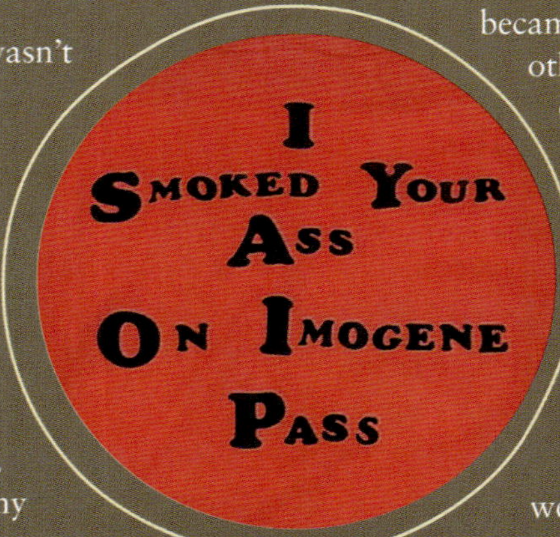

For many years, it was a family event for me, with my sister and her family from Tucson, my brother from Phoenix, my sister and family from Mancos, Colorado, and often my sister from the East Coast all meeting in Ouray for the weekend.

My sister Annette Mullikin (the one from Mancos) and I became a bit competitive over the years at Imogene and other Colorado mountain runs. One year I may have crossed a line when I became too excited about beating her, conveniently ignoring the fact that she was pregnant at the time. When she beat me the following year, she created a red T-shirt with black lettering that said, "I Smoked Your Ass On Imogene Pass."

From then on, that shirt became a much-coveted traveling trophy. It got passed back and forth each year, depending on who won. But we're not so competitive anymore, and I'm honestly not sure who earned it last.

A tiger's story

CORY (SHEELEY) ROBERDEAU

I **GREW UP IN FLAGSTAFF AND STARTED BACKPACKING** in the Grand Canyon with my dad, Tom Sheeley, when I was seven. Every spring break, we did the same 80-mile trek—my dad and I and his guy friends.

One of them, a super-strong former Army Ranger named Damon, was always goading us to go faster (while smoking cigarettes). We held him in high esteem. He told us one year, "I did this race, and it was the hardest thing I've ever done." Of course Dad and I had to try it.

We started doing the Imogene Pass Run in 1997, when I was 17. I have medals from those early years, not because I was particularly fast but because there were only about three girls in my age group. I have registered for and completed the race 10 times. Damon never did it again.

In 2010, I was diagnosed with leukemia. That was a bummer, being sidelined; I didn't do Imogene that year. It was just important to me to get over chemo and back to real life.

When I returned to Imogene in 2011, one of the Flagstaff people I ran into said, "Oh, it's your first Imogene after chemo! I remember that." She had survived breast cancer. What I remember from that year is that I weighed less, so it was easier to carry my ass over that hill.

The song that got me over the Pass:
"Come on up to the House" by Tom Waits

In 2012, my husband, Gene, and I ran it wearing tiger shirts. We chose to wear them because we are solid middle-of-the-packers, and at that pace, it's about having fun. We bought the shirts in a Cleveland Walmart when we were there for a friend's wedding. I remember us seeing them and saying simultaneously, "For Imogene this year!"

It's such a friendly race. You end up talking to people as you're climbing, saying, "Oh my god, this is so hard, why am I doing this? Why aren't I back in Ouray drinking coffee?" As we climbed, I felt instantly drawn to these two women who were walking together. We kept trading places on that hill, as you do. They must have commented on our shirts near Tomboy Basin,

With Gene at the Pass, 2012.

and that launched a natural progression to "Where are you from? Flagstaff? Me too!" It was Dawn Begley and her mom, Pat Taylor (see page 9).

I've never done Imogene with my mom. I wanted to be encouraging because we could see they were taking it step by step. I remember Pat coming up to the Pass. We were telling her, "You can do it!" She was doing an amazing thing.

I loved them; they had a powerful bond you could just feel. Dawn looked at her mom with love and pride in her eyes. They had a great attitude about the challenge; like us, they were there to celebrate life. You could see they had a long history of having fun together.

Imogene has been such a part of our lives. It marks the end of summer, a change of seasons, the promise of fall, and all the fun that comes with that, like new backpacking permits for the Grand Canyon, the Soulstice race in Flagstaff, and street runs in the Valley of the Sun. It's a celebration and the culmination of all the endless training on summer days when you'd rather be tucked in at Pay-N-Take with an IPA.

We have a four-year-old daughter now. We go hiking each weekend. I hope she's drawn to the outdoors and athletic endeavors, like I've been. The harder you push yourself, the tougher the climb, the more rewarding the view. At Imogene, you see things nobody else gets to see. When you stand at that starting line, you have to appreciate the fact that out of the billions of people in the world, these 1,200 friends are here, and we're all going to live this beautiful morning together.

BY EMY TICE

I DECIDED TO RUN THE IMOGENE PASS RUN FOR THE first time in 1999. I turned 30 a few months before the race. At that time, there were both running and walking categories. The walking category had a total cutoff time of seven hours. There were no cutoff times at Upper Camp Bird or the Pass. You could still get into the run a month or so after registration went live. It was mainly a local Colorado event, and local residents were always guaranteed a spot, even at the last minute.

I ran Imogene 10 times officially and 11 times total, in consecutive years. The one year that I didn't run it officially, I was having knee problems. My osteopath asked me to stop running early in the summer because we thought I would need knee surgery for a meniscus tear. Through visualization and physical therapy, I let my body repair my knee itself and was released to run again—the day before Imogene. I had already given up my spot (at that time, you could sell your spot and transfer registration), so I paced my friend Joyce Bassett instead.

There was too much snow on the Pass to go over to Telluride that year (2006), so runners did a loop above Upper Camp Bird and came back down the same route into Ouray. The total run was around 12 miles. I paced my friend up, waited for her to return from the loop above Upper Camp Bird, and then paced her back down to the finish, completing about 10 miles.

For my first Imogene, my two friends (Kim Culbertson and Jennifer DeMott Miller) and I trained really hard all summer, hoping to beat the goal of four hours. We were running up to 30 miles per week by the end of the summer and were in great shape. We even squeezed in long runs through amazing parks while we were traveling in Europe that May.

Once we reached the steep grade at the start of our first Imogene, though, we realized we hadn't trained correctly. We thought that since we lived at 7,000 feet, simply running our trails would be sufficient. Unfortunately, we hadn't spent enough time training at higher elevations, so we all ended up hypoxic above Upper Camp Bird.

It was a strange feeling to have my brain send a signal to my foot to step in front of me and instead have my foot step out to the side and throw off my balance. It was also strange to feel agitated when someone came within a few feet while I was passing or being passed. I remember getting to the false summit above Upper Camp Bird and seeing the true Pass above. I was so disappointed! We ended up finishing the run around 4:23. We didn't meet our goal, but we were happy with the results.

I ran Imogene the first few years with these same two friends, until their lives changed to include other priorities. I've run it with friends, in close proximity to friends, or alone with my music on for inspiration. I have run Imogene so sick (from a cold) that I ended up walking a majority of the uphill and most of the way down. After that year, I swore I would never run it unless I was in top health, because that was unbelievably miserable. I kept that promise.

Over the years, my training evolved to include more high-altitude hiking and less running, or minimal training altogether. Some years, I had a more competitive focus with a goal in mind, and other years I was just there to enjoy the journey and beauty around me. Some years, I kept my head down and pushed hard, and other years I stopped and took pictures of the changing leaves and breathtaking scenery.

SOME YEARS, I HAD A MORE COMPETITIVE FOCUS WITH A GOAL IN MIND, AND OTHER YEARS I WAS JUST THERE TO ENJOY THE JOURNEY AND BEAUTY AROUND ME.

I've been passed on the last two-mile stretch of the climb by participants over 70 who were in amazing shape, and I have passed younger participants who probably didn't train much.

Some years, I ran fast downhill, and other years I stopped at every aid station to hang out for a bit, chatting with volunteers and thanking them for their help.

Some years, the weather was warm and beautiful, while others it was brutal and cold. One year, there was snow on the Pass, and we started the downhill by "skiing" down the first portion from the top. There was a singletrack pounded out in the powder, and if you wanted to pass someone, you had to go around in the deep snow. We decided just to slide down as if on skis (even making "jump turns" with our feet), avoiding the singletrack altogether.

One year, I watched a runner fall off the edge on the Telluride side and tumble down the talus slope for about 20 yards. Amazingly, he popped right back up onto the trail and kept running. A little blood didn't hurt, I guess.

One year, a friend with diabetes ran IPR. She turned her insulin pump to a higher setting for the run, to give herself a little energy kick. This is not recommended, however, and she passed out on the downhill because her blood sugar was too low. Needless to say, the medics would not let her finish the run. She begged and pleaded, but they didn't give in.

One year, a friend didn't make the cutoff at Upper Camp Bird. She missed it by about two minutes. They wanted her to turn around and return to Ouray. She handed them her bib and said she was going to continue even though she was disqualified. On the last $2\frac{1}{2}$-mile climb, she passed several people who had made the cutoff. She felt vindicated by beating them to the Pass but mad that a DQ would show in her results. She has not run IPR since.

***

I watched the run become more elite. The walking division was eliminated to allow more room for competitive runners. Then the race organizers decided that, for the safety of volunteers, they wanted to include a cutoff at Upper Camp Bird. This made the run most conducive to elite runners. The last few years I ran Imogene, the cutoff was in place. I worked hard on the first $7\frac{1}{2}$ miles to ensure that I made the cutoff; after that, I could relax a little more to enjoy the last $2\frac{1}{2}$ miles up.

My husband traveled with me and my friends almost every year to support us in the run and to shuttle us from Ouray to Telluride or back. One year, he rode his mountain bike up from Telluride to support us on the trail. Unfortunately, he got a flat tire on the way down and missed my finish that year. He was my greatest source of support and was very understanding about the intensive summer training schedule.

I ran Imogene in 2009 for the last time when I was 40 years old. I was in the best shape I'd been in since I first ran IPR at 30. I traveled there with my friend Jeff Stein, but we did not expect to stay together during the run. Running with headphones, I got in a zone. I pushed hard and had a great split time at the Pass, where I waited a few minutes for Jeff. He showed up and took off quickly with the intent of beating me to the finish, which he did (by about a minute). He's lucky I waited for him at the top! I ran fast downhill, and my splits got faster as I neared the finish. I set a personal record that day.

I spent 11 years straight waking up early every Saturday morning in the summer to do long training runs or hikes. I ran until dark (and sometimes after) during the week to get in the mileage. After that, I was burned out and needed something new to focus on. My knees were starting to ache from all the running. I decided that after 10 runs and a PR in number 10, I would go out on top.

I love that Imogene is part of my past, and I wouldn't do it differently. It was interesting to watch the relatively young event ev[illegible]e into what it is today. It helped me grow as a human being, t[illegible]ing through the many trials and tribulations Imogene c[illegible]vide.

[illegible]en tempted a few times in the years since to sign up for the [illegible]t was always glad I didn't. In fact, I have not been back to [illegible]de for IPR weekend since. I may consider going in the future [illegible]port all my current Imogene-running friends… but I have to [illegible]er the PTSD, first.

Birthday treat

BY JOANNE KEENE

THE IMOGENE PASS RUN ALMOST ALWAYS FALLS ON my birthday weekend. Whether it's having to give up a traditional birthday or not being able to walk down stairs on my actual birthday, Imogene has brought so much pleasure and pain to this day of celebration.

During my first Imogene, in 2010, we started a tradition of the beer "hand-up." We pack a cooler the morning of and hope we have someone who is either pregnant, injured, or just not interested in running to man the cooler at the finish line.

Then, the fun starts. The first finisher receives the first beer hand-up. There are many considerations given to the type of beer we choose and who is given what beer. My husband, John Comer, turns up his nose at anything not hoppy. Our friends Josh Biggs and Aaron Borling are convinced there's only one beer—yellow beer. Others are just so happy to finish that they will drink anything.

My husband, John, receiving the hand-up in 2011.

In 2010, I was so thrilled to be done that I barely noticed Josh (see page 149 for his story) dressed in a gorilla suit at the finish line and instead, headed straight for the cold beer my husband was holding out. As I recall, it was an ice-cold Dale's Pale Ale.

Some hand-ups can be sloppy. Some can be a bit dramatic. Mostly, it's a way to celebrate the finale of an amazing race that brings our community of Flagstaff together in a different town.

Me just before the 2012 hand-up.

Being a birthday girl during Imogene has made for some amazing races and postrace celebrations. Next year, Imogene will be the day before my 45th birthday. I'm going to celebrate by running 17.1 miles over one of the most beautiful and unforgiving mountain passes in the world. I will enjoy the last day running in that age group, accept a beer hand-up at the finish line, and go soak my legs in the river.

THE IPR BEER HAND-UP

Some hand-ups can be sloppy. Some can be a bit dramatic. Mostly, it's a way to celebrate the finale of an amazing race that brings our community of Flagstaff together in a different town.

Tayloe Dubay for the miss (above) and Engracia "Cha-Cha" Dang with a successful two-hander, 2011.

3 Age Groups, 3 Imogenes

LINDA SHERMAN

THE FIRST TIME I RAN IMOGENE, I WAS UNDERSTANDABLY nervous. Although I had considerable running experience, including a few marathons, running up and over a pass at more than 13,000 feet elevation was daunting. Would I be able to meet the challenge of this historically difficult race?

Before that first Imogene Pass Run, in 2001, I'd been warned by friends that there was a false summit, but when I arrived at the rock wall below, I thought the top was right around the corner. Imagine my surprise when I turned that corner to see Imogene Pass looming high above, with a line of runners below it (walkers by then) looking like an expedition up Mount Everest!

Well, I had to just suck it up and continue. After the Pass, things went better, since I am a stronger downhill runner—gravity is my friend. I was in my element as I raced down the hill, passing many runners. Looking down on Telluride as it loomed larger and larger served to spur me on. Crossing the finish line was a huge relief, but at the same time, a huge rush of emotion to know that, yes, I had lived up to my own expectations.

From left: Durango's Linda Johnson, Flagstaff's Nancy Taylor, and me, top three in our age group in 2010.

Now that I'm (somewhat) older, I sometimes think of this moment when I'm facing other challenges. It gives me courage to attempt some very difficult but potentially rewarding activities in life.

Predictably enough, after forgetting the pain, I had to do another Imogene Pass Run. I waited until I entered another age group. This time, weather was not my friend. The year was 2004, and although the day was clear and cool, there were two feet of snow on the Pass. Rick Trujillo, one of the race organizers, had gotten his truck stuck in the middle of the road near the top the day before, so we had to detour around it. Earlier runners had formed a path through the snow that we all stuck to, since passing another runner meant floundering through the unpacked powder.

Once we reached the Pass, things opened up a little, but we had to watch our footing, as there was ice blanketing the rocks on the other side. I managed to stay on my feet until about a mile or so before the finish, when I caught my toe on a rock. Down I went. Charley horses immediately attacked both calves. It was a few minutes before I could continue, but I finally made it past the finish line. The medical tent was quite busy after that run.

My last run came after I entered the next age group. The weather was fine, and being a more experienced Imogene runner, I paced myself well, was ready for the climb to the Pass, and stayed on my feet all the way down.

Unfortunately, 2010 turned out to be my last Imogene, due to joint issues. I still miss it.

The rewards of accomplishing that run create memories to last a lifetime. Why would anyone miss the pain and agony involved in this tortuous race? Because there are very few other places where a person can challenge themselves and feel the wonderful rush of feelings of accomplishment as they pass that final finish line. Yes, a feeling of pride in oneself is totally acceptable here. It can set a tone of determination for the rest of your life.

Q: How often should you consider running Imogene?
A: I recommend every five years, or the number of years it takes to change age groups. That's just about long enough for a runner to forget how much Imogene hurts.
—Abe Springer

SLOWER, BUT STILL KINGS OF THE MOUNTAIN

BY KERMIT SMITH

I KNOW MANY PEOPLE HAVE HORROR STORIES OF their first Imogene Pass Run—the altitude, the unknowns, the steep and endless climb, the treacherous descent. I have mostly fond memories of my half dozen or more trips up and over the Pass, and those started with my first IPR in 1989.

I ran that year with my buddies Rich, David, and Neil. Their last names are not important, and I certainly wouldn't want to tarnish their fine reputations by questionable association. No matter. All four of us somehow managed to spend three nights in my old eight-foot cab-over camper. We were definitely traveling on a budget. I remember being quite intimidated upon our arrival in Telluride. With cool weather, overcast skies, and a light rain falling, we started wondering just what in creation we had gotten ourselves into.

We left the camper in Telluride at what I believe was the city-operated campground at the south end of town and booked a ride to Ouray in a private "taxi," a Chevrolet suburban operated by an obvious local. The trip took way less time than any of us thought it should; a prompt pit-stop seemed to be the common goal of all when we arrived at the motel in Ouray. We then participated in the official race-sponsored carbo-loading dinner and attended a formal race orientation.

Due to many factors, including a healthy fear of the unknown, we managed to finish the race in good shape. We were of course much younger and had worked pretty hard to be in condition to accomplish the task. As it turned out, our training served us well. There was plenty of apprehension the morning of the run, but once we got settled in, our conditioning kicked in and the event went off without any glitches.

My memory says there were fewer than 400 runners that year. Wow, how popular it's become. It turned out to be a comfortable day, and we ended with a great feeling of accomplishment coupled with some relief. I'll always remember the cheers of support at the aid stations and from the communities of both Ouray and Telluride, which were especially gratifying at the finish. We felt like we were kings of the mountain the evening after the run, which naturally required several libations and a fine dinner to properly honor ourselves. That became an important part of our memories of the effort.

One year, I was not able to participate in the libations or the memory-making, so my buddies did so for me. I had been diagnosed with cancer and was undergoing chemotherapy in September. My buddies Rich Haag,

From left: Rich Haag, Dave Klensin, and Tom Grabarek toasting me at the top, 2002.

Tom Grabarek, and Dave Klensin toasted me at the top. We had run together for years, from Imogene and the Grand Canyon to marathons around the country. They took mini bottles of Jack Daniels and were all together at the Pass. They cracked the bottles open, slugged 'em down, and took off downhill. The high, I'm told, lasted a nanosecond.

It meant a lot that they were thinking of me that day. I'm thankful for the support I received from many quarters during that period, and specifically my running friends for their consideration to acknowledge my recovery process in a special manner of their choosing.

Memories fade and become confused, but I remember fondly the personal association with many Flagstaff friends and acquaintances whom I would sometimes see only at Imogene each year. The Flagstaff trail-running community is always there in force, with natural attrition due to age, health, and change of residence, supplanted by a generally younger, eager, talented new guard.

After a hiatus of maybe 10 years, I managed to will my older (not old!) body over the Pass again in 2017. As a matter of personal pride, I wanted to complete Imogene after I turned 70. Once more, there were a few Flagstaffians from my earliest years of participation still doing their same Imogene thing. Although we had slowed down some, it sure seemed that most still were doing their thing just a little faster than me—especially Nat White… what a competitor and inspiration to so many!

When I ran my first IPR, my buddies and I surprised ourselves with our performances. By 2017, I surprised myself just by finishing. When I think back on what a significant part of my recreational and personal life Imogene has been for so long, I'm greatly appreciative that I was able to achieve my goal of running it after age 70. I can celebrate the good health to be able to train for and participate in such a beautiful, tough race that holds such lasting memories for me. I believe Imogene will continue to create memories for years to come.

From left: Rich Haag, Tom and Ellen Grabarek, me, and Dave Klensin, 2004.

WE FELT LIKE WE WERE KINGS OF THE MOUNTAIN THE EVENING AFTER THE RUN, WHICH NATURALLY REQUIRED SEVERAL LIBATIONS AND A FINE DINNER TO PROPERLY HONOR OURSELVES.

I CAN CELEBRATE THE GOOD HEALTH TO BE ABLE TO TRAIN FOR AND PARTICIPATE IN SUCH A BEAUTIFUL, TOUGH RACE THAT HOLDS SUCH LASTING MEMORIES FOR ME. I BELIEVE IMOGENE WILL CONTINUE TO CREATE MEMORIES FOR YEARS TO COME.

part 5

Love Bleeds

Endurance, trial, tribulation, and yes, blood

At Imogene, there will be blood

BY JASON WOLFE

MY EXPECTATIONS COMING INTO THE 2013 IMOGENE Pass Run were… complicated.

I had finished second the year before and wanted to believe I had a shot at winning this one. But I was struggling with asthma. About 10 minutes into every run, I would start to hyperventilate and break into gagging and coughing fits. Kinda scary. The night before Imogene, I did a 10-minute shakeout with my wife, and it was sketchy at best.

At that point, my plan was to start the race very conservatively and just see how it went.

The next morning at the start line, Ouray was surprisingly warm. The gun went off and I stuck to my plan. Keep it slow. See how it goes.

Flagstaff two-fer: Sara Wagner and I both won the 2013 IPR.

A couple miles passed and I wasn't having too much trouble breathing. Only a couple coughs, but no "fits"… yet. I continued to "run the fine line" aerobically and before I knew it, I was at the front, running stride for stride with the 2012 champ, Daniel Kraft of Grand Junction, Colorado. We were cruising at a pretty good pace and soon I started to build a bit of a lead. I was running very hesitantly, but I was able to continue up the mountain at a good clip.

Soon enough, I was about $2^1/_2$ miles from the 13,114-foot Pass. I continued to push but could feel my lungs rattle a bit, so I began to pull back. I had about a three-minute lead, so my thought was to relax and not risk a coughing attack. The last two miles going up were SLOW. Anybody who has done Imogene knows what I mean. For me, it meant running somewhere in the neighborhood of 15-minute miles. This was partially intentional due to my hesitation to push my breathing too hard and partially that I was just feeling the difficulty of the race.

When I hit the summit, Daniel had made up the gap and was about 20 seconds behind. No bueno.

I knew this was going to force me into a battle downhill that I'd been hoping to avoid, since I wanted to race again in a few weeks at the Ultra Race of Champions… oh well. It was time to get to racing.

We both sped down the mountain at a dangerous pace. No matter how hard I pushed down the technical, washed-out mountainside, Daniel was right there. Finally, with about three miles remaining, I realized that I had a lead of a few minutes and I was dropping 4:50 miles.

"I'm gonna win!" The thought quickly rushed through my head.

At that moment, my right toe caught a rock. CRASH! I was on the ground cramping and bleeding. What a turn of fate.

"I'm gonna lose!"

Not ready to give up, I picked myself up and limped down the trail. Quickly looking back, I could see Daniel reeling me in. That's when the adrenaline kicked in. Within a few strides, I got back to rolling down the mountain.

As I flew downhill, I kept feeling water splash on my legs. But there wasn't any water on the trail. Then it hit me—that wasn't water; it was blood squirting out of my knee and onto my other leg.

"Well," I thought, "that can't be good."

When I got to the finish, 73 seconds ahead of Daniel, the volunteers and spectators all seemed pretty concerned about my knee. I nodded my head a lot, but in the back of my mind I was thinking, "Yeah, yeah, I've fallen on the trails before. I'll be fine."

After about the 10th person brought it up, my wife walked over.

"Jason," she said, "it looks really bad."

She isn't one for coddling me, so I took her concern pretty seriously. I bent over, looked at the bloody mess, and peeled back the now loose skin off my kneecap. Surprised at the severity, I thought, "Yikes, that is kinda bad."

Reluctantly, I admitted, "OK, maybe you're right."

I made my way to the medical tent and eventually the emergency room, where I received 10 stitches in my left knee.

Much like my knee, the race was ugly. But it was a win.

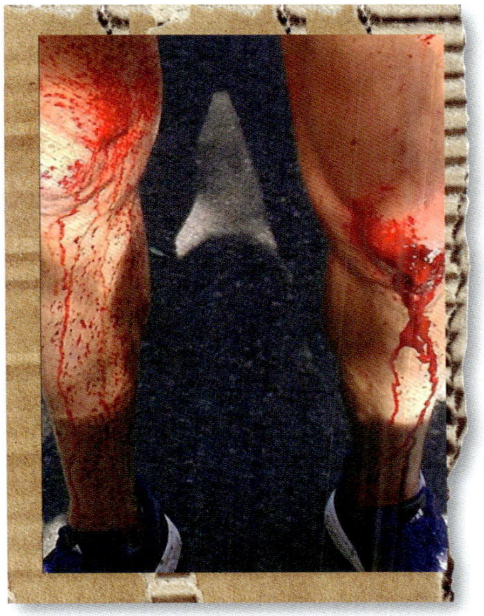

Imogene at a blistering pace

BY DARA MARKS MARINO

A version of this essay originally appeared in the High Country Running column of the Arizona Daily Sun *on September 8, 2013.*

TWO NIGHTS BEFORE THE 2010 IMOGENE PASS Run, I chased my two-year-old daughter up and down the street to keep her entertained as my husband, Troy Marino, my parents, and I waited for our dinner at a restaurant in Ouray. That was when it hit me: I had trained for Imogene by doing little more than chasing my toddler around. This was less than encouraging. Sure, McKenna kept me running at all hours of the day (and night), and hiking with her in a backpack was surprisingly effective uphill resistance training. Still, I imagined that most of the other runners had spent more time running trails and getting solid nights of sleep, and less time running "toddler 10Ks," as I liked to call our forest forays, or taking sleep breaks during the night.

My fears for the epic 17.1-mile run mounted. But come race day, I was relatively calm. I went through my pre-race rituals of eating an oatmeal breakfast, foam rolling, greasing up my toes, arches, and forefeet with Bag Balm, and finally doing some light warm-ups before heading to the start line.

I placed myself mid-pack for the start, just behind where they stage the runners who have a goal of three hours as their finish time, since my goal was 3:10 and I really didn't want to get sucked into starting too fast.

I followed my race plan and worked my way steadily forward through the crowd. By Mile 5, I felt great, and I was somewhere in the top 10 among women. Mile by mile, I continued to pass more runners until we neared the top, when I was suddenly the fourth-place woman.

Playing with my daughter on her balance bike (once I heale

My plan for the way down was nothing more than to be smooth, steady, and sure-footed. Somewhere around Mile 12, I felt what seemed to be a pebble in my right shoe. No worries, just a pebble; surely it would shift in my shoe and not be a big deal. I passed the 14-mile marker and thought to myself, "Woohoo! Fourteen miles! I'm doing awesome! I've now run farther than I ever have before! I'm amazing!" and instantly found myself face down in the dirt; bruised, cut, shaken, and very humbled.

As I dusted myself off, I thought, "Yep! That's what ya get! Time to focus, Dara."

It took some time to get moving again, but eventually the cuts and bruises gave way to the endorphins and adrenaline. However, that darn "pebble" was starting to cut into my foot, and it seemed like I now had one in my left shoe, too.

As the finish line neared, I knew that third place was right ahead of me. I was catching glimpses of her around corners, and spectators were telling me she was just a few seconds ahead. I put my head down and ran for all I was worth. I kept telling myself to forget about that rock-turned-boulder in my shoe, and that I didn't care if I would have a shoe full of blood after the race—just run hard.

Ultimately, I was not able to catch third place before the finish line, but I did far exceed my goal time by finishing in 2:58 and change. As soon as I got to the benches after the finish line, I removed my shoe and discovered that there was no rock.

There also was no more heel attached to my heel.

What felt like a rock was actually a blister on the sole of my foot that had completely torn off the entire surface of my heel. I had not put any Bag Balm on the soles of my heels, since I had never had a blister there in training. I guess when your maximum weekly mileage is less than the length of your race, you haven't exactly uncovered all the possible issues!

The medical staff on site were great, expertly cutting away the peeled-off skin and bandaging it up with the materials used to treat burn victims. When I removed the bandages a few days later, the skin underneath was so new to this world that I had the sensitivity of McKenna's newborn skin; even our tile floor felt icy cold in that spot.

Nonetheless, I "healed" up in no time. And now I can truthfully say I ran Imogene at a blistering pace.

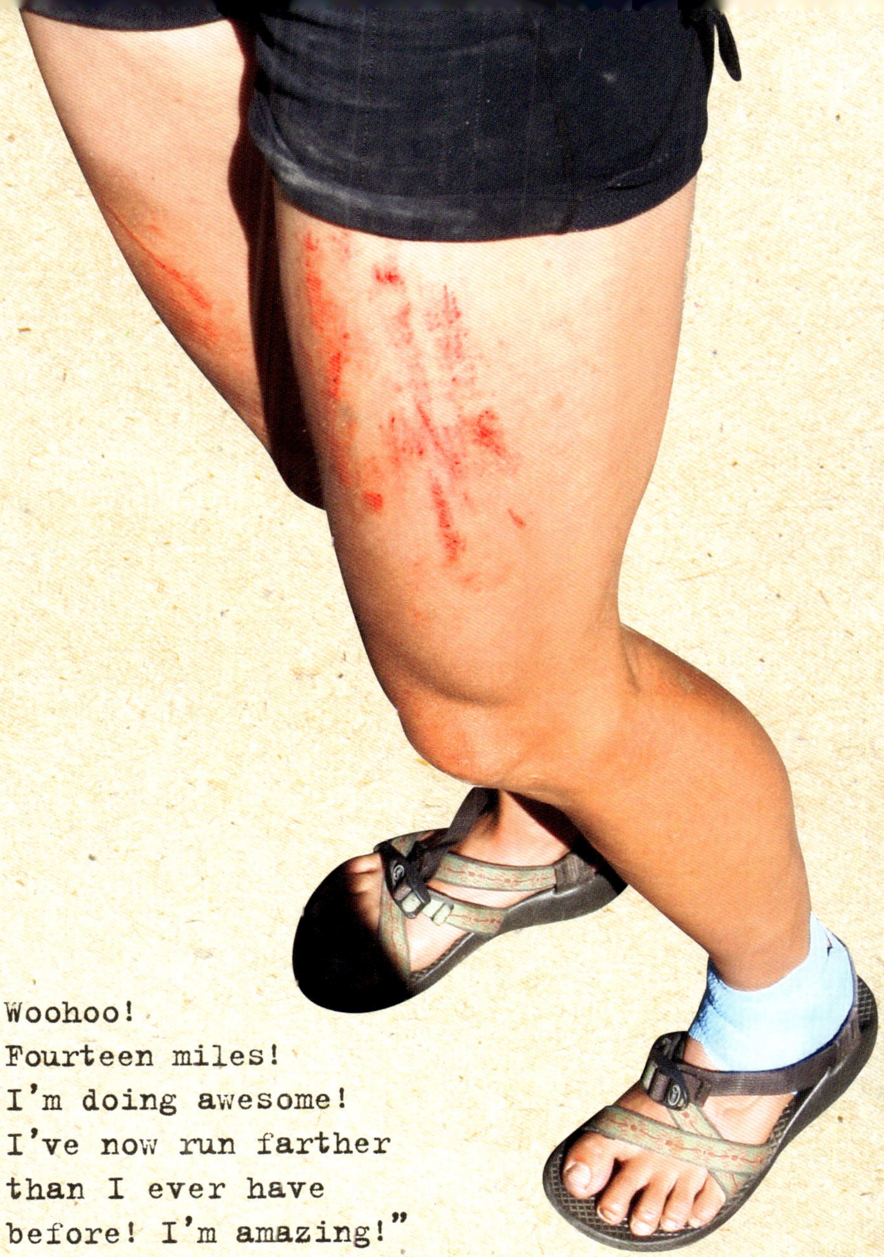

Woohoo!
Fourteen miles!
I'm doing awesome!
I've now run farther
than I ever have
before! I'm amazing!"
and instantly found myself
face down in the dirt; bruised,
cut, shaken, and very humbled.

Train for the downhill

BY MICHAEL OLSON

RUNNING WAS MY FIRST LOVE. OK, THAT IS NOT true. It was basketball. But by ninth grade, it became apparent I was not going to play in the NBA, so I started running cross country in the fall of 1981, and running became my second first love.

I ran cross country in my freshman year at Northern Arizona University, but as many college students do, I soon found other challenges for my lungs (if this is a PG-rated book, then you can say the word "marijuana"), which led me to quit my career as a competitive runner. Once I graduated and grew up, though, I resumed racing. I became an accomplished triathlete who even won an age group national championship (35–39) a few years before running Imogene.

Although most of my hard workouts were on the track, I had always loved trail running. I was talked into doing my first trail race, the Soulstice Mountain Trail Run, in October 2002, and won. Track work had not impeded my trail running but helped it, as I was able to distance myself from Ian Torrence, a nationally ranked trail runner, in many of the hilly sections.

Fun with my family.

I'd heard about the fabled Imogene Pass Run from running friends, old-school Flagstaffians like Paul Brinkmann, and casual runners I knew from the Flagstaff Athletic Club. Unfortunately, the fall season was prime time for triathlons, so this race was never on my schedule until my success at Soulstice. After that win, I vowed to see what all the Imogene hype was about.

•••

The training seemed simple; run uphill. A lot. So in the early summer of 2003, after a winter of light training, I picked the biggest hill around, Humphreys Peak, and began to train. The initial workout was to run from the trailhead to the saddle and take it easy on the way back down. Injuries always seem to happen when running downhill, and everyone runs the same speed down a hill anyway, right?

Once I was able to do this in about 52 minutes, I decided to start at the bottom of Snowbowl Road. I figured this would be 11 miles of uphill, simulating the hard part of Imogene. The downhill would be easy—just let your legs go. I did this workout every weekend in August and kept getting faster, while always relaxing on the downhill. By September, I felt ready to break 2:30 at Imogene.

Imogene couldn't be more Flagstaff if you picked up the mountain pas

Train for the downhill: What goes up, must come down. And the latter ain't easier than the former.

The trip was planned as a four-day weekend, with the last two days to be spent with my fiancée, Natalie Jacobs, soaking in Ouray's famous hot springs, eating everything, and drinking good wine. This sounded like the fun part of the trip, after spending the summer training so austerely.

•••

The race began quickly, and I was in oxygen debt within a quarter mile. Once training took over, I settled into about 10th place. Being used to the altitude, I started picking people off one by one until I was sharing the lead at Upper Camp Bird with a guy named Bernie Boetcher. Bernie was the favorite, so I was pleased to be with him. We stayed together until the Pass, where I took a few seconds to grab some water as Bernie disappeared in the fog (literally) down the hill.

At this point, I just let my legs go, as this was the easy part and it was all downhill now. In the worst-case scenario, I would take second place overall, but my goal was still to win. After the incredibly steep and uncomfortable first mile, though, I knew something was wrong with my feet. The heels felt funny, like someone was lighting a match to them. I slowed slightly, but kept my mind on winning. By the time the trail leveled out a little, I was unable to strike my foot to the ground in a normal fashion. The pain in the heels was too great, so I began running on my toes.

Running on your toes is not very efficient or fast, and pretty soon a runner passed me. When I tried to stay with him, I realized the pain that was occurring in my calves from an unnatural running form. My mind settled on third place… until I was passed again. Yikes!

As we neared Telluride, I went into survival mode. I could not wait for this race to be over. Everything was burning: quads, calves, hips, shoulders. I'd forgotten about my heels, as they were numb. I ended up finishing in 2:34, just a few minutes off my goal time and in fourth place overall. Bernie had outpaced me by seven minutes on the downhill. The lesson was this: When racing an uphill/downhill race, remember to train for both.

•••

The first thing that struck me as I crossed the line was the crowd we had, all cheering for each other at the finish. Though I could barely stand, I felt compelled to stay and yell every time I heard, "Flagstaff finisher." Imogene couldn't be more Flagstaff if you picked up the mountain pass and moved it right in front of Buffalo Park. When I got home that week, people I didn't know congratulated me on the street. It was overwhelming.

When I peeled my shoes off after the race, I found I had lost all the thick skin on both heels. Unable to walk, I was also unable to soak in the hot springs or enjoy the rest of the trip as planned. I did enjoy the wine and food part, though.

While I have incredible and vivid memories of that trip, I've never been back to Telluride or Ouray since. Something about the run seemed surreal, almost like it happened to someone else, so I just left it alone. I need to get back there soon, though. I may even take another shot at Imogene—with better socks.

…nd moved it right in front of Buffalo Park.

FLAGSTAFF IS FAST!

Top 25 IPR finish times by Flagstaff entrants, 1992 through 2017

Flagstaff Men

RANK	TIME	NAME	YEAR	AGE
1	2:09:28	MIKE SMITH	2011	31
2	2:17:07	MIKE SMITH	2009	29
3	2:17:23	JASON WOLFE	2013	37
4	2:18:17	JASON WOLFE	2012	36
5	2:21:51	ANDREW BENFORD	2015	27
6	2:22:28	JASON WOLFE	2010	34
7	2:23:24	CHRIS GOMEZ	2016	34
8	2:23:29	TIM MARTIN	2005	31
9	2:26:05	KALIB WILKINSON	2015	31
10	2:26:33	KALIB WILKINSON	2014	30
11	2:30:53	ERIC BOHN	2009	28
12	2:30:55	ERIC BOHN	2011	30
13	2:31:36	CHRIS GOMEZ	2015	33
14	2:33:30	ERIC BOHN	2012	31
15	2:33:48	JOHN GRIFFITH	2015	27
16	2:34:06	BRIAN TINDER	2013	33
17	2:34:15	SEAN MAHONEY	2014	26
18	2:34:37	MICHAEL OLSON	2003	38
19	2:34:38	ERIC BOHN	2013	32
20	2:35:11	MARK ULM	1999	33
21	2:35:27	SETH WATKINS	2016	34
22	2:35:54	AUSTIN HORN	2016	19
23	2:36:12	ERIC BOHN	2010	29
24	2:36:24	SETH WATKINS	2017	35
25	2:37:26	TOM SABOL	2005	30

Flagstaff Women

RANK	TIME	NAME	YEAR	AGE
1	2:48:32	SARA WAGNER	2013	41
2	2:48:37	JENNY MCCARTHY	2011	31
3	2:49:52	KATE McGEE	2017	44
4	2:51:04	SARA WAGNER	2012	40
5	2:53:48	SARA WAGNER	2011	39
6	2:55:57	MICHELLE WESSON	2013	38
7	2:56:58	SARA WAGNER	2008	36
8	2:58:40	DARA MARKS MARINO	2010	35
9	3:00:45	KRISTI KNECHT	2015	32
10	3:02:57	KATHERINE LANDRY	2015	31
11	3:03:15	SHERRY JOHNS	1993	38
12	3:05:50	SONYA LUCATERO	2015	26
13	3:06:39	MICHELLE WESSON	2015	40
14	3:08:25	MARGARET GROVE (MONTFORT)	2009	49
15	3:09:39	CAILIE BUCKINGHAM	2013	30
16	3:09:47	JEAN MARIE RIECK	2015	29
17	3:10:00	PAIGE HELLER	2009	32
18	3:10:39	ROBIN LYON	2011	40
19	3:11:17	KARA HUFFMAN (TATE)	2009	38
20	3:12:18	JEAN MARIE RIECK	2014	28
21	3:12:38	ALEXANDRA MYERS	2013	22
22	3:12:40	BECKY CAIN	2001	23
23	3:12:43	NOREEN SMITH	2007	46
24	3:13:28	PAIGE HELLER	2008	31
25	3:14:11	BECKY CAIN	2002	24

Compiled by Eric Bohn and Julie Hammonds

Flagstaff's Joshua Washburn (718) and other runners soon after the 2018 IPR start.

I did IPR in checkered Vans

BY MELODY DELMAR

IT WAS TIME TO GO. I HAD PREPPED EVERYTHING the night before, laid out and packed up all my gear for the race. Now my clothes were on and I was looking for the last and most important race item: my running shoes. A wave of panic electrified me as I emptied my bags and searched the Telluride hotel room in a frenzy. And it was time to go. I grabbed my keys but found nothing in my car. Defeated, I told my boyfriend, "I left my running shoes at home."

•••

All that training; so much hard work, on so many trails. I was so angry with myself that I couldn't cry. I mean, do I cry? Do I laugh? No. This was not a laughing matter. It was time to go. We had to drive to Ouray so my boyfriend could run.

My heart was broken. In Ouray, I didn't bother to change out of my running clothes. I almost started crying as everyone gathered at the starting line. It was right in my face. Putting on a smile for my boyfriend, I wished him well and saw him off. But walking back to my car, I was so disappointed.

Standing at the car door, I paused a moment and looked down at my shoes, my checkered Vans. I knew the rule: Never wear new shoes on race day. The race had already started. But there sat my race bag, packed and ready to go. I had done all that training for the 2010 Imogene Pass Run—my very first.

F--- it, I thought, grabbing my bag. I can at least try. I'll go as far as I can, and see how the shoes feel. If it doesn't work, I can always drop out.

The guy dismantling the starting line said yes, I could go, my time would still be recorded. Nervously, I began to run, sheepish to be so far behind, in last place. As I started up the road, I noticed quizzical glances and (to my surprise) cheers from onlookers to keep going. I remember hearing one enthusiastic shout of encouragement by some guy in the dissipating crowd. I was too embarrassed to acknowledge it.

At the road to Imogene Pass, I was relieved to see other racers. In my excitement, I wanted to make up time, though I remembered to keep a moderate pace. My Vans gripped the dirt road with a thick, thudding cadence as the incline began to elevate. To my surprise, my feet felt fresh. I felt strong.

When I safely made the cutoff time at Upper Camp Bird, I still felt great, and my heart was in it to keep heading for Imogene Pass and down to Telluride. In the steepest section of the climb, I passed a couple wearing Vibram Fivefingers (when they were becoming a thing). I felt a little relieved, validated to be doing the race in an "old school," flat-footed shoe. I was waiting for someone to point out my poor choice in footwear or maybe silently judge me as a newbie. Mostly, I didn't care, because I was ecstatic that my old Vans were taking me up this beautiful trail and allowing me such an incredible racing experience along the way.

Beaming, I started up the final stretch to Imogene Pass. A medical volunteer sitting at the top shouted, "ALRIIIGHT, running the IPR in her VAAAANNNSSS!!" When I laughed and awkwardly said, "I forgot my shoes," he clapped. I'd made it to the top, pain free!

Adrenaline and excitement drove me on, down toward Telluride. I kept thinking, I can't believe I'm running this race in these simple shoes. I couldn't wait to find my boyfriend and tell him the good news.

After passing the tunnel, I picked up the pace. The trail was pretty rough with loose rocks. Letting gravity pull me along turned into a scary dance of navigating the trail with caution, especially in shoes not designed for the feat. Because I still felt great, excitement got the best of me; my foot caught on a rock, and I flew.

Dusting off, I checked for injuries. Just below my left knee was a spot that soon swelled to the size of a golf ball. Nothing felt bad or broken, just creaky. I walked a little (although bothered by the golf ball below my knee) and gradually started to run, with no pain. I sped up once I saw the first glimpse of Telluride, again excited.

Running into town was the best. I could hear the announcer welcoming runners. At the last turn, a guy shouted, "Heyyyy! I was looking out for you! I saw you start the race and wondered if you made it, and you did, WOOHOO!! I was cheering you on!" He must have been the guy who encouraged me starting out. As I waved and acknowledged him (unlike before), I noticed he was holding his daughter. What a sweet sight.

I MADE IT!!! At the finish line, I teared up, looking for my boyfriend. Then I remembered my knee. It was bleeding, and the size and awkwardness of the injury scared me a little. Maybe adrenaline had numbed some pain. Giving up my search, I made my way to the medical tent. The medic said the golf ball was a hematoma, a kind of bruise that becomes raised and swollen, "Like boxers get." The prescription was for him to push it back down. Awed by this rugged technique, I felt no pain, just thankfulness that it was not more severe.

Patched up, I hobbled out of the medical tent. The race was truly complete when I found Phillip. That's when I finally burst into tears, overwhelmed by a feeling of accomplishment and relief. We made our way to the cold creek, where we could sit and share the trail's joyful and perilous moments.

Removing my Vans to dip my feet in the water, I felt the usual wear from a trail race, with no trace of shoe-related injuries. What an amazing experience my absent-mindedness had given me. As we laughed at my perilous choice to trust these unlikely shoes, I was ever so grateful to them for taking me on a beautiful ride.

Adrenaline and excitement drove me on, down toward Telluride.
I kept thinking, I can't believe I'm running this race in these simple shoes.

MY ONE AND ONLY IMOGENE

BY RANDY MARLATT

IN 2001, I HAD JUST TURNED 50, AND LIKE MANY OTHERS who reach that milestone, I felt compelled to challenge myself with something I had always imagined impossible. My many running friends often talked about doing the Imogene Pass Run, so I became intrigued with this iconic race. I was not a runner. But I wondered, is this something I could do too? I made the decision to go for it.

My attempts at running in the past had always been unsuccessful, so I had to start at square one with short runs around the block. I added brisk hikes and then intermittent jogging up the Humphreys Trail on the San Francisco Peaks to simulate the altitude and steep terrain of Imogene. I had a full-time job, so finding time for training was difficult, and runs were limited to the weekends. I stuck to this regimen for months but was never able to run more than seven or eight miles. I began to wonder if it was crazy to even attempt this. I had no illusions that I could run the entire race—just finishing was my goal.

The day before the race, my good friend Mark James and I piled into his car with a pop-up camper in tow. Our drive to Ouray was a great time for us to reconnect after having lost touch for quite some time.

Upon arrival, we immediately set up the camper at a campground. Hungry from hours of driving, we went to buy groceries for dinner and breakfast. We were shocked to find the tiny local food market had closed at 5:00 p.m. We had no food, and my mind went into panic mode. I flashed back to the first time I hiked the Grand Canyon, when I was 20. I ran out of food the second day of a five-day trip and had to survive on donated dried fruit! Concerned that we would have nothing to fuel our bodies for the run, we drove to a local coffeehouse and were relieved to find they also served food.

Back at the campground, a fellow camper informed us there would be a prerace meeting that evening in a local hotel. What? How had we missed that critical piece of information? We walked to the hotel and entered a large room packed with hundreds of runners who, to our surprise, were eating a spaghetti dinner! The room was filled with noisy conversation and laughter, and we recognized many people from Flagstaff, including Ken Walters, Tom Sheeley, Jim and Holly Garretson, and Tom Grabarek.

After dinner, we were given instructions on what to expect and how to prepare for the race, including tips on prerace hydration. I figured, the more hydration the better, so I drank large quantities of water. I was later punished for that decision when I had to run to the bathroom all night long, depriving me of much-needed sleep!

The morning of the run, I was surprised at how nervous Mark was, but as a lifelong runner, he took these races very seriously. I was nervous too. Was I really up for this? We checked in and pinned our numbers to the front of our shirts, chatting with people we knew (the Flagstaff running contingent was approximately 130, the largest group of entrants from a single city).

As race time drew near, we gathered at the starting line in the middle of town, almost 1,000 runners strong. It was quite a

sight! I tried to get as close to the front as I could, but it was nearly impossible. The start was a slow jog (except for the front-runners), and as we headed up the dirt road at the base of the mountain, we slowed to a walk in areas due to the congestion. About two miles into the race, the runners and walkers began to string out, and I was able to get into a slow, comfortable pace. I stayed focused on challenging myself instead of the other runners.

Many runners casually talked in the first couple of miles, but after that, there was an eerie silence. We trudged along in a human column miles long, the only sound our heavy breathing. The road got steeper and steeper, and just when you thought it was as steep as it could be, it got worse! Near the top, a guy next to me suddenly screamed, "Ahhhhhhh!" from the pain and exertion, then looked at those of us near him and said, "Y'all know you feel the same way!" We all broke out laughing.

It was too steep to run, so I maintained a fast walking pace that even enabled me to pass a few joggers. The temperature began to plummet, but I felt prepared with insulated tights, a fleece jacket, windbreaker, hat, and gloves. As I neared the Pass, it was so steep we were nearly walking on our toes. The cold became uncomfortable, and my fingers grew numb even with gloves on.

I came across another Flagstaff friend who was stooped over, grasping his calves in pain due to horrible cramps. A long string of mucus hung from his nearly frozen nose. I asked if he needed help. At the prerace meeting, we were warned that hypothermia was a danger if we stopped, but he assured me he was fine and waved me on. Not too far away was an aid station that could help if he needed it. Aid stations were spaced every 2 1/2 miles on the way up. They provided first aid, water, Gatorade, energy bars, and fruit. The volunteers cheered us on with great enthusiasm, which we greatly appreciated.

When we reached the Pass, we were asked to expose our number so they could keep track of us. At this point, I had hoped to make a bathroom stop. To my disappointment, there were no portable bathrooms, so I decided to find a place farther down the mountain. I grabbed some Gatorade without slowing down and sipped on it as I headed downhill. Three people dressed as salmon were coming up from the other side, "swimming against the current" just to keep us smiling. I later found out they were Telluride residents who did it for a lark.

Surprisingly, I still had plenty of strength, but the downhill run was the true test. Training on Humphreys Peak, I was plagued with knee pain, especially on the downhill. It would take up to a week to heal before I could train again. I'd felt like I was getting nowhere, but miraculously, on my last training hike, the knees held up. But that was an eight-mile trip, and this was 17.1 miles. I feared that halfway down, my knees would fail and my chance of a decent time would be ruined.

At first, I walked quickly with long strides, conserving energy and lessening the shock on the knees. I again found myself keeping up with the runners on the steepest downhill section, but as the road became less steep, I realized that in order to stay with them I had to run. Deciding to go for it, I got into a comfortable rhythm—not fast, but steady—and the knees continued to hold up.

About three miles down, I started to feel that familiar knee pain, but I pushed through it and was amazed when it did not worsen. My bladder by this time was screaming. I kept thinking I would find the perfect tree to stop at, but when I reached that tree I would push on, looking for another. I'm a lot more competitive than I thought!

Fatigue set in, and it was now no longer a challenge of the body, but a challenge of the mind. Approximately two miles from the finish, I seriously considered walking as my energy ebbed, but around the last bend I could see Telluride, and I told myself, You can do this! I was in a group of other runners going the same speed, so we stayed evenly spaced for the next two miles. I felt no need to compete with them.

FATIGUE SET IN, AND IT WAS NOW NO LONGER A CHALLENGE OF THE BODY, BUT A CHALLENGE OF THE MIND.

When the road finally transitioned from dirt to pavement in town, the finish line was only a quarter mile away. Feeling a surge of energy, I ran faster there than any other part of the race. People lining the road were cheering and clapping, and being new to this, I wasn't sure if I should acknowledge them. Should I smile and wave back? I decided to focus on the finish, and when I passed the line, I felt an enormous sense of relief and accomplishment.

An older woman grabbed me by the shoulders and looked into my eyes as she congratulated me. I felt faint for a moment, and I think she could see that. She held on to me until she was satisfied I was OK. To my relief, I spied a line of portable bathrooms just beyond the finish line. Somehow, I had completed the race without stopping even for a moment. Now, I could allow myself the luxury of relieving my aching bladder!

•••

I walked to a grassy area to stretch and spotted Mark. He was shocked to see me. He had finished the race an hour earlier and didn't expect me to finish for another hour or so.

Mark and I were the last people to get on the first bus. The long, slow trip back to Ouray took forever, and the bus smelled of sweat and fatigue. But we runners passed the time reminiscing about the race and feeling good about what we had accomplished.

Back in Ouray, we enjoyed a long soak in the hot springs with dozens of other runners. It felt good to finally relax.

As I walked away from the hot springs, I decided I would do this again. And next time I would train harder and strengthen my knees further. I might even try to knock 20 minutes or so off my time. But the 2001 Imogene Pass Run turned out to be my one and only long-distance run experience. In the following years, my business and personal commitments did not allow the time needed to train for another race.

I was OK with that. I had set a lofty goal at age 50 and accomplished it. I added running to my regular exercise routine. And the memories of Imogene would always be there to sustain me when I needed a reminder on how to handle some of life's most difficult challenges. ⊠

Third time's the charm

BY CHRISSY SPEER

THIS WAS MY SECOND TIME AT THE IMOGENE PASS RUN. The first time had gone so smoothly, and I'd had so much fun, that I had decided to do it again. This time, I talked my husband, Rob, into running it too.

All went well on the trek up the hill, and I caught my husband at the Pass. Feeling good, I planned to make up some time on the downhill. I was on autopilot and cruising at a faster speed than normal when I tripped. I thought I was going down but managed to stick the landing, recover, and keep running.

My girls let me use the stroller, thank goodness!

"Shit, that was a close call," I thought. "I wonder who saw that slick move?" Not two miles later, at Mile 15, I tripped again, only this time, I went fully airborne. After a hard landing, I had to lie on the ground for a solid 15 minutes. Some people stopped to see if I needed help, but I said no. I could tell my right ankle was messed up pretty bad, and a huge gash in my left knee was gushing blood, but naturally I was most concerned about the fact that I had torn up my new running tights.

As I sat beside the trail, pissed off and wondering what the heck I should do, it occurred to me to wonder how far I had gotten ahead of Rob. How could he not have caught up with me by now? Where was he?

What got me off the ground was the fact that if he caught up with me, he was going to make me call for help! NO WAY was I getting carried out of there on an ATV or stretcher. I stood up and started walking, then running. Adrenaline took over, and I made it the last couple miles and crossed the finish line!

About halfway through the postrace beer, I told my friend Tracy, "I think I hurt my ankle." She took one look and answered, "Um, you need to go to the first-aid tent!" Once I sat down in the tent, I realized I couldn't walk another step. Somehow, someway, I had run those last two miles, but now I literally could not walk a single step on that leg.

I'm not sure who first suggested that I get in my daughter's BOB stroller to be wheeled back to our condo, but that was my ride. The picture made its way around town real fast, and we still laugh about it today! Later, an MRI showed three torn ligaments in my ankle. I was in a boot until Thanksgiving.

I haven't run Imogene again because my medical drama didn't end there. Nine months later, an X-ray revealed a 20 cm mass in my chest and a completely compressed left lung. It turns out I had advanced Hodgkin's lymphoma—and most likely had it during my race. My friend Andrew Overheiser likes to remind me that I ran Imogene on one leg and one lung so I need to do it again! I plan to race again next year… five years after my cancer diagnosis. They say the third time is the charm, right?

As we neared Telluride, I went into survival mode. I could not wait for this race to be over.

– MICHAEL OLSON

I qualified for the Imogene Pass Run and made it through each of the aid stations, but secretly I was wishing a bear would come out of the woods and eat me right then!

—ADAIR SCANTLEBURY

THERE'S ALWAYS SOMETHING WORSE

BY LIZ BRAUER

IN 2009, WHEN I WAS ON MY FIRST LONG IMOGENE PASS Run training run up Weatherford Trail, two guys started up from Schultz Tank at the same time. It turns out they were Rob Hall and Todd Schultz, whom I didn't know back then.

They quickly disappeared, but we finished at the same time, about 4½ hours later. Schultz Tank is at 8,000 feet. I'd gone 16 miles and gained 2,900 feet of elevation. I asked how far they went, and it was either Humphreys Saddle or Humphreys Peak, which would be 22 miles and 5,800 feet of elevation gain.

My partner, Anne Hart, was there too, hiking to recover from a bout of pneumonia she'd caught almost a year earlier at the Paralympics in Beijing, China. We started chatting.

"You must be training for Imogene," Anne said.

"No, we're doing the TransRockies," Rob replied.

"That sounds worse than Imogene."

"There's always something worse," he replied with a wry grin.

I wasn't familiar with the TransRockies, so I looked it up when we got home. I decided it was basically six Imogenes in a row. Indeed, there is always something worse.

Finishing with mincemeat mitts and a smile

One year, I took a tumble less than a mile from the finish. About five of us had settled into a rhythm together when suddenly I tripped and was down. I stayed there for a few minutes. Most all the runners who passed my prone form asked if I was OK—I'm not sure they really cared. They could see I was alive and the long-awaited finish line was in their sights, but at least they were kind enough to ask. I finally managed to uncramp enough to get to my feet and shuffle off to the finish line with a couple of bloody hands, a few tears in my running shorts, and (mostly) a smile on my face. I was then very kindly and gently escorted off to the first-aid station, where a couple of quite young, attractive, and caring nurses picked the rocks out of my hands for what seemed like a long time. From my perspective, they could have cared for me and my mincemeat mitts for at least another hour or two. Who doesn't appreciate a little attention? I'm sure I milked my wounds for all they were worth for weeks afterward. —Kermit Smith

part 6

My Own Private Imogene

Quirky tales from people who do this race like nobody else

Run. Laugh. Repeat.

BY JENNY McCARTHY

THE IMOGENE PASS RUN ITSELF WAS BRUTAL, beautiful, humbling. There are a lot of details I could expand on—having to pee my pants on the early morning school bus ride over to Ouray (I'll never forget that), laughing with Rob Hall at the starting line about what the f--- we were doing there, experiencing the unexplainable feeling when I reached the top, being confused as to why they were serving chicken soup up there, falling in slow motion really hard on the descent, and feeling the euphoria of running fast downhill with Telluride in view, completely depleted and overjoyed.

•••

Winning was fun, but by far the most important and memorable part of that weekend and the summer was the time spent laughing with my friends Mike Smith, Ryan Stevens, Chris Gomez, and Brianna (Bri) Torres.

From left: Prerace fun for Bri, Ryan, Chris, and me (Mike took the picture).

2011 was a weird but wonderful summer. Bri and I moved back to Flagstaff having no real idea what we were doing with our lives. I'd quit an on-paper "dream" job in San Diego; Bri was in similar circumstances. We moved in together. We got restaurant jobs. We were 31 and shunned all real responsibility. I wanted the opposite of the sedentary office-job life I'd been living. We were lost, but happy to be back in Flagstaff.

Bri and I put our energy and attention toward what we love most: running in the woods and playing in the mountains. For some reason, we agreed to let Mike Smith coach/torture us. Looking back, I can't believe we listened to the ridiculous training he wanted us to do; but we did it—and it worked.

The entire Flagstaff trail-running community was on a high leading up to Imogene. Most of us had participated in the TransRockies Run in Colorado a couple weeks before (Bri and I ran as partners). We'd all bonded at hyper speed while participating in this absurd hobby. You're usually too tired to be guarded or keep a wall up, so friendships come fast and easy, which everyone ends up realizing is the whole point of the sport anyway. It feels like making friends when you're a little kid—completely pure.

It seemed as if every runner from Flagstaff was making the trek up to Telluride, so we all knew it would be a great time regardless of how the race went. Bri, Mike, and I made the beautiful drive north and met up with Chris and Ryan. We all stayed together in a hotel. Chris and Bri were not running; they came to support us (and drink a lot of tequila).

When we first got there, the day before the race, we went for a hill-less shakeout run, which, for some reason, felt worse than any run I had ever been on. Afterward, I was semi-panicked at having to run up to 13,114 feet, but we had a couple beers and a big dinner and didn't take anything too seriously. Chris and Bri started drinking tequila pretty much immediately; Mike, Ryan, and I were jealous. We discovered the gondola between Telluride and Mountain Village and rode it a number of times—too many times—then went to bed relatively early.

I got a lot of clarity about what I wanted and was reminded of what is important: my relationships, getting outside, feeling small.

Most of the specifics of the race are hazy. I spent a good part of the incline wondering why I was doing this, which is standard for me. Then I got a little teary at the top and remembered that feeling was why. I mostly just remember my interaction with Ryan. We spotted each other a few miles into the race, and I was lucky enough to run with him for a while. Ryan had been my "short course" running buddy for many Flagstaff races over the years. By that I mean whenever there was an option to run a 5K instead of a 10K or longer, we took it. And then we laughed at all the suckers who ran longer.

Now it was our turn to run long (and Bri and Chris's turn to laugh). Ryan must've thought I had a chance of racing up front (or he thought I was dying; not sure which), so he gave me a box of coconut water midrace; typical, generous Ryan. After I drank it we laughed a bit more and enjoyed the incredible view together, and then he said, "Go."

We discovered the gondola between Telluride and Mountain Village and rode it a number of times—too many times...

We still laugh about it years later, but I'm pretty sure his friendly face and unexpected support during that increasingly painful uphill drudge were the only reasons I won. (See Ryan's take on it, page 183.)

•••

Mike also won, and sharing in that with him was incredibly special. We got to be the first Flagstaff winners together. He coached me through that summer, but he's also my best and oldest friend. We've known each other since we were 14, growing up in small, adjacent towns in the woods of central Massachusetts. He's the reason I ended up in Flagstaff four years earlier. I wasn't running then; I was more or less a vagabond. Mike gave me a floor to sleep on for three months when I was unsure what to do next. He's family. The whole experience of Imogene and our success felt like a manifestation of the love and trust I have in Mike and our friendship. It was just joyful to experience it with him.

When the race was over, we joined the rest of Flagstaff in the town square for the award ceremony. It felt like there were more of us than people from Colorado. Then Mike, Ryan, and I joined Bri and Chris in the equally physically demanding "tequila drinking at altitude" portion of the day, which Bri and Chris had been excelling at. We rode the gondola another 700 times. We met up with the rest of the Flagstaff running crew in downtown Telluride and celebrated with them. At one point there was a lightsaber fight. All day, there was a tremendous amount of laughter and love, that post run-in-the-mountains fog/exhaustion after hours of being wholly present. Slaphappiness and the feeling that you are exactly where you want to be with the people you care about most. That was Imogene.

Few memories make me smile as wide as that weekend. It was so silly and so difficult. Imogene was a bookend to this confusing, magical, much-needed summer. I got a lot of clarity about what I wanted and was reminded of what is important: my relationships, getting outside, feeling small.

We all knew in the moment that it was a special, fleeting time in our lives. We didn't need it to become a memory to take on that importance. I'm grateful for that. I can't think of Imogene without feeling love and joy from and for my friends and the greater Flagstaff trail-running community. The experience is a gift I truly cherish. *Thank you, Imogene.*

STORY AND ILLUSTRATION
BY SARA KNIGHT

I got this idea during your average, run-of-the-mill case of midwinter depression. I was only seeing the sun during a too-short lunch break, and was hardly salvaging my mood with a few measly endorphins worked up on the treadmill at the gym after dark. So, while sitting on my bed one night, watching Netflix and eating my feelings from a giant bag of chips, I decided I needed a goal. A goal to get me up off my butt. Ah ha, well of course! Why not do the Imogene Pass Run? How hard could running 17 miles over a mountain pass possibly be? Over the next 9 months or so I got outside and got myself running, and hiking and biking, and before I knew it, I was standing in a crowd in downtown Ouray wondering what on earth I had gotten myself into.

An Olympian sighting

BY MYLES SCHRAG

AROUND FLAGSTAFF, SEEING TOP ENDURANCE athletes training is as commonplace as seeing actors in LA or politicians in DC. But the Imogene Pass Run is different. It attracts strong and talented runners, but not the fastest in the world. It is communal—note that it's called the Imogene Pass "Run," not "Race"—and focused on all of us, not the elites.

That's why, three miles above Telluride at the 2013 IPR, focused on securing my footing, I sure didn't expect to look up to see Janet Cherobon-Bawcom—a Flagstaff resident who a year earlier took 12th place in the 10,000 meters at the London Olympics—cheering us on.

I kept pushing downhill, but now I was smiling. I had to share with somebody.

"Did you know she was in the Olympics?" I asked the runner closest to me.

He didn't answer. Maybe he thought the altitude was getting to me.

Did LeBron clap for you at your last city-league basketball tournament? Did Bryce Harper high-five you at your slowpitch softball game?

Me neither.

My Own Private Imogene

MY FAVORITE IPR MEMORIES

My name: ______________________________

First Imogene year: ______________________________

Other years I've run it: ______________________________

How I first learned of Imogene: ______________________________

____

Favorite snack at the Imogene Pass aid station: ______________________________

A mantra that helped me reach the finish line: ______________________________

Favorite Imogene weekend travel memory: ______________________________

____

Favorite Imogene on-the-course memory: ______________________________

____

Imogene New Year... What does it mean to you?

____

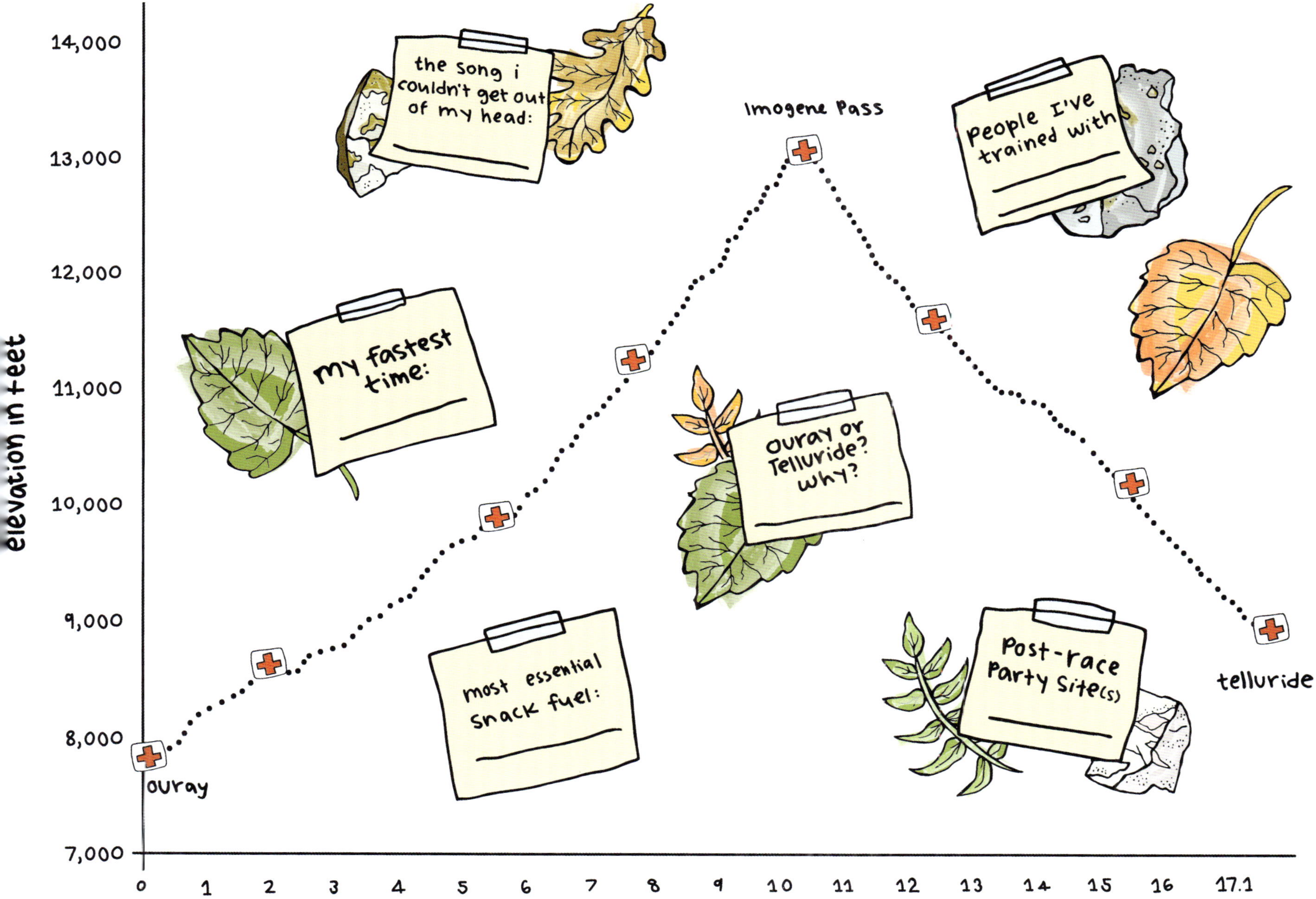

elevation in feet
14,000
13,000
12,000
11,000
10,000
9,000
8,000
7,000
0
1
2
3
4
5
6
7
8
9
10
11
12
13
14
15
16
17.1
ouray
Imogene Pass
telluride
the song i couldn't get out of my head:
people I've trained with
my fastest time:
ouray or Telluride? why?
most essential snack fuel:
Post-race Party Site(s)

Racing on Colorado's turf

BY ADAM OWENS

THE PILGRIMAGE TO COLORADO FROM FLAGSTAFF is exciting and, if I'm honest, also intimidating. A tad melodramatic, perhaps, but I compare the journey to that of medieval bands of marauders marching to battle across a desolate landscape to fight for glory on another tribe's turf.

Call me overly competitive, but from the elite Flagstaff trail-runner's perspective, this fight for glory is an annual attempt to prove we can outcompete Colorado runners in their own mountains. Like many Flagstaff runners, I regularly advocate that Flagstaff is the best place to train in the country. We have a long track record at many different distances to provide evidence for that assertion. When I competed in my first Imogene Pass Run in 2018, I wanted to add to the resume of Flagstaff-based runners and show that just because our mountains aren't as high as Colorado's, our talent and work ethic in the sport is stronger.

I realize a trail race is primarily a personal challenge; in this case, literally a mountain to overcome. Still, this is where my mind went as I prepared for race day. It is not the Olympics, but the mental preparation for this race is greatly assisted by the pride of representing Flagstaff's running community on a prestigious stage like Imogene.

In the six-hour drive I made to Telluride alone, I felt all sorts of emotions… excitement mostly, but I also felt a looming sense of uncertainty for how this race would play out. As a first-timer to the race and never having seen the course before, I didn't know what to expect. After a rough night's sleep from prerace anxiety and camping just outside Ouray on a cold night, I made it to the start feeling lethargic, but my confidence in my training calmed me.

> The pain cave: It's a place to go, not a place to live. It's that dark bubble you have to explore so you realize the value of light.

The course immediately put my body into lactic stress leaving Ouray with a steep hill in the first quarter-mile. The course continued to ascend more gradually, but every step up equals less oxygen to breathe. My lungs quickly recognized the math was inescapable. I hung with the top 10 for the first six miles. Around there is where I started to be absolutely humbled by the intense climb, and I realized that just because I was fit didn't mean I was ready for this kind of race. It's a different animal, requiring just as much preparation in the weight room as on the trails. I skipped out on strength training in order to get in extra miles, which in hindsight was a big mistake.

The other factor was the mental game, which is always unpredictable on any given day. My confidence sank throughout the climb, realizing that I lacked the strength in my legs to compete with the top 10. As a result, I started to walk more than run up the Pass. As I lost the motivation to dig deep the more the race went on, I started to enjoy the scenery by simply being more observant rather than remaining in this dark bubble referred to as the "pain cave." It was maybe a sacrifice in my overall performance, but I don't regret taking the slight step back to relax and appreciate this beautiful moment surrounded by awe-inspiring picturesque

The mental preparation for this race is greatly assisted by the pride of representing Flagstaff's running community on a prestigious stage like Imogene.

nature scenes. I love the alpine backcountry, and it was a beautiful, sunny day.

Between miles 7 and 9, I reached this euphoric and contradictory phase of marching up in the shadow of the biggest mountains I have ever seen and trying to hold my place in the race, while also relishing the moment I was in for the pure love of a new, grandiose landscape that is very different from our own San Francisco Peaks.

Once I neared the end of the climb, I decidedly switched gears and picked up the pace to reach the Pass in under two hours. I was also excited, because I knew all along that I am a better downhill runner. After taking the customary 360-degree turn to fully embrace the view from the top, the heat of competition was once again at the forefront of my mind and I was on a mission to release the power I had trained for all summer by "bombing" down the Pass into Telluride as fast as humanly possible.

The first quarter mile downhill is arguably the hardest section of the course to stay on your feet. Many runners lose their footing and fall, sometimes costing time or even causing injuries. I witnessed this happen to the man in front of me, and it was nerve-racking. But it didn't slow me down.

As a result of having grown up running and hiking the rocky trails of Virginia, my feet have an instinctual way of finding traction among the highly tactical nature of the trail. The seven-mile descent was a blast—everything I had hoped to squeeze out of my body. I managed to not only stay on my feet, but I blew by several competitors who had beaten me on the uphill. I finished 21st overall, third in the 25–29 age group, and most importantly to me, I was the fourth Flagstaff local to cross the line. Not a bad day, but it was humbling to be outcompeted by so many seasoned mountain athletes, most of whom were at least a decade older than me.

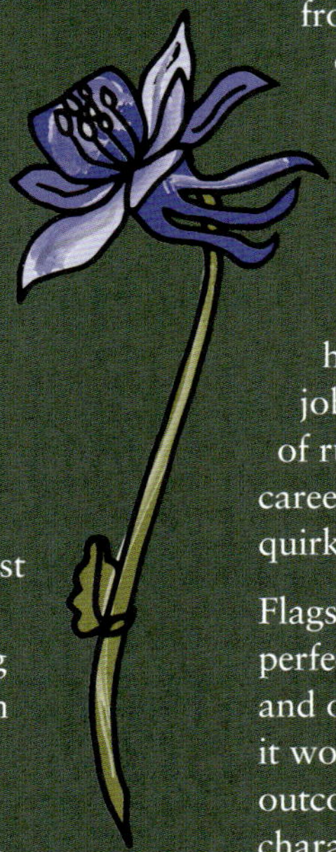

Being humbled is always a good thing in this sport, and since I train alone, it's a motivating experience to know I can do a lot more in the coming years to compete with these aerobic beasts. A race like Imogene is not my strong suit, given that I come from a background of track and road running for the past decade, but it's an event I have become more and more passionate about excelling at.

That passion is critical to staying motivated for months of rigorous training in the mountains and doing the little things that get your mind and body ready for this race. I attribute the vibrant Flagstaff trail-running scene for helping me sustain this passion while working a full-time job. I want to make my contribution to the inspiring group of runners who live and train here. Many of them forgo better career opportunities elsewhere in order to live the dream in this quirky town dubbed "poverty with a view."

Flagstaff runners have a love affair with Imogene because it's a perfect stage to display this undeniable pride for our mountain and our community, the potential sacrifice it takes to make it work here, and our desire to prove that we can collectively outcompete any town in Colorado in their home state. We characterize ourselves as fearlessly tough warriors who can handle any terrain, weather, and competition with confidence and tenacity. If you look at the 2018 results, you'll see that no single town in Colorado is represented more among the top 25 finishers than Flagstaff. I have fallen in love with Imogene for making me proud of my running accomplishments, but also for making me proud of the place I call home.

To Imogene, with love,
Adam

Why don't you just meet me in the middle?

BY TODD SCHULTZ

WHEN OUR FAMILY MOVED TO FLAGSTAFF IN 2012, I immediately sought a new group of like-minded athletes to train with. I was lucky enough to quickly connect with local masters legends such as Ian Torrence and Rob Hall. Rob and I discussed the Imogene Pass Run often on our long trail days around Flagstaff and in the Grand Canyon.

At some point, I realized that Telluride is roughly halfway between Flagstaff and Colorado Springs, the current home base of my best friend and adventure partner since 1987, Lt. Col. Richard F. Benz, US Air Force. We stupidly learned to rock climb together without instruction, often putting ourselves in very dangerous situations due to our naiveté. We once spent a night on Half Dome in Yosemite Valley in T-shirts, having badly misjudged the amount of daylight on a glorious October day in the early 1990s. That harrowing 24-hour experience cemented what has become a lifelong bond.

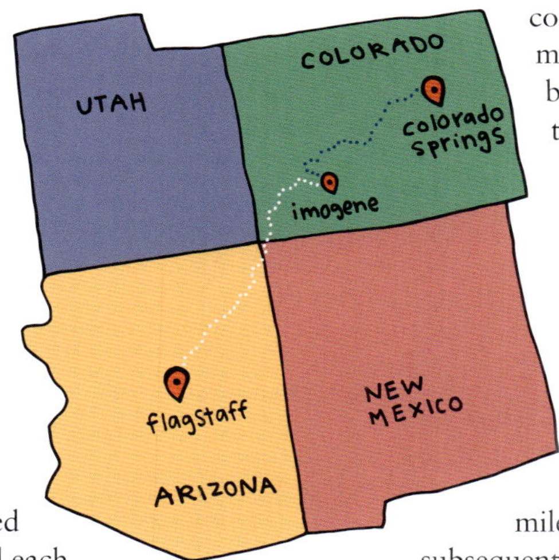

Over the last 30 years, we have celebrated each other's achievements and supported each other during times of great tragedy and loss. In 2012, Richard actually crewed and paced me through the Leadville Trail 100 run (putting in over 30 miles himself). I'm positive this day at Leadville was just as hard as mine.

I attempted to pay him back a couple years later by pacing him at the Leadville Marathon. He had recently lost his father and was also suffering from severe back spasms. He wanted to complete the race for his dad, so I poked and prodded him along (between stops to lie on the rocky ground trying in vain to get his back to quiet down). He got inspired about three miles from the finish line and we ran hard into Leadville, Richard in tears from sadness and pain. He finished the race for his dad in style, and I was honored that we did it together. Years later, Richard would find out he had three broken vertebrae at the time; yes, the guy is that tough.

Realizing the Imogene Pass Run was a convenient meeting point for both Richard and me was a very welcome discovery. We have busy lives and family commitments; getting together for adventure time is not easy these days. Since we started in 2014, we've tried to make it to the IPR every year.

It's a tough race—the toughest of that distance I've ever done. There are several miles on the course that are so steep, it is helpful to put your palms on top of your knees and push as hard as you can, alternating left, right, left, right. Even then, it can be difficult to cover a single mile in under 25 minutes. That difficulty, and subsequent inevitable suffering, is a reminder for my old friend and me of adventures past. It's also a reminder that we can still head into the mountains and show the younger generation how it's done.

Richard and I will continue to head to Telluride every September for Imogene as long as our bodies will allow. And one day when we cannot run the race anymore, I'm sure we will still meet in Telluride to volunteer and scream for the throng of Flagstaff friends we both have.

Getting a friend into the race

AN EMAIL EXCHANGE AMONG NAT WHITE, MICHELLE WESSON, AND JOHN JETT

From: Nat White	Sent: Monday, June 4, 2018, 6:07 p.m.
To: John Jett	Cc: Michelle Wesson
Subject: Nat White Plans to Run 2018	

Hi John,

At 77 years plus, I plan to run with no injuries between now and September 8. Hope arrangements are going well. I know this is very irregular, but I have pasted an email below from my friend Michelle Wesson, who is currently our top female 40–45 10K runner in Flagstaff, "the Running Nation." I'll let the pasted email speak for itself.

Thanks,
Nat White

Hi Nat,

Thank you for offering to put in a word for me in hopes I can somehow get into Imogene this year. I ran Imogene in 2013 and carried some of my dear friend's ashes to the top. (Pat Taylor ran Imogene the year before and passed away from a brain tumor shortly afterward.) As I let her ashes go, tears in my eyes, a gentleman at the top grabbed my shoulders and said, "Go, girl, you're number three!" I had no idea! I was just enjoying my run up the "one hill" with Pat in a ziplock baggie tucked into my sports bra. As I ran down, there you were, playing "Amazing Grace." I cried almost the whole way down.

I ended up as third overall woman that year and told myself I might not run Imogene again because that had to be one of the greatest experiences of my life… but Pat's daughter Dawn encouraged me to do it again. That experience was not nearly as grand, but still an experience nonetheless. This year, I set my alarm for 4:00 a.m. on June 1. I had family in town for my son's high school graduation that same day and had a lot on my plate. I woke up at 7:00 a.m. on June 1 and cried (I know, again) because I missed it! It was sold out.

I expected that I didn't get in, but you gave me a glimmer of hope today when you said you could put in a good word for me. Then you somehow referenced my being competitive and getting old—hahaha, I think only runners get excited about getting older! Anyhow, thank you for offering to help, and if I do somehow have the opportunity to run Imogene this year, I know I will hear "Amazing Grace" in my head the entire way.

Thanks Nat!

Michelle Wesson

On 6/5/2018 7:00 a.m., John Jett wrote:

Hi Nat

Happy to have you back this year. Train well and see if you can beat your record! Your friend is welcome also, and an invitation has been sent to her.

Thanks

John Jett

Tue, 5 Jun 2018 14:51:07 -0700

John, thank you so much. Run for a new record? Time will tell, and it is telling me a lot these days.

Thanks,
Nat White

13 ways of looking at a marmot

BY MYLES SCHRAG

Climbing ever higher above tree line, a person seeks something—anything—to distract the senses from shredded legs, the occasional grunts from your fellow gluttons for punishment, and nearly a mile at 21 percent grade still to go to reach the Pass. I found my distraction in the cuddly form of Imogene's chubby buddies, scurrying just off the narrow trail to the many holes they had burrowed and shrieking at us as they ran.

Call this list my marmot musings—an Imogene mantra of sorts that helped get me to the top.

1. Was that M&M I ate back at Upper Camp Bird the red pill? Because listening to these little dudes talking definitely makes me feel like Alice in Wonderland.
2. I think that one just whistled "Stayin' Alive"... flawlessly.
3. I think that one just mocked my 26-minute-per-mile pace. I saw the smirk. I'm alright... I think.
4. Even Carl Spackler would love these adorable, gopher-looking creatures.
5. A marmot would totally be my mascot if I ever had an Imogene softball team.
6. Would Marmot the clothing manufacturer outfit the Imogene Fighting Marmots? What would they look like in down jackets?
7. Do they tidy up the mountain before Imogene each year?
8. These industrious furbearers should run a summit aid station and offer marmosas. Could they pour champagne without opposable thumbs?
9. It's really fun to say "marmot" slowly: Mmmmmmarrrrr-mot. Now say it even slower.
10. What do they do when more than a thousand people aren't running through their yards?
11. What else might I notice if I chose to think and feel beyond my pain? Thank you for opening my mind, Mr. Mmmmmmmmmmmarrrrrrrrrr-mmmmmot.
12. I-HEART-Imogene, sure. But give me a marmot for a pet.
13. I'll take that one in the yellow vest. And get me another red M&M at the summit aid station.

I don't think you're ready

BY ALICIA HENDRICKS

HEY, WE SHOULD GO WATCH MICHELLE AT THE IMOGENE Pass Run!" my husband said in the summer of 2018. (Michelle Wesson is an active runner in Flagstaff who has received medals for her Imogene finishes.)

I thought, Damion doesn't know me very well… I'm not just going to sit there. Maybe I'll run it, too!

•••

I started running with the dog every morning, on a trail near my house. One day, I decided to try Elden Lookout Road. Pizzicletta happened to be giving out free pizzas to anyone who could make it to the top by 8:30 a.m. I made it in time! After that, I knew I could do it.

Once I'd done a little training, we were talking with friends about the run when my husband said, "I don't think you should do Imogene. I don't think you're ready." That's when I realized how stubborn I am. I had the strongest desire to prove him wrong, and just to prove myself!

I scoured the internet for tips and ideas for taking on a mountain like that. Luckily, I came across a training program from Dara Marks Marino. It was a 13-week program made specifically for people in Flagstaff to train for Imogene. I bought it and dedicated myself to her plan, each month becoming stronger and more proud of myself.

I ran every peak in Flagstaff! But starting in May, many parts of the Coconino National Forest near Flagstaff were closed to all entry, due to extreme fire danger. Between fire restrictions and then monsoons, it was always a challenge to find an open, safe trail. But I met many people out there who were training for Imogene as well. They inspired me, gave me tips, and assured me I would be fine.

•••

The weekend for Imogene finally arrived. My husband and his father, Jerry Travens; Michelle Wesson and her husband, Neil; and my best friend April Thompson (who is battling stage 4 breast cancer) and her husband, Kevin, were there. Though she had every reason not to go, April said, "My best friend is conquering a freakin' mountain, and I wouldn't miss it for the world!"

We drove Imogene Pass in our Jeeps the day before while Michelle told us all the ins and outs of the run, the best part being her advice about that last singletrack before the summit. She said, "This is the part where you might want to poop yourself." After seeing what we would actually be running, my husband was even more nervous and stressed for me. I was just glad to drive it and get a chance to truly enjoy the beautiful scenery.

The song that got me over the Pass:
"I Will Survive" by Gloria Gaynor

Never having run a race of any kind before was nerve-racking. I planned to use a pacer so I wouldn't get caught up in the excitement of the start and go too fast. I had my playlist ready, and off we went. Within five minutes, though, my headphones broke. I was thinking, OK, it's all you now. So in silence, I ran. It was interesting to me that no one talked. All you heard was breathing and footsteps. I guess everyone knew the pain that was to come.

So I ran on.

Coming to the first checkpoint, I had no idea what time it was. I asked, "Did I make the cutoff?" They said, "Oh yeah, you have a half hour to go." I was so happy, I got teary-eyed. I knew everyone would be excited I had made it when they got the notification.

I had given myself two hours to get from Upper Camp Bird to the top, not knowing how I'd do. That next couple of miles is where you truly find yourself. You just hike, and your mental strength takes over. I took all the energy I could from every person who was rooting for me. I pretended my friend Michelle had a bungee cord attached to her and was pulling me up the hill. Every corner you turn, you see another hill. The elevation starts to mess with your head, your stomach hurts, and when you finally reach that singletrack to the top, you do want to poop yourself! But you hear the cheers and that cowbell. There were men standing at the final ledge to help people over, and boy, do you need that hand! When I made it to the Pass, I looked at the time. I was 3:08 into the race.

From left: Damion and me, with April and Kevin at Imogene Pass. As April said, "My best friend is conquering a freakin' mountain!"

Woohoo! I had done better than expected. I was so emotional, it was a struggle not to cry. I stopped and treated myself to a banana and some pretzels. Then it was time to head down. I'd heard about some falls on the unstable, rocky terrain going down, so I decided to take it easy on the first couple switchbacks. The downhill was long, but less painful than the uphill for sure. I finally took a moment to look up and enjoy the views!

When I got close to the finish, there were people at every turn cheering us on, and boy, do you need that, too! Around the last turn, I saw Michelle. She was cheering people on and waiting for me (she had finished in 3:20, earning a second-place medal). She started running with me, telling me how proud she was. My emotions were going crazy. Next, I saw her husband, Neil, and my father-in-law. Then at the street, I saw April and Kevin with their signs! Oh my gosh, I couldn't stop the tears. Finally, my husband started running with me to the finish, telling me how proud he was, both of us crying. He pointed out that I made it in under five hours. For me, that was a huge accomplishment.

Imogene is something I will never forget. Just the memory.

That next couple of miles is where you truly find yourself.

My mama ran up a mountain today

BY EMILY R. HOPPE

This essay originally appeared in the High Country Running column of the Arizona Daily Sun *on July 7, 2013, with the title "Overcoming Jitters to Conquer Elden."*

AFTER A STANDARD NIGHT OF FALLING ASLEEP in one child's bed at 8:00 p.m., waking up 30 minutes later, putting the second child to bed, falling asleep there until 10:00 when I crawled into my own bed, only to be awakened by child No. 1 at 1:30 a.m. in a scream-fest, I was lucky just to drive my car safely to the meeting place.

I haven't run well-rested in about three years, so a zombie-like state of putting in my contact lenses, pulling on my running clothes, and tiptoeing around the house is my normal.

I'm Mama to two beautiful girls (3 years and 19 months), a professional flutist, and a running junkie. I don't look like a runner. I'm squishy around the edges. I have asthma that has me chained to steroid and albuterol inhalers. I'm a solid mid-packer, but I manage 40-mile weeks. Running is my meditation. So on this morning at 4:30 a.m., I persuaded my body to ingest some breakfast, laced my shoes, and met my new training partners at 6:00.

I tend to be a loner when it comes to exercise. But as I knock on the door of my 40s, I long for the companionship of amazing women who inspire me to strive for greatness. When the opportunity arose to run with a fine group of ladies, I jumped on it. They are multitaskers of time, dedication, devotion, love, and life who are training for a big event while offering support.

> I felt like I could run forever. What's even more amazing: I was having the time of my life.

This would be my first attempt running Elden Lookout Road, up the west side of the mountain, and I was nervous. Nauseous nervous. That maybe-I-should-turn-my-car-around-and-drive-home kind of nervous. What if I didn't make it to the top? What if I had an asthma attack halfway through? Do I stick with my "eat a Gu every 45 minutes plan," or will I need more calories? It didn't help that my GPS decided to die that morning when I strapped it to my wrist. As a certified type-A personality, this was nearly enough to make me bag the whole thing.

Here's my real motivation: I am training for my first Imogene Pass Run. Somewhere in my perfectionist brain, I made a pact with the devil and decided that an Elden run would be the deciding factor of my viability for the Herculean feat of Imogene. I had only decided the night before to march my body up Mount Elden, so my normal dissertation-style research project of determining route, elevation, terrain, and total mileage was sabotaged.

We met with a joyful "good morning" and set the ground rules (run your own pace, wait at the top), and off we went. In an instant, I settled into a comfortable pace. I felt like I could run forever. What's even more amazing: I was having the time of my life. My breathing was rhythmic, my cadence well-paced. My legs felt loose and strong after I jogged/tiptoed around each switchback.

When I came to the last steep section before Oldham Park, which almost forced my body to a standstill, I urged my legs to keep going and stay fluid and tried to allow air to flow into my lungs. I stopped for a second to gaze at the small meadow, snapped a picture on my phone, and texted it to a friend. "Almost there, just have to get to those trees!" was the caption. I'm not sure why I felt so strong, but at that moment I felt like a superhero.

I learned a few things about myself that day. I soul-searched. I envisioned finishing Imogene. I made plans for the future and smiled at my past. I felt an inner strength reminiscent of when I finished my first and only marathon. I was in awe of the city below me. The houses looked so small, and I wondered if families were making pancakes, drinking their coffee, reading the newspaper, and enjoying the cool breeze of another clear-sky Flagstaff morning.

I returned home to bubbles, painting, repetitions of "Don't bite your sister," and reading *Pinkalicious*. For those few hours on Mount Elden, I worried about nothing other than putting one foot in front of the other. The adrenaline was still pouring through my veins. Later that day when I took the two lights of my life to the park, I overheard my Hello Kitty–clad daughter tell another little girl, "My mama ran up a mountain today."

Just typing that sentence brings a Cheshire cat–like grin to my face. That is why I run.

My Imogene Mantra:

"As long as you're still moving forward, you are doing just fine!"

FIRST YEAR/SNOW YEAR, THREE MORE RUNS THEN VOLUNTEER

BY DARLENE RYAN

I'VE BEEN A RUNNER EVER SINCE I CAN REMEMBER. Growing up in a small village in western New Mexico, I was literally always running late to school. I was active on the high school track team starting in eighth grade. When my family moved to Flagstaff in the mid-seventies, I joined the team at Coconino High School.

As an adult, I always enjoy running alone, left to my own thoughts and immersed in my surroundings. I heard of the Imogene Pass Run through a friend and neighbor in early 2006. She talked me into training with her, and when June 1 came, she reminded me to register (that's when you had more than a week to sign up!). I had no idea what I was getting myself into and no idea there was such a huge Flagstaff contingent taking part in this event every year.

With our husbands planning to go along for moral support, we rented a condo and drove to Telluride. My friend was hesitant to do the race, as she was healing from plantar fasciitis, which she had developed during training. It rained and rained in the days leading up to Imogene, and there was talk that for once, the race could be canceled. But the night before, everyone was told to head to Ouray in the morning and plan to run. For the first time in its history, the race would be rerouted. It would start and end in Ouray, due to snow at the Pass.

The next morning, I got up early, dressed, and headed to the bus alone. It was wet and cold. I entered the bus and saw a few familiar faces. We waited until everyone got aboard, then headed to Ouray. I slept most of the way.

At the school in Ouray, everyone was moving so fast. Lines for the bathroom were seemingly endless. A woman looked at me and said, "The demographics for this race sure have changed over the past years, don't you think?" I told her I didn't know, as this was my first time.

It turned out to be a beautiful day. Not knowing what was involved, I mostly fast-walked, running the flat areas. I was taken in by the stunning beauty of the area and the route. There were people all along the roadside, cheering the runners with cowbells and claps. The aid stations provided water, Gatorade, and trays of salty and sweet treats.

We worked our way past Lower Camp Bird and up, then veered right to about 10,800 feet elevation and looped back down. At some point, I decided I could run all the way back. On what turned out to be a clear and sunny day, I was overcome by heat—I was substantially overdressed. Back in Ouray, I followed other runners to stay on course. My husband met me at the finish, and was I ever happy to see him!

I did the run three more times after that. The second time, I went to experience the full course. I stopped and took

My Imogene Mantra:
Praying the "Hail Mary"
at least 100 times.

photos of the spectacular scenery and runners, and I even saw a fox. On the third run, I set out to beat my previous time (which I did). The fourth time, I ran to accompany a friend.

Each run was so grueling I swore I'd never do it again. Imogene is the most difficult thing I've ever done, but I still yearn for just one more.

•••

My husband and I have also volunteered twice for Imogene. The first time (2014) was at Tomboy aid station, on the downhill. This was a good warmup for the Pass (where the action is), which we did the following year.

Volunteering required us to get up very early to head over to orientation and then bum a ride up the mountain. That year at Tomboy aid station, the weather was unseasonably warm, and I took it upon myself to ask the runners if they'd like a "refresher." If they said yes, I would splash cold water on their back. One person wanted it in their face. Peter mixed up gallons of Gatorade and put hundreds of filled cups on a table others carried closer to the course to hand out.

At the Pass, everything is served—and then some. There were massages for those with cramps, and hot broth for anyone who wanted it. Unfortunately, that year someone forgot the paper cups, and the hot broth melted the plastic cups.

While volunteering, we noticed the elite runners didn't stop for anything, looking over their shoulder to see who might be gaining. Everyone else managed to enjoy the party. Many runners just hang out at the Pass, chatting with friends, having their photo taken with the sign, seemingly unconcerned about time until they decided to head down to Telluride.

The weather couldn't have been better on both occasions. Runners and volunteers alike had an amazingly upbeat attitude. And being from Flagstaff, it was great fun to see familiar faces!

The rabbit in the hat

BY ANNE LEOTA HART

THE IMOGENE ALLURE, THIS MYSTIQUE THAT LURES so many to take on the physical, mental, and emotional challenge of running 17.1 miles—ascending out of Ouray at 7,810 feet elevation, crossing over the 13,114 Imogene Pass and dropping down to 8,750 feet to end up in Telluride, in who knows what kind of weather—what is this quest that has enchanted so many Flagstaffians?

With my spouse, Liz Brauer, 2009.

When my spouse and I moved to Flagstaff in 1997, we had never heard of Ouray and had no idea about this race or who the heck Imogene was. Liz was a runner, but I wasn't anymore (long story involving vanishing knee cartilage). After she connected with the running community, it became obvious that to get real running "creds" in this town, you had to experience the Imogene Pass Run. Running was not an option for me, but I wanted to feel the Imogene magic. I was unable to be the magician, but at least I could be the rabbit that gets pulled out of the hat! So I've been part of my spouse's crew in her three races (so far): 2009, 2016, and 2017.

Crewing for a runner takes many skills. You have to be able to:

- arrive at least a day early to scout the layout at the start and along the course.

Scouting the course in 2009, we drove partway up the jeep trail and missed the first turnoff. This photo was taken far off the course. Liz is pointing to nothing, really. My grandfather loved for people to point in photos, so that's why she's pointing.

- get up at ass-crack dawn with a functioning brain and be upbeat and perky, even when one is a night person.

From left: Me, Liz's sister Lois Colberg, and Liz at the start, 2017.

- maintain calm and be motivating or supportive or all three at the same time as needed.
- carry extra clothing, gear, and assorted "stuff" for comfort in the cold morning hours before the start, which are then removed in the last minutes.
- organize what's needed at the finish (like recovery equipment, clothes, snacks, and beverages).
- drive through the incredible beauty between Ouray and Telluride without getting distracted and off schedule.
- check and double-check to be sure the bathing suits are packed for the requisite stop at the Ouray Hot Springs postrace (crew members need a hot soak too).
- and, the greatest challenge: find a parking place in Telluride on race day (do you pay, or do you spend your limited time searching for a free place?).

Some of my favorite things about being part of a crew have been:

- attending the pre-race orientation banquet and information session and seeing all the runners (newbies and repeaters) lined up for their packets, race shirts, and coveted bibs.
- listening to the conversations about weather reports, shoes, rain gear or cold-weather gear, water storage systems, Gu, electrolyte replacements, and the likeliest places to fall on the course.
- soaking up the crackling electricity at the starting line as runners begin their journey.
- feeling the energy drain away as the start line is deserted and Ouray returns to its quiet, small-town vibe.
- watching the runners fade into tiny, colorful dots as they go up the hill outside Ouray and gradually disappear into the mountains.
- making the drive from Ouray to Telluride through such incredible beauty.
- my most favorite: waiting along the last mile (dropping into Telluride before Oak Street and the finish), cheering, clapping, ringing a cowbell, and asking a few times, "Are you OK?" when exhausted runners fall at that little bump created by a drainage pipe near where the road turns to pavement (you know the one). It's a great spot to watch the bloodied and the bent and to soak up the amazing, triumphant feeling of those who realize they're going to make it.
- walking in the crowds of runners and spectators around the finish area, catching wisps of laughter and postrace stories of triumph, pain, and fear overcome, along with the proverbial question, "Will you do it next year?"

The bloodied and the bent: Your perfectly fit body after 17.1 miles of high-altitude running.

I learned some very unexpected and valuable life lessons from being at Imogene. From the wise and humorous words shared in the prerace orientation, from the buzz of runners' chat before and after the race, from the cheers of supporters lining the course into Telluride, and from the postrace soak in the Ouray Hot Springs, my most memorable lessons are:

- "The mountain don't care" (PLAN AHEAD, BE PREPARED, PRACTICE SELF-RELIANCE)
- "Incessant forward motion" (THE IMPORTANCE OF PERSISTENCE, ESPECIALLY WHEN THINGS GET HARD)
- "You've got one more mile to the finish" (THE VALUE OF BEING TRUTHFUL)

I treasure each and every time I was in the Wonderland of Imogene. I loved being able to say, "I am from Flagstaff." And I still dream of making that journey on foot over the Pass one day to become part of Imogene lore.

Crew has learned to relax (Box Canyon).

THE DUDE WEARING SANDALS

BY JOHN WHIPPLE

I HAD RETURNED TO FLAGSTAFF AFTER YEARS ON THE road, touring with my music. I was in bad shape. Trucker bod. Stomping out rhythms as a one-man band didn't burn enough calories to make up for all that free beer and pub grub.

Flagstaff shamed me into fitness. On every trip through town, there would be beautiful people running and biking around, the weather always so welcoming. Come outside and play! I gave in to peer pressure and started running.

Early in 2012, my friend Matt Brydenthal convinced me to try the Imogene Pass Run. That seemed a worthy goal to set my sights upon. I had no fantasies of winning, but I thought I could finish in some respectable manner. The toughest challenge was figuring out what to do about shoes. I had been living barefoot for years. Being a musician and occasionally self-contracting odd jobs, I could set my own dress code. Mine did not include any footwear.

I've always been this way. Shoes seem so alien to me. I don't like being cut off from the world, with all my experience of it entering through the senses in my head. I like to connect with the ground below me and experience the world through my entire body.

My feet were certainly tougher than most. I ran barefoot across town without much fuss. I did a fair amount of hiking barefoot. I have even climbed mountains barefoot. Still, I knew there were limits. I am not a goat. I would not be able to run over a rocky Colorado mountain pass in bare feet.

I had some running shoes from years before. They were pretty much new, as I almost never wore them. I tried them, but they killed me. The cramped toe box was murder. My feet were probably a size wider than when I bought those shoes. After going barefoot for so long, these feet have become such outliers that it's nearly impossible to find shoes that fit. Shoes are all designed for the thinner and more fragile feet of the modern human. Even sports sandals are murder. All their "support" counters the muscles I've developed to support myself.

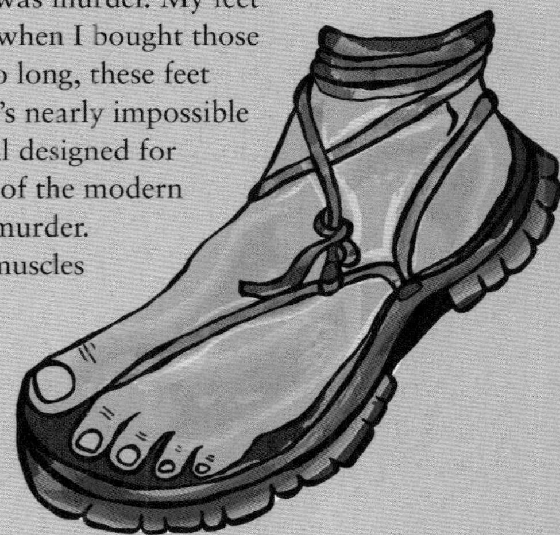

I had built some lightweight huaraches based on what the Tarahumara Indians of Mexico's Copper Canyon wear. Their flat soles were about an eighth of an inch thick. It was enough to blunt the impact of small rocks, but when I tried them in the San Juans, I realized I was going to need something sturdier to withstand the impact of all the large rocks.

AFTER GOING BAREFOOT FOR SO LONG, THESE FEET HAVE BECOME SUCH OUTLIERS THAT IT'S NEARLY IMPOSSIBLE TO FIND SHOES THAT FIT.

Matt and I arrived in the San Juan mountains about a week early to fish, camp, and prepare for the run. Just days before the event I was worried. I had given up on the running shoes, but I knew I needed something more than bare feet. The next time we went into Telluride, I found some old hiking boots that were just about my size. I had no interest in the boots themselves, but their soles were thick and sturdy. Back at our camp, I took a knife to them and carved out the soles. Lacing my flimsy huaraches to the boot soles, I had my solution; something sturdy enough to stomp over the rocky terrain, with enough freedom for my toes to splay out like they're accustomed to.

The modified sandals served me well during the run. I was able to complete the course without being cramped in shoes or being punished by the thousands of rocks. In passing, a lot of runners commented on them. At the aid station on Imogene Pass, a guy announced loudly, "That dude is wearing sandals!" I was the only one.

Some runners expressed shock at the sight of my sandals. It was hard for them to believe someone could take on the mountain with such footwear. I looked at their high-tech trail runners with equal disbelief, knowing I couldn't possibly wear those.

Still, we were helping each other up the mountain. We were sharing the struggle. We were sharing the suffering, too, but it was a joyous suffering. When I reached the top of Imogene Pass, the weight of the mountain was lifted off my shoulders and I was given the sky to ride down on. A lace broke, and I fell. I got a little bloody, but I got up. I made a quick repair. I could see the rooftops of Telluride below me. I crossed the finish line and felt that triumphant exhaustion all us runners shared. I immediately pulled off my sandals, to my great relief. The warm pavement was a welcome sensation for my bare feet as I returned to the lifestyle I had adapted myself to.

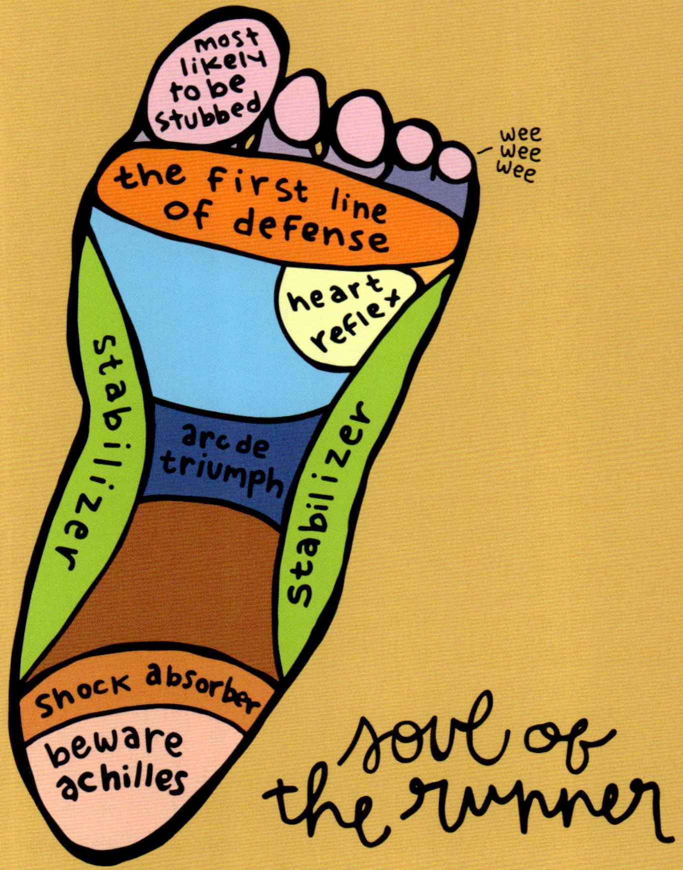

Human bodies are far more adaptable than we give them credit for. I'm not sure we have discovered how far the mind can change the body. Though I've always hated the cold of winter, this year I made a point to take it on and will go running in little more than a pair of shorts. It sucked at first, but now I hunger for it. Plenty of people I have told about the Imogene Pass Run react with groans. To them, it sounds like torture, but we who have done it know it to be a joyous adventure. We have changed our minds, and our minds changed our bodies. The best thing is that what the body learns, it won't let the mind forget.

A primate's perspective

I was IPR's high-fiving finish-line gorilla

BY JOSH BIGGS

Two bits of trivia about me: 1) I'm perennially injured for the Imogene Pass Run. 2) I usually travel with a cheap gorilla suit in the back of my car.

IN 2010, THESE TWO FACTS CAME TOGETHER TO create one of my strangest IPR experiences (and definitely my smelliest).

About the first item: I train too hard and hurt myself or get sick. I make it to the start line about a third of the times I register. By the time there's a problem, the hotel has usually been booked, so we drive up to Telluride anyway, to cheer on friends and take in the western Colorado autumn.

In 2010, I injured my knee… or was it my Achilles? Because I couldn't race, I spent the day at the finish line, harassing Imogene finishers. That's where the second item comes in: Not many people know about my gorilla suit anymore. I used to break it out at parties, weddings, or sometimes just for a late-night walk through downtown Flagstaff.

In 2010, I added the Imogene finish line to that list.

Instead of running over a mountain, I spent my morning high-fiving dozens of runners and hugging a few more as they neared the end of their race in Telluride. The suit sheds, so not only does a gorilla hug smell like rubber, body odor, and old beer, it deposits tufts of black hair on recipients, especially if they are sweaty.

After 17 miles, trust me… the recipients of my hugs had tufts of black hair stuck to them.

Some folks were excited to see me, running faster or jumping in for a victory dance with the gorilla. More memorable were the racers who were not. They were suffering through it, and no matter how much I jumped around, they kept their eyes firmly on the trail. Better yet, they'd throw a bulldoggy stink eye my way. As one racer passed me closely, I heard him mutter under his breath, "Fuck you, gorilla."

I ran down Oak Street in the suit with some friends as they finished. Running in the suit is a disorienting, stumbling experience, especially on the steep grade. The mask gives tunnel vision, and the large rubber gorilla feet flop around. Having seen so many runners wipe out at the finish line, I remember thinking that rather than stressing an Achilles, getting plantar fasciitis, or straining an IT band while racing too hard on the mountain, this would be a more memorable way to injure myself at a race—going down dressed as a primate.

Clockwise from top left: Ben Keeler and Carrie Butler; Greg Szymanski and Sheri Young; Margaret Montfort and Krista Star; Mary Mohr.

Clockwise from top left: Chrissy and Rob Speer; Fon Cordasco (in blue) beside her dad, Roger Hartman (black cowboy hat) and members of the Fon-tourage in 2013 (see page 176); Jerry and Sandy Diehl; Sharon Moore; Alicia Hendricks and April Thomoson.

COLOR YOUR OWN IMOGENE!

Notes

part 7

Advice From the Lovelorn

What we've learned from our grand romance

A mindset shift, a lasting gift

BY STEVE SUE

WHEN I FIRST STARTED ATTENDING TEAM RUN Flagstaff workouts in 2010, I came across runners of all ages and skill levels who were driven to take on new challenges. Whether knowledgeable long-time runners or newbies fresh out of the organization's Step Into Running program, they always seemed to be searching for more difficult races.

Many of my friends on those Tuesday-evening workouts talked about the Imogene Pass Run, how fun it was and how everybody in Flagstaff wanted to participate in it. These people were weirdly inspired by this race. Against this backdrop of optimism and enthusiasm, my reaction was, um… less than excited.

All I could think about was how difficult climbing to 13,000 feet sounded. That's not for me, I decided.

And, you know, of course that's what I decided. That's how I lived my life then. I didn't want to challenge myself—in school, in work, in my personal life. If there was an easier class or an easier route, I took it; this Imogene thing was definitely not the easier route to anything. Above all else, I did not want to fail. Better to say, "Yeah, I could have done it but chose not to" rather than try it and not succeed. Better to be considered lazy than incapable. I believed that.

That's how I lived, and it wasn't getting me what I wanted. I'm a creature of habit, but I slowly realized I needed to make a change. Maybe, I thought, my running life was a good place to start. Finally, in 2014, with years of people's encouragement and joy swirling in my head, I thought maybe I should give this Imogene thing a shot.

When registration morning came around, as always, on June 1—or as I like to call it, Flagstaff's summer Christmas—I signed up for the run.

That was a huge step. Once I committed, I made failure a possibility. But I also opened myself up to the fun and satisfaction experienced by my friends. People told me Elden Lookout Road was similar to Imogene. So, I ran it. Monday-night group runs met at Buffalo Park and dropped down to Lower Oldham Trail Loop. Tuesdays were TRF workouts at the Northern Arizona University track. I trained harder that summer than for any past race I'd ever run.

•••

The night before the race, crashing in the living room of friends who had rented a Telluride condo, I didn't get a great night's sleep. But I still had my plan, and I was excited to execute it.

The next morning, I felt good for the first three miles. But soon, my stomach started doing flip-flops. Slowing to a walk, I barely avoided throwing up. I tried to run again, but that just made my stomach worse. I realized I needed to walk to keep incessant forward motion happening. My summer of training hadn't included exactly what I needed to do right now… walking. Walking, as it turns

Flagstaff's summer Christmas: June 1, Imogene registration day. For some, the gift of three months of hard-core training; for the rest, a lump of coal inscribed, "Wait 'til next year."

out, is really important for Imogene. Now my short legs and I were going to have to shift plans. Failure was definitely very much on the table.

Anybody who does Imogene comes to the realization that walking with urgency (speed-hiking is often the term used) is necessary to meet the cutoff times and get to the Pass. Everyone around me certainly seemed to know that. I was getting passed by everyone, and I felt horrible. However, I could see the top. And I told myself, "When I get to the top, I'm going to feel better. I just know that." I had no logical reason to think that was true, but I sincerely believed it. With several miles and thousands of feet of climbing still to go, though, in that moment I was still miserable. I kept trudging along.

Along the way, I saw Flagstaff participants and spectators cheering everybody on with signs and loud voices. I did get to the Pass, and once there I realized that Darlene Ryan, a friend from TRF workouts, was volunteering. She asked if I wanted my photo taken. To this day, that photo is my profile picture on Facebook… and I did start to feel better.

That first quarter mile on the Telluride side is steep, but I told myself I could do this. We have rocky, steep trails in Flagstaff, including Lower Oldham. Other runners were cautious, almost tiptoeing, but I was taking the bad lines and passing them. I felt great. That continued all the way down the mountain.

When I finally reached the finish line, the elation of having been moving quickly for the past hour gave way to relief. The stomach problems that were out of mind returned, and I threw up three times. To this day, that's absolutely the hardest race I've ever run. That includes eight marathons and the Stagecoach 55K. I consider Imogene, even at just 17.1 miles, easily a marathon effort.

•••

I'm a numbers guy, so I looked at my splits later. It took me 3:24 to get to the top, and 1:11 to reach the bottom. As I read the results, I was the 995th person who reached the Pass that year out of 1,220 people who got that far, and my time from the top to Telluride was 440th best. I finished 786th overall, meaning I passed 209 people on the downhill. That felt great, but Imogene was not about beating other people—not by a long shot. Imogene was about overcoming my own fear of failure, about having to adjust when the plan changed and not taking the easy way out.

Imogene gave me a new approach to races and life. When I'm struggling, I remind myself I'll feel better later on, but I need to keep moving for now. Imogene spurred me on to accept other challenges; professionally, personally, and in running. I even began to understand that sometimes the greater joy is accomplishing something after I fail at it the first time.

This was a realization—to see failure as part of a process toward achievement, not as an endpoint I should be ashamed of. Perfection isn't important. Shoot, it's the trying that makes anything any fun at all. We're human beings, driven not by instinct but by trial and error.

That is the only time I've ever run Imogene, and though I'll never say never, I don't plan on signing up again. I'd like to shoot for a better time, but I have other goals and challenges right now. I've done Imogene, and it turns out that when I chose Imogene, she gave me a great gift.

THE DIRECTION I CHOSE

BY PATTI QUIGLEY

"You have brains in your head. You have feet in your shoes.
You can steer yourself any direction you choose.
You're on your own. And you know what you know.
And you are the one who'll decide where to go."

That's what Dr. Seuss told us in *Oh, The Places You'll Go.*

From left: Me, Mary, Marsha, and Sharon in Ouray, 2014.

WHEN I BEGAN MY RUNNING JOURNEY IN MY EARLY 50s at Flagstaff's annual Machine Solutions Run and Walk, I did not realize how much my future would change. I developed a passion for running and made new friendships. As the years passed with active memberships in Team Run Flagstaff, Northern Arizona Trail Runners Association, and the Flagstaff Trail Divas, I began hearing about a Flagstaff rite of passage called the Imogene Pass Run.

Could I even think about doing this race? Was I strong enough? I had already pushed myself and boosted my self-confidence with numerous 5K and 10K races and half marathons, but Imogene? The Pass was over 13,000 feet, and that in itself was intimidating to me. But I heard stories from past participants of how wonderful this race was to run. I decided (with some trepidation) to register.

I felt that in order to be successful, I needed to start training more aggressively with longer runs and hikes, hill training, and elevation training. My running buddies provided support to make this experience more fun. I elicited training tips from fellow Trail Divas Marsha Jensen and Sharon Moore, past IPR participants. I shared my goals with Jesse Coddington at New Roots Personal Training, who developed a strength program for conquering that "one long hill." My fellow gym mates Rob and Alice Berger provided additional tips based on their multiple past Imogene races.

In Telluride, I met up with my friends Mary Mohr and Marsha Jensen before the race. I remember at packet pickup, the three of us looked up toward the Pass and felt a combination of awe and intimidation about the upcoming event. We wanted to all start together, but we knew the ending would be an individual accomplishment.

I cannot describe fully the feeling I had after I made the first cutoff at Upper Camp Bird. I had set the first goal of the race and achieved this milestone. I ran and walked to the Pass, where the majestic mountains surrounded and embraced me with congratulations in making it to the top. I was in shock as I finally did what many Flagstaffians have done when I crossed that finish line, with my husband waiting and cheering me on.

My Imogene Mantra:
"You can do it."

This story doesn't end here. I returned to Imogene two years later, but this time I was not successful in completing the race. I made it to the first cutoff feeling nauseated and light-headed with headache. Although the medical personnel told me I could go on, I decided to listen to my gut and end the race. I could have lamented not continuing; however, I focused on the positives of attempting IPR for the second time, being in the mountains and with my running community, and staying healthy. On a side note, the four-wheel-drive EMS truck that hauled me back to Ouray was an exciting ride back down the rocky, steep, and uneven road. If I had continued, I wouldn't have had this experience!

I proved to myself that with proper preparation, any goal can be achieved. I had trained hard for my first Imogene, not knowing what to expect from myself. The physical and mental challenges were immense, especially for a newer, older runner like me. Yes, the mountain beat me the second time, but the spiritual gains from both years outweighed the "did not finish" status. Plans may change, so be happy for the experience, and journey toward adventures. I made the decision to attempt something out of my norm and prove to myself anything was possible. In memory of the late Dr. Nate Avery: Live your Best Life Ever!

No chicken noodle soup for me, thanks

BY RACHEL (TABER) HART

MY FIRST IMOGENE PASS RUN WAS PROBABLY SIMILAR to everyone else's (although I'm a vegetarian, so I didn't have the chicken noodle soup at the finish line, or the bacon-wrapped something at the top!). I went into it with the idea that I was going to enjoy myself and not make it a race. My goals were to have fun and make the cutoffs. I did both with ease. As I crossed the finish line, it was hard to stop due to the downhill grade, but thankfully, there was a crowd who helped me, and no one got knocked over in the process. The pin is the best finishers gift I've ever received. But my strongest memories from that 2015 run are:

- Around Mile 3, I started to alternate slow running with walking. I remember very clearly that I wanted to take pictures. I'm so glad I did!

- When we reached the switchbacks, I was having a hard but great time. I turned to the girl behind me and said, "I may ask you to push me up this thing." I was joking! But the girl said, "I make it a point to not touch people."

- I cried when I reached the Pass. I had my picture taken, took another lady's picture, and off I went, down the hill. I probably spent the first half mile on my rear. The dirt was really loose, and I'm not too great on downhills to begin with. Around Mile 14 was an aid station with candy–lots of candy! I took five jelly beans and ate them one by one. They were the most delicious jelly beans I've ever had.

- Back on the trail I went. When I curved around the corner to the pavement, my legs were tired, but I picked up speed thanks to the crowds of people cheering us on. It was the best and the highest I felt the whole run! I hear my name and looked to the right, and ther were my friends. One of them took a perfect snapshot of me smiling and looking strong.

I GOT IN AGAIN TWO YEARS LATER, but when a training injury got worse and worse, I decided not to race. We went to Telluride anyway, to support the droves of runners we knew. On race day, I left breakfast early so I could watch the finish. Seeing that the first female finisher was from Flagstaff was a bittersweet moment that brought tears to my eyes. I wanted to give Kate McGee a hug, since (unlike some runners I've met) I do make it a point to touch people, but I worried that might seem a little creepy on my end.

At the time, I knew we would soon be moving to Wisconsin. Watching everyone finish, I thought sadly, I'll never be able to do this run again because there's no elevation training where I'm going. But when a man from Green Bay crossed the finish line, my faith was restored: I will run this mountain again. I am so excited for my next Imogene, whenever it comes!

- As we were walking around afterward so I wouldn't stiffen up too badly, we saw a grilled cheese sandwich cart. Holy cow, that grilled cheese was sooooo good.

My family has never missed a race or run in the nine years I've been racing. They are my rocks, my biggest fans.

GENERAL NON-PROFESSIONAL BUT EXPERIENCED THOUGHTS ABOUT RUNNING IMOGENE

BY NAT WHITE

I gave this presentation at the Run Flagstaff store to local runners who were preparing for the 2013 Imogene Pass Run.

Your motivation for running Imogene influences your overall training plan.

- If your goal is to be first in some category, that requires a more technical and strategic approach, and a long-term running background.
- If your goal is to see what you can do all-out, that requires good overall conditioning with long runs and strategic training over a four- to five-month period.
- If your goal is to complete the run as a personal challenge, that requires lots of power hill hiking and long, slow runs over three or four months.

Your training plan should be capitalizing on your strong points and strengthening your weaker points. Your strategies must take account of your training and running background and your age.

For most runners, the run has four elements that you will encounter and need to train or prepare for, plus gear:

- continuous running uphill
- significant uphill power walking
- altitude
- continuous downhill running
- gear

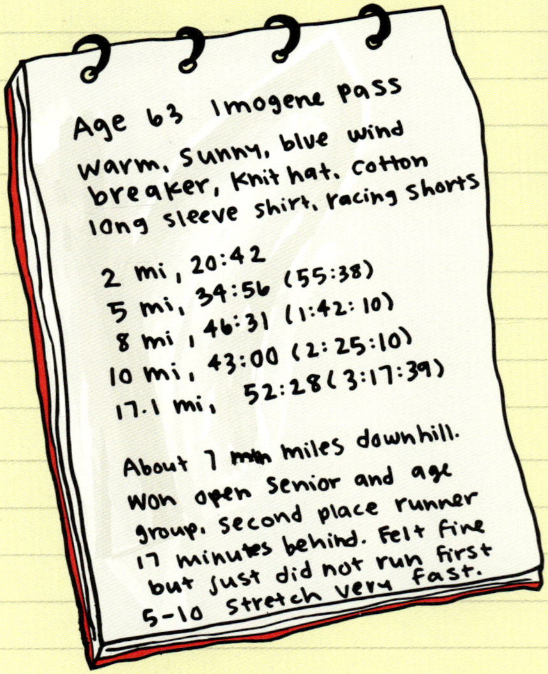

Things I have done that probably were not the most efficient training:

- Run until tired every day.
- Focus on lots of mileage.
- Long, hard runs high on the Peaks.
- Training at high altitude.
- Sleeping at altitude.

Things that worked better for me:

- Early on in the training I start with a guess as to easily manageable weekly mileage and divide this distance into one longer run and all the rest shorter runs.
- I may increase the weekly mileage or not, but I do increase the distance and intensity of the longer run over time.
- On the shorter runs during the week, I might emphasize repeat hills, or downhill running or power walking or just easy running.
- I will do some fast-slow running once a week.

Train rested, with the primary goal of a more intense weekly long run.

Favorite training spots:

For long runs: Mount Elden Road, Inner Basin Road, Schultz Pass Road east to west, cinder cones north and west of Winona, Snowbowl from Aspen Corner to midway up the Agassiz ski run switchbacks.

For shorter runs: Lowell Flagstaff Urban Trail System, Buffalo Park, the many roads and trails on Observatory Mesa, and some track runs.

Equitable sleeping arrangements

BY KERMIT SMITH

One of my fondest memories is of my wife and me sharing the same condo in Ouray, in the late 1990s and early 2000s, with the same three couples for about four years in a row: Rich and Jennie Haag, David and Linda Klensin, and Tom and Ellen Grabarek. Ellen was a regular IPR participant along with us four guys. There were a variety of sleeping areas, from master suite with full bath, to regular bedrooms with a shared bath, to the sleeper sofa in the den. We managed to all cycle through each different sleeping space due to our consistent participation at Imogene. The homemade celebratory dinners, cocktail hours, and reminiscences about the day's challenges were always the highlight of the weekend.

From left: Rich, Tom, Ellen, me, and David, 2004.

DON'T UNDERESTIMATE OLD GUYS ON THE DOWNHILL

BY STEWART AITCHISON

W**HEN I MADE THE APPOINTMENT FOR MY ANNUAL** checkup with my family doctor in early 1994, I had no idea the lesson I was about to learn.

While I was being poked and tested, my doctor, Walt Taylor, told me how he and his wife, Nancy, had been participating in the Imogene Pass Run for a number of years. He said a large group of people made the annual trip from Flagstaff to Colorado, and it was always great fun.

That wasn't what I focused on, however. I immediately got to thinking: Walt is 10 years older than me. Well, if this old guy could do it, I told myself, surely I could easily complete the course.

My training began. Finally, the end of summer came, and we found ourselves at the starting line in Ouray facing that steep initial climb. The starting gun went off, and the running crowd began its slow slog uphill. Geez, this was going to be really hard.

Walt was taking his time, barely shuffling. "I'm not too fast on the uphill, but I'm really good on the downhill," he calmly said.

After a mile or so, Walt and I were beginning to get warmed up and finding our individual paces. After a few more miles, I was way ahead of Walt but could still see him back in the crowd. Up and up we all went. Once above timberline, I looked back and thought I could see him. He was much lower down. I finally stumbled to the Pass aid station. While there, I took a short break, as so many participants do. I scanned back down the trail, but no sign of Walt.

Off I began down the steep other side toward Telluride. The loose gravel made footing treacherous, and although gravity was pulling hard, I was extra careful not to slide and fall. It was touch-and-go trying to run fast while not losing control. My quads were burning, but seeing the town below spurred me on.

About halfway down the mountain, I heard footsteps quickly coming up behind me. Suddenly, Walt zoomed by, and as he disappeared down the trail, I heard: "I'm really good on the downhill!"

No matter how hard I coaxed my body, there was no way to catch him. I guess it's true: Old guys rule.

Lessons learned from the mountain

A REMINDER OF MY STRENGTH

BY KRISTINA LEE KAISER

A GROUP OF GIRLS I WAS RUNNING WITH TALKED ME into doing my first Imogene Pass Run in 2013. They had been doing the race on and off for years. My boyfriend at the time came to watch, and we shared lodging with some of my runner friends. My knee and glute had been hurting for a few weeks, so I saw a physical therapist two weeks before the race. The PT told me I had a significant muscle imbalance as a result of injuring my knee when I fell on a rock while trail running a few months prior.

The scenery during the race was breathtaking. Inspiring views of the rugged terrain, coupled with running among so many joyful racers, including many from my hometown, made the long uphill to the Pass attainable. The adrenaline of the race took my mind off any knee pain, and once I came around the corner with the finish line in sight, the supportive spectators cheering us racers on gave me a much-needed kick. With the race finished and the adrenaline gone, my knee began to swell and ache. But I did finish, and with a race time I was pleased with. (In the 2013 results, I'm "Kristina Saxton.")

Afterward, I craved a turkey sandwich, so while I iced my knee, my boyfriend drove us to a local deli. I bought my sandwich, then limped back to the car, using the partially open window to help myself get into the car. He intended to roll down the window, but instead he accidently rolled it up on my finger. Seeing this, he panicked, and for what seemed like a few minutes (but was really just a few seconds), I shrieked, "Roll it down! Roll it down!" I teased him for weeks that his strategy to make my knee quit hurting was to make my finger hurt much worse.

My second Imogene race the next year was much different. A couple weeks after registering for the race with my boyfriend, I found a lump in my breast. I suspected immediately that it was breast cancer, since I'd been getting ill more than normal for the previous few months. Exactly two months before the race, the diagnosis was confirmed, and a few weeks before the race, I had two lumpectomies to remove the cancer.

Imogene was smack in the middle of 6 ½ weeks of radiation. I planned to arrive in Colorado a couple days early but was told I couldn't skip the radiation that was scheduled the day before the race. The oncologist nurse told me I could run Imogene but added, "We don't yet know all the side effects of radiation." During the race, I found one: elevation! Just one year earlier, the trek up to 13,100 feet hadn't affected me at all, nor had my run up 12,637-foot Mount Humphreys, the highest natural point in Arizona, a couple of weeks prior to starting radiation. But this time, about a mile from the Pass, I felt dizzy and somewhat disoriented. I thought I might pass out and was certain there was no way I would make it to the top. I remember seeing my boyfriend ahead of me and wishing he would read my mind that I needed help. I so badly wanted him to take my hand to give me a mental boost up that last mile.

And he did seem to read my mind. While I watched him climb the mountain ahead of me, which by itself motivated me to keep going, he stopped in his tracks and looked back for me with a smile. I looked at him with desperate eyes, hoping he would understand that I needed help. He stopped and waited patiently for me to reach him. I felt a huge wave of relief as he took my hand. Just having him by my side, even though he wasn't physically pulling me up the hill, relaxed my entire body and mind. I knew I could get to the top, slow as I was.

I did not let that confidence extend beyond my goal of reaching the Pass. I was certain I would stop there and wait for someone to drive me down the remaining seven miles. But something remarkable happened when I saw the familiar downhill: a wave of happiness, relief, and energy came over me.

My boyfriend and I started down the mountain. After a few miles, he tweaked his knee. He'd had two knee surgeries previously, one in each knee, so when I saw him start limping, I stopped to ask if he was OK.

"Keep going," he told me. I did, and finished the race only about eight minutes slower than the previous year. I was holding back tears of relief, overwhelmed with emotion, and slightly annoyed that I was slower than my 2013 time. Looking back on the race, I realize how ridiculous that was and how big of an accomplishment even attempting the race was.

A few minutes later, my boyfriend crossed the finish limping but with a smile on his face.

•••

For the next couple of years, I took time off from racing to recover from breast cancer, focus on moving in with my boyfriend who was now my fiancé, and blend our families.

Then, in 2017, several of my friends from the same running group were doing the race again, so I signed up for a third time.

I invited my fiancé to go with me. We'd been having difficulties in our relationship, and I thought a getaway would be good for us. But things continued to fall apart, and I left for the race without him.

I was under a different kind of stress this time, the heartbreak kind, not the physical of my two earlier Imogenes—or so I thought. I cancelled the place I had rented for the two of us and made plans to sleep on the couch at the place where two of my good friends were staying. I caught a ride with another friend, teary-eyed on part of the drive there.

During the race, my body felt very tired, but I chalked it up to emotional stress. The biggest annoyance to me was that I had to stop a few times to pee, but when I tried, hardly anything would happen. Thanks to adrenaline, it didn't register in my mind that I likely had a bladder infection. For the mile before reaching Imogene Pass and then at the top, I held back tears from all the stresses of the past year, but also because there is something deeply moving about reaching the top after climbing so long and hard for a few miles.

I started down the hill I was now very acquainted with, relieved that there wasn't anyone running right beside me so I could finally let out the tears I'd been holding in for too long. I saw a photographer focus his camera lens on me, so I tried to turn my ugly, stress-relieving sobs into a half smile. I never looked for that photo, but I'm sure it wasn't pretty.

I finished the race, my slowest of all three times, slower even than when I was in the middle of radiation treatments. A beautiful light rain began to fall, but I was unusually chilled.

I couldn't get warm no matter what I did—even after enjoying two cups of the warm chicken noodle soup they always have for finishers. I watched some of my friends finish, then went and mostly rested on the couch in my temporary home. I caught a ride back to Flagstaff with my friends the next day, feeling rundown and worried about the future of my relationship. I went to the doctor and was prescribed medicine for what I had suspected—a bladder infection.

Despite this, I had a wonderful experience bonding with supportive friends, running among many other joyful runners who were also attempting this challenging race, and once again taking in the magnificent views of the San Juan Mountains. The Imogene race always seems to bring people together.

•••

All three Imogene races provided lessons I needed to learn. The first taught me that I need to prepare for big things by strengthening my weaknesses, that everyone makes mistakes, and that there's humor in most moments, even the painful ones. In the second, I learned that I don't have to prove anything and that all challenges eventually come to an end, including illness. The third time I did IPR, I learned that I have wonderful, supportive friends.

Racing conditions, including how we feel mentally, physically, and emotionally, are rarely ideal. Enduring such a tough event when our conditions aren't perfect makes us more resilient and is part of what calls us to this mountain race. Imogene is an invitation to dig deeper, to embrace the pain.

When life feels hard, I have a tendency to want to push myself physically, because it helps me work through problems. Imogene is one of the most mentally and physically challenging races a person can do. Imogene reminded me of just how strong I am.

From left: Me, Laureen Simpson, and Staci Whitman, 2017.

ENDURING SUCH A TOUGH EVENT WHEN OUR CONDITIONS AREN'T PERFECT MAKES US MORE RESILIENT AND IS PART OF WHAT CALLS US TO THIS MOUNTAIN RACE. IMOGENE IS AN INVITATION TO DIG DEEPER, TO EMBRACE THE PAIN.

Plotting for Imogene

BY LIZ BRAUER

I **DON'T REMEMBER HOW I FIRST HEARD ABOUT THE** Imogene Pass Run, but in 2009 I decided to give it a try. Because, why not? It seemed a bit crazy, but not crazy crazy.

I was 49, so I needed to be prepared to get through it without suffering too much. I was particularly worried about the 2:30 cutoff at Upper Camp Bird, 7.6 miles and 3,400 feet of elevation gain from the start. I am not a fast runner, and I knew the altitude and distance would make the first cutoff a challenge. The 4:30 cutoff at Imogene Pass was not as concerning to me.

Being self-coached and having no idea how to train for a race like Imogene, I asked other runners what they did. Most everyone said, "Oh, you'll do fine; you will make the cutoff with no problem." The first cutoff had just been reduced from three hours, and I thought they were being overly optimistic. Someone suggested training on Snowbowl Road, which I tried a couple of times. It was horrible: traffic and no shoulder. Maybe they actually said Elden Lookout Road, but I don't like running on dirt roads, with the dust from vehicles. So that left the trails.

I hadn't done a lot of trail running on the San Francisco Peaks, so I didn't know the trails very well. I pulled out my "Flagstaff Trails Map" from Emmitt Barks Cartography and started plotting profiles. I put the distance in miles on the x axis and the elevation in feet on the y axis. I started with the uphill to Imogene Pass, then added Weatherford, Humphreys, Inner Basin, and Waterline. I would study the map and add more trails and more points. It got quite elaborate, but here is a simplified version (facing page).

My conclusion was that the Weatherford Trail from Schultz Tank to the intersection with Inner Basin was the best match for the first 7.6 miles of Imogene. They have almost the same starting altitude and steepness. When I ran that section of the Weatherford Trail in 2:20, I knew I could make the Imogene cutoff. I remember looking at my watch and saying, "Ha!"

In fact, on race day, I met the first cutoff with 15 minutes to spare and the second cutoff with almost 90 minutes to spare. I finished the race in just under five hours (faster than I thought I would), 49th in my age group.

I went on to run Imogene in 2016 and 2017, this time with the help of a coach, Emily (Harrison) Torrence, then with McMillan Running. Training was so much easier; just follow the plan. Interestingly, I ran fewer long runs and more hills and speedwork in 2016 than in 2009 and finished with a faster time—just under 4:30. In 2017, my focus was the Stagecoach Line 55K three weeks later, so Imogene was more of a training run. That year's result was slower than the year before, but I did have my most favorite time ever: 4:44:44.4 for the 44th Imogene.

When I ran that section of the Weatherford Trail in 2:20, I knew I could make the Imogene cutoff. I remember looking at my watch and saying, "Ha!"

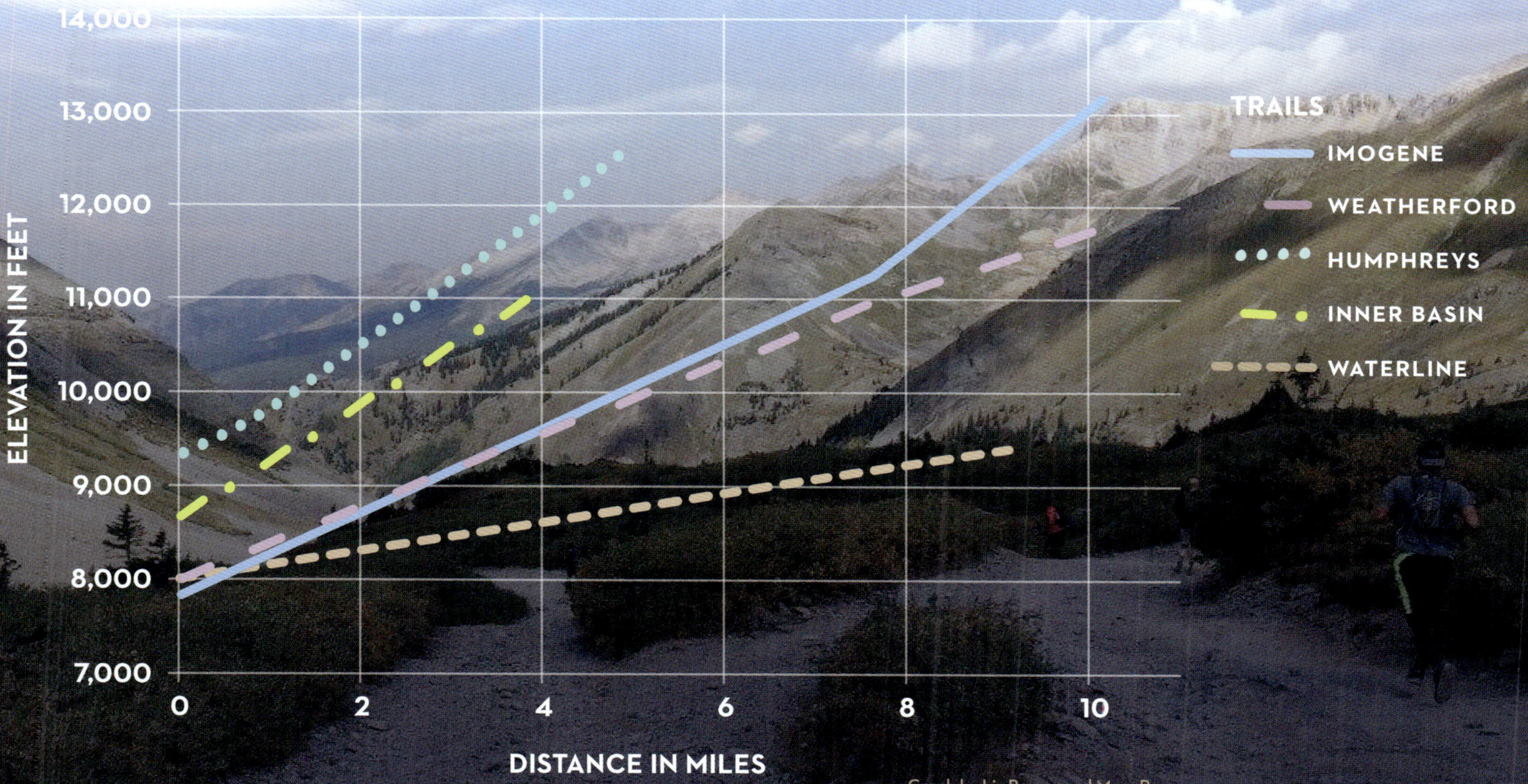

Graph by Liz Brauer and Mary Ross

I pulled out my "Flagstaff Trails Map" from Emmitt Barks Cartography and started plotting profiles. I put the distance in miles on the x axis and the elevation in feet on the y axis. I started with the uphill to Imogene Pass, then added Weatherford, Humphreys, Inner Basin, and Waterline. I would study the map and add more trails and more points. It got quite elaborate, but here is a simplified version.

part 8

Best Life Ever

Stories of love and remembrance

MY IPR (INDIVIDUAL PERSONAL REFLECTION)

BY JERRY DIEHL

MY NAME IS JERRY DIEHL. I WAS A LATE BLOOMER for the Imogene Pass Run, starting in 2006, when I was in my 40s. Back then, you could mail in your entry form with no worry as to whether or not you'd get in. It gradually got more popular over the years. In 2013, Outside magazine included it in their online article "The Trail Runner's Bucket List." These days, the race fills up in under 20 minutes.

It hurt us a bit in Arizona when registration went from midnight to 6:00 a.m. Colorado time on June 1. Before the time change, everyone in the Mountain time zone was asleep when registration opened, but for us it was only 11:00 p.m. With the change, Coloradoans had more of a jump, as it was 5:00 a.m. in Arizona. Calendars were marked, phone trees were established, alarms were set. No one wanted to be left out.

Our family caught the IPR bug mainly from three people: Fon Cordasco, Maureen (Mo) Meyer, and Jan Newton. All were very close friends (more like family) who had done the IPR numerous times and thought I would enjoy it. Dozens of others we knew had run it, but these three were our pillars. Fon had completed more IPRs than any person we knew. My wife, Sandy, and I affectionately called her "the Queen of Imogene"!

When I started, I went solo. My family got hooked later. To me, the Imogene Pass Run is an "Individual Personal Reflection" (that's my version of IPR). I call it that because almost everyone carries a story, a life lesson, or a personal possession from Ouray to Telluride. Throughout my years as a state police officer, I carried a little stuffed bear whenever I had to travel for work. I took pictures of Busby the traveling bear in many unique places. It was a way I could let my family know I was always thinking of them, and they were always with me. Busby has been over Imogene Pass many times.

As we venture through the 17.1-mile trek, those same stories, lessons, and personal possessions we carry become the past and the future. By the way, I say "almost" everyone because most first-timers are focused on 10 miles straight up and 7 miles straight down. They usually don't learn until later that the IPR is a spiritual event, as well as a physical one. The number of people who complete it and don't end up in a happier place is very few.

TRADITIONS

The traditions that take place on the first Saturday after Labor Day are a huge part of the IPR. Traditions obviously vary from person to person and family to family, but here are some that always put a smile on my face.

One of the first was getting up early on the Friday before, getting a Macy's Special extra hot, then hitting the road. Through the years, that was tweaked a bit. Sometimes Fon's husband, Billy Cordasco (BC), and I would get two Macy's Specials each; one to chug, the other to get us into Colorado. This changed slightly when we decided we needed more time in Telluride. In the later years, our trips moved up to Thursday. This meant afternoon coffee, and lunch on the way.

Flip-flops were another traditional must. Don't know for sure who started it (probably BC!). Even our youngest son, Sean, always made sure his were packed for the trip. If we weren't wearing them on the way, they were on before we hit the streets.

Speaking of the streets: cruzin' the town on foot checking out the farmer's market and the shops was another traditional must. The day you arrived dictated what you were doing first, but make no mistake, you were going walkabout. If you came in Friday afternoon, the first priority was getting your bib, as they generally closed shop around 2:00 or 2:30 p.m. That always turned out to be fun, as you would meet the massive Flagstaff contingent as well as folks you hadn't seen since the last Imogene. If you didn't get your bib then, you had to wait until race day.

The biggest, most meaningful activities revolved around families and friends. The pre-IPR dinner on Friday night and the post-run celebration dinner on Saturday were huge. Everyone brought their favorite foods, and we all sat around sharing stories and memories. Families from all over Flagstaff were there. The Averys, the Cordascos, the Meyers, the Contos, the Quigleys, the Bednars, the Phillipses, the Hendrickses, the Johnsons, the Tullosses... the list is endless! To name the number of friends running solo would be quite daunting. Conversations went all over the map, including motivational talks for all the first-timers following in the footsteps of friends and family.

Above: Telluride before the race-day crowd. Right: One tradition for Billy and me on every hike that put us near the top of a picture was what we called "touching the sky." To the right is Billy in 2016.

It became a tradition for all Flagstaff participants and any supporters to meet in the street at the end of every IPR and get a massive picture taken underneath the Imogene banner strung across Colorado Avenue. Awesome!

Coffees at Cowboy Coffee (after the picture, of course) was another ritual. It started out with mainly BC, Fon, Sandy, and me, but grew as the years went by. Nothing like a mocha to get the blood flowing after crossing the finish line.

Another great tradition: cooling off in the San Miguel River. I believe this was another one from Fon, starting off small then growing by leaps and bounds. The best spot was smack dab in front of the Manitou Lodge. A lot of us stayed there anyway, so it only seemed logical to hit the river in that spot. We'd all laugh at each other as we got in, and laugh some more as we worked our way past freezing our butts off. As we numbed up a bit and our muscles relaxed, we dove right back into the day's events.

It is quite the scene, young and old, family and friends, IPR participants and supporters, all there and all enjoying each other's company.

SNOW YEAR

My earliest solid memory of Imogene was the year we all got turned around, 2006. Due to the heavy snow that hit the mountains, we started and completed the event in Ouray.

That stuck out for a couple reasons. The first was that it had never happened before. The next was what it did for my understanding of what the Individual Personal Reflection was all about.

While some participants complained about being turned around, not getting their money's worth, it not being a legitimate race, and having to ride the bus back to Telluride, the family and friends I know and love were there enjoying the day. They were thankful and eager to share their stories.

Fon said it best: "The IPR is a RUN, not a race! It says so right on your bib!" Fon had always called the IPR her "new year," and I finally began to understand why. Although some set out to win, and most everyone tried to do their best, there was still a bigger picture. Family, friends, life. What a difference it made, that Individual Personal Reflection.

After everyone finishes, we gather beneath the sign. Some hardy runners then soak in the river, but everyone enjoys the hot tub.

This was 2017. Standing (from left): Becky Myers, Maya Huffman, Sean Diehl, Hannah Doskicz, Will Jenney, Paulina Jenney, Rachel Diehl, Keith Harris, Rae Johnson, Wendell Johnson, Joel Giannola, Mike Tulloss, Billy Cordasco, Duane Weston, Josh Weston. Kneeling (from left): Amy Stilley, Jerry Diehl, Sandy Diehl, Heidi Conto, Carrie Butler, Caleb Cordasco, Jackie Thomas, Kim Marr, Margaret Donnelly.

A PACK FROM START TO FINISH

In August 2012, Dr. Nate Avery, a friend and a man I credit for saving my life, died in a tragic accident. That same year, Fon Cordasco was diagnosed with stage four cancer and began undergoing surgeries and treatment. Last, my beautiful bride, Sandy, finally got the bug, and registered for Imogene. Because of these significant events, the 2013 IPR had a new meaning, a new focus, and once again, family and friends pulled together.

The training for 2013 was different, too, as I remember. This marked the first year we trained together in large groups, sometimes 10 or more. This was fun, as it created a larger pool of stories to lift each other up on the rough days.

When race day came, over a dozen of that core group lined up in Ouray, ready to go. Sandy and I, Mo, Fon, Kim Marr, Annette Avery, Margaret Montfort, Deanne Despain, Heidi Conto, Jen Bednar, Mike Tulloss, and several others (sorry I can't remember all of them; it's been awhile) traveled as a pack from start to finish. It didn't matter how long it took; we did it as a group. We ran, we walked, we laughed, and we cried. Heck, we even stopped along the way to strike some yoga poses. (Well, I didn't, but I was there, haha.)

A high moment for the 2013 crew (for names, see page 180).

As we passed Mile 9 and the summit came into sight, we could hear this "hooting and hollering" as well as an extremely loud cowbell coming from the top. We figured it was just a highly motivated aid station worker, cheering people on. But when we cleared the false summits and approached the Bataan Death March section (as Fon always called it), that voice materialized into a big man in a cowboy hat. The bell ringer was none other than Fon's dad, Roger Hartman. He had plotted to work the summit aid station just so he could surprise Fon.

Man, I wish I could describe all the emotions that exploded from everyone. Roger walked that last section with Fon, and when we reached the Pass, the views—and the visits—were unforgettable.

From Mile 0 to 17.1, we remained together, survivors, supporters, family, and friends, start to finish. And speaking of the finish: as we came down the hill, more friends and family joined the group, so that by the time we crossed, our numbers had more than doubled. Fon's son Caleb met us at the tunnel and stayed through the finish, and our son Sean, joined in as well. He dang near had to run to keep up (in flip-flops of course), but he stuck right with us. It was truly a memorable day!

BC'S DB-4

Fon passed away in late June 2016. We trained for the run, but a lot of us weren't "feeling it."

Even though he had done the IPR, BC was never much into it. He preferred being "the sheriff," hanging around the finish line, cheering all who came across. His was a face we all looked for as we crossed—he was always there.

We and others had been talking about how difficult it was becoming to get an IPR bib. Well, a year or so prior to 2016,

BC started going up to Imogene Pass from the Telluride side the day before, as his own version of the IPR. He liked that it didn't take him away from the finish line on event day.

This spurred more and more interest, as folks who didn't necessarily want to do the IPR didn't mind hiking up the back way. We got quite a following for it in 2016, when many of us opted out of the IPR to do what became known as "BC's DB-4, Telluride to Imogene and back."

BC and Fon, 2013.

In memory of Fon, Sandy and I had T-shirts made for everyone who committed to the walk. I'm not sure how many people actually went up and back with us, but we made several dozen T-shirts and they're all gone. Some DB participants went on to do the IPR the following day. Awesome!

Last, but by far the coolest to me, Chris Gomez volunteered to carry Fon's bib during the run. (Fon had registered for the 2016 IPR just over a month before she died.) Chris finished second overall that year, wearing Fon's bib. As he approached the finish line, he unclipped it and proudly held it high for all to see.

Fon had completed her last IPR. As I looked around at the crowd gathered at the finish, there were very few dry eyes among those who understood the significance.

Individual Personal Reflection (IPR):
The story, life lesson, or personal possession almost everyone carries from Ouray to Telluride.

PASSING THE TORCH

Our oldest son, Will, did his first IPR in 2017. He was joined the next year by our oldest daughter, Paulina, as she completed her first in 2018. Ours weren't the only ones; several of our friends and families had sons and daughters picking up the guidon and carrying on.

Our youngest daughter, Rachel, hasn't caught the IPR bug yet but is all about hanging with family and friends there. Sean is a different story. He would have attempted it last year if we'd let him. He turns 16 this year, so who knows? I have no doubt that when he gets the green light, he'll be ready to go.

Looking back on these stories, I find myself smiling once again as I move from the past toward the future. So many precious memories—gifts to share over and over again. It's almost like having Christmas each September. I can honestly say I have received many more gifts than I gave at Imogene, the most recent being our kids joining us. Kind of a special thing, to see the torch passing to another generation. Will all the traditions stay the same? Probably not, but that's OK. Will the fun remain? Absolutely! This is why the IPR itself will forever be my Individual Personal Reflection. ☺

Gomez, Flagstaff runners honor Fon Cordasco at Imogene

BY MYLES SCHRAG

This article originally appeared in the Arizona Daily Sun *on September 13, 2016.*

FON CORDASCO FINISHED HER 21ST IMOGENE PASS Run on Saturday.

When Chris Gomez of Flagstaff turned onto Oak Street into Telluride as the runner-up at the 43rd IPR, he held his friend's bib high for all to see.

Cordasco's presence was felt by many in the always-formidable Flagstaff contingent. Gomez's gesture was a poignant reminder to them and everyone in attendance just how linked Cordasco was to the 17.1-mile race connecting Ouray to Telluride over Imogene Pass.

Chris Gomez (left) shared Fon Cordasco's bib with Billy Cordasco after crossing the finish line in 2016.

A Flagstaff native, Cordasco had participated in every IPR since 1998, including the past two years while undergoing chemotherapy. She was registered for this year's race before she succumbed to cancer this summer.

Gomez met her when he was an oncology nurse during her treatments, and he wore her bib alongside his own on Saturday morning. Gomez reached the Pass in third place, but he said his head was "fuzzy" at the top and even though he is a blistering downhill runner, he was struggling.

He took over second place with about five miles to go, then literally called on Cordasco to help him down the rugged seven-mile descent to the finish.

"I was not my normal self that morning and had to work through a lot of cramping to get down the hill and maintain second place," he said. "I audibly kept telling myself, 'Fon, push me down this hill.'"

Knowing he had second place in hand as he neared the bottom of Tomboy Road, Gomez unpinned Cordasco's bib, made his left turn into town and shared the moment with the crowd lining Oak Street.

Cordasco, whom Gomez said claimed the motto "It's a Wonderful Life" after her diagnosis, championed mass Flagstaff participation going back to her first IPR in 1995. This year, there were 121 Flagstaff competitors out of 1,176 recorded times, a whopping 10.3 percent of the total number of finishers.

Nat White, who set the 75-plus men's age group record in 4:28:24, remembered how Cordasco and others would "encourage to the point of recruiting" their Flagstaff friends to run IPR. White noted that race director John Jett referred to "Flagstaff, the Running Nation."

"I was thinking of Fon," said White, who dedicated his course record to Cordasco in the post-race ceremony. "She would say IPR is my New Year's, where one year ends and training for the year begins."

White began Saturday owning the 65–69 and 70–74 age group records, but Bob Evers of Park City, Utah, bested White's 65–69 mark, meaning White returned home still holding two IPR age group records.

Family and friends of Fon Cordasco hiked to Imogene Pass the day before the 2016 IPR, carrying her prayer flags. Back row (from left): Billy Cordasco, Keith Harris, Ken Phillips, Margaret Montfort, Jerry Diehl. Front row (from left): Tom Myers, Sandy Diehl.

"In the earlier years, I did it to see if I could go faster each year," White said. "This year, I ran it just to see if I could do it… It's a beautiful run if you have time to look around."

Flagstaff nabbed three of the top 10 overall finishes. Gomez's 2:23:24 was almost eight minutes behind repeat winner Timmy Parr of Leadville, Colorado. Seth Watkins of Flagstaff ran 2:35:24 for eighth place, while Austin Horn's 2:35:48 was good for 10th overall and victory in the men's 15–19 age group.

Horn, a former Coconino High standout, shaved 29 minutes off his inaugural IPR last year. He had several motivations for a strong performance. He is running the Flagstaff Sky 55K in three weeks and wanted one final test before his first ultra. Also, he placed second in his age group last year.

"One of my main goals was to get first this year," he said. "I wanted the free entry into next year's race, so I don't have to wake up to register at 5 a.m. next year.

"I had no idea I was in 10th place when I finished. It was a huge surprise to see all my training in the mountains this summer start to pay off."

The mild conditions made for a fast day for others as well. Todd Schultz of Flagstaff ran a PR in 3:11:33 to place 74th overall and third in the men's 45–49 age group.

"The story at Imogene regarding the course was how benign the conditions were," he said. "Not cold, not hot, not windy, not rainy, nothing extreme whatsoever. You could concentrate on running the race without any of the environmental hurdles a mountain summit can throw your way."

Maryjane Robinson was the first Flagstaff woman to finish. She was 180th overall with a time of 3:32:01, good for sixth in the 35–39 age group. Following close behind was Margaret Montfort, who ran 3:33:17 to win the 55–59 age group.

"The feeling I had at the finish line was completely different than last year," said Gomez, who finished fifth in 2015. "I was tired but not as exhausted."

Running inspired will do that. It's a wonderful life, indeed.

Fon-tourage, 2013. From left: Annette Avery, Kim Marr, Krista Star, Sandy Diehl, Deanne Despain, Jen Bednar (1629), Margaret Montfort, Fon Cordasco (1235), Mike Tulloss, Heidi Conto (in front), Adrian Meyer (886), Maureen Meyer, Jerry Diehl.

SNAPSHOTS

MEMORIES OF FAMILY, FON, AND FRIENDS

BY MARGARET MONTFORT

2005

THIS WAS MY FIRST IMOGENE PASS RUN. I WAS filled with such excitement and nervous energy lining up at the starting line. I looked up at the mountain, thinking, "Everyone is smiling so it must not be too bad!" I truly don't remember much about the race other than catching up to Fon Cordasco, a talented Flagstaff runner and Imogene veteran. I asked her, "How much farther 'til the finish line?" She smiled and said it was another mile.

Over that last mile, we gradually increased our speed. I'm not sure if it was the adrenaline of knowing that we were nearing the end or that sneaky, competitive side that comes out during races, but before long we were sprinting full speed to the finish. We both crossed with the same official time: 3:36:08. We laughed and hugged and went to greet our families.

2009

Imogene was a distant second on my mind. I was training to run a 3:30 marathon to celebrate my upcoming 50th birthday. I hadn't thought about how the training would affect September's Imogene because the goal was the Tucson Marathon in December. I boarded the bus in Telluride with coffee and sandwich in hand, and sat next to a friendly woman who had spent summers in Telluride with her grandparents. She was running Imogene for the first time. The woman told me how she and her husband had sold all their belongings and were on a cross-country tour. It was so much fun sharing stories with her, I don't think I had even finished my coffee as we pulled into town. Soon, everyone was leaving the warmth of the Ouray Community Center to head to the starting line.

That was my fastest Imogene race. Several years later, a coworker was getting ready to run his first Imogene and asked what my married name had been. Googling to find my past Imogene times, he found Margaret Grove, 3:08:25. He also found an article written by the woman I had chatted with in 2009. Turns out, that woman was Sarah Lavender Smith. She was a strong runner and coach herself with a blog, The Runner's Trip, devoted to that journey. Her Imogene entry even mentioned me.

> *"A groggy but good-natured Morgan [Sarah's husband] drove me to Telluride at 5 a.m. Saturday morning to catch a bus to Ouray. He was supposed to run, too, but three weeks ago he fractured his big toe on a training run. It was hard to say goodbye to him; I wished he were boarding the bus with me. In his absence, however, I was more inclined to strike up a conversation with others, and sure enough, I met a few people who reminded me of how friendly the trail running community is.*
>
> *"First, I met Margaret Grove of Flagstaff on the seat next to me, and our conversation about our families and running made the hour-long bus trip fly by. (Turns out she's an extremely talented runner, finishing way ahead of me and winning the 45-49 age group.)"*
>
> Source: www.therunnerstrip.com/2009/09/imogene-pass-run-race-report

2014

My youngest daughter, Tess, was finally old enough to run Imogene. That was also the second year of the "Fon-tourage." A group of Flagstaff friends joined Fon, my identical-time buddy from nine years earlier, as she hiked Imogene while undergoing chemotherapy for colon cancer. Along with Tess, my niece Krista was also participating. Krista had done Imogene with me the year before as part of the first Fon-tourage. Spending time at the Ouray Community Center with Tess and Krista was such a wonderful feeling. I was getting to share my favorite place with not only two family members, but also with dear friends in the Fon-tourage, which included several others who were doing Imogene for the first time.

Shortly after leaving Upper Camp Bird aid station, my niece started experiencing severe muscle cramps. I told Tess to go ahead with the Fon-tourage and Krista and I would keep plugging away. As we watched them go ahead, I was torn between experiencing the Pass with Tess and wondering if Krista and I would even make it to the top. With Krista sitting beside the trail, I dug deep to find any and all inspiring quotes that would help her get going again. A sweet woman stopped and asked what the problem was. She quickly pulled out several salt tabs and told Krista to take them. Also, she said, stop at the Pass for chicken broth at the aid station. I had run Imogene multiple times by then and I never knew about the chicken broth. The salt tablets and the chicken broth got Krista going again. Every year, I now stop at the top of the climb for a cup.

2016

Fon did Imogene with a smaller group in 2015. She was signed up for the 2016 Imogene Run but sadly, cancer took her away in June of that year. The 2016 Imogene Run was a way for all of us to honor Fon. It started with a large group of Flagstaff friends going up to Imogene Pass from the Telluride side—the second year in a row for what we called BC's DB-4 Telluride to Imogene and Back. We held a string of prayer flags over the Imogene sign on that Friday. After that, Billy and I headed down to pick up bibs. John Jett, the IPR race director, allowed us to pick up Fon's bib so Chris Gomez could wear it on race day (see page 189 to read about his emotional runner-up finish).

2017

While participating in the third annual Day-Before-Race, we reached the Pass. As we posed for pictures with the spectacular scenery as our backdrop, we watched Caleb Cordasco summit to surprise his dad, Billy (see photo, page 187). Caleb and several of his friends had hiked the steep last two miles to the top after setting up an aid station for all of us to enjoy on the trip down.

Caleb hiking two technically challenging miles was an indescribable feat when you consider that on New Year's Eve 2014, he suffered a compression burst fracture of his spine and crushed the calcaneus bones in both feet after falling 45 feet at the climbing gym. It was highly questionable whether he would walk again after the accident. Now, here he was standing at 13,114 feet with his dad at one of his mother's favorite spots. We placed a Best Life Ever (BLE) sticker with Fon's beloved columbine on the Forest Service sign Fon and thousands of other IPR participants had reached over the years during this run.

There was not a dry eye on the Pass that morning.

A FLAGSTAFF REUNION

The Imogene Pass Run is about so much more than just a 17.1-mile race over a mountain pass. It embraces the love of the Flagstaff running community and allows us the chance to get together and enjoy the beauty of the Colorado mountains and our dear friends and family, old and new.

She signed up

BY RYAN STEVENS

JENNY PUT HEADPHONES ON, PULLED UP HER HOOD, and turned away from me. She pretended to look out the window, even though it was dark outside. We sat so close to each other on the small benches of the yellow school bus that, with each curve in the mountain road, our shoulders would bump. Jenny kept her head turned away. We are good friends.

The animated Midwesterner seated directly in front of us was completely turned around, facing me. It was probably 7:00 a.m. in his hometown, but it felt more like 5:00 a.m. to me, being from Arizona. Every one of his questions, stated too loudly, was inappropriate. "How much did you train for this? What's your weekly mileage? I trained on flat surfaces. Do you think I'll be OK?" Jenny just stared out the window.

It was my first Imogene Pass Run. Year: 2011. I had learned my first Imogene lesson: bring headphones on the bus ride from Telluride to Ouray. Jenny looked so blissful, hood up, headphones on.

When we got to Ouray, I felt awake and charged. I had remembered to use the bathroom before boarding the school bus. Jenny, however, was trembling. "I have to pee so bad!" She ran off the bus and squatted behind a tree. Jenny had learned her first Imogene lesson: pee before you get on the bus. I laughed, and felt vindicated.

•••

Two hours later, Jenny and I were running hard, shoulder-to-shoulder once again. We were just past Upper Camp Bird—when things get real. I hadn't thought about her place until this moment. "Are you in first?" I asked casually. "I think so!" she responded. I had a small and completely unnecessary backpack on. It contained one coconut water. I grabbed it and handed it to Jenny. "Drink this!" She gave it back to me. "Can't… open… it." I gave it a shot. It wouldn't open. The problem was mental, not physical. I focused hard, used my teeth, and it finally opened. I gave it back to Jenny. She drank some coconut water and handed it back to me. That was the last time I saw Jenny until the finish line.

•••

Nobody from Flagstaff had won Imogene. Then, in 2011, Jenny McCarthy won. And we soon found out our good buddy Mike Smith won too, in one of the top three fastest men's time ever recorded. In my experience that year, the celebration after that Imogene Pass Run was second only to the Ironman World Championship: the finish line was a constant stream of inspiration; the crowd was deeply supportive and vibrant, if not inebriated; the runners all kicked back and enjoyed the post-finish bliss in downtown Telluride; and the mountain views knocked my socks off. Everything was so memorable.

My first year of Imogene, Chris Gomez didn't run. But he was there. Everyone thinks he walks on water, but that day, he was more walking on whiskey. I can say that; I'm married to him. After cheering that year while sharing a flask with our dear friend Brianna Torres, one thing was for sure: Chris was going to run Imogene. I didn't know, however, that he would inspire me as much as he did.

My second attempt at Imogene was my personal best. I mostly ran the uphill with my buddy A.J. That year, "Fight Song" by Rachel Platten was a popular hit. It was apparently A.J.'s mantra as he ran up to the Pass, secretly reminding himself, "This is my fight song, take back my life song." He was in great shape that year. He totally crushed me on the Humphreys-Weatherford-Kachina loop on the San Francisco Peaks a few weeks prior. But Imogene is no training run. After the race, I only remember him saying one thing: "Fuck off, Rachel." I laughed. It made my abs burn. Another year was in the books. And I was hooked on Imogene.

Then came my regret. I only ever regretted running Imogene once. That was in 2016. It wasn't the race. It was the finish line. Because Chris is always ahead of me (except for one special race where I will always cherish the memory of passing him), he got to the Imogene finish line way ahead of me. The only thing better than running that year would have been witnessing Chris's finish. He was second overall, but that wasn't the reason. The special part was that he got to wear Fon Cordasco's number.

I only ever regretted running Imogene once. That was in 2016. It wasn't the race. It was the finish line.

The year prior, I waited in the packet pickup line with Fon. She recounted the years when the weather was so bad that they sent the runners back to Ouray. She talked about her favorite years too. "Always drink the soup at the Pass. You need the sodium," she told me. The next day, I ran my personal best time on the course. And I drank the soup at the Pass.

That next June, I signed up for Imogene again. Fon, I was soon told, would be in hospice care over the summer. She brought so much love and friendship to so many people in Flagstaff. But the most inspiring story to me personally, perhaps in all of sport, isn't found in the Imogene races she ran. It was the one she didn't run. Prior to the race, when Chris told me he'd been asked to wear Fon's number, I was so confused. Why did she have a number? "Because she signed up!" he said.

It didn't hit me for a moment. Fon signed up for Imogene? Facing a terminal recurrence, she still made sure she was registered for the Imogene Pass Run. To this day, I tell this part of her story. She signed up.

Everything about that simple act is inspiring to me. Her faith. Persistence. Resilience. Her dignity. It is the preeminent example of why I look to sport to inspire my humanity.

That year, I would've given anything to watch Chris, who inspires me daily, remove Fon's race bib at Mile 17, hold it high above his head, and run down Oak Street to Fon's finish line. In second place overall. In honor of one of the greats.

It should come as no surprise that Chris and I tell everyone about Imogene, and try to bring as many of our family and friends to it as we can. This past year, our friend Leah Rosenfeld joined us. She asked how we would get from Telluride to the start line in Ouray. She asked about the school buses, and if she needed to know anything about the race.

"Yeah," I said, "pee first and bring headphones."

"And drink the soup at the Pass!" Chris chimed in, smiling, remembering.

Over the years, Chris and I have missed a few Imogene races. Injuries. Work. Not in shape. Excuses. But now, when there is something worth doing, nothing stops us from pressing forward. When things get hard on the trails, or off the trails, I remember the most important life lesson from all of my sport experiences, highlighted in my heart forever because Chris became a part of it: no matter what happens, we will sign up. ©

Of Fon, Nate, and Flag... BLE

BY MYLES SCHRAG

A version of this essay appeared in the High Country Running column of the Arizona Daily Sun *on September 26, 2016.*

HOW DO YOU TELL THE STORY OF A BEAUTIFUL LIFE? On Friday, September 9, the day before she defended her Imogene Pass Run 55–59 age-group title, Margaret Montfort hiked seven miles and more than 4,300 feet up, and the same amount back down.

She joined a contingent of around 20 people to pay respects to their friend, Fon Cordasco, who lost her battle with cancer less than two months earlier.

Seven of that larger group that left Telluride, Colorado, reached the top of the Pass: Tom Myers, Keith Harris, Ken Phillips, Jerry and Sandy Diehl, Billy Cordasco, and Montfort. They brought prayer flags with symbols of Fon's life, and lingered long.

Once there, they realized it would be fitting to place a Best Life Ever (BLE) sticker with Fon's Rocky Mountain columbine on the iconic "Imogene Pass Elev 13,114 ft" sign.

Her favorite flower at the top of her favorite race.

Fon Cordasco, 2013.

There was only one problem. Sandy had already given away her two BLE–Fon stickers to a couple from Austin, Texas, doing a Jeep tour. The couple was curious about the group and was genuinely moved by Fon's story.

Montfort realized she had a sticker on her visor. She peeled it off and placed it on the sign.

Montfort said she told Billy, Fon's widower, that she wondered how wise it was to exert herself so much when she would be running up and over that same pass in less than 24 hours.

"I said, 'Billy, I may have made a mistake,'" Montfort said. "But you know what? I wouldn't trade it for the world. Friday was much more important."

Unlike his wife, Billy is not a runner. He ran Imogene once—just two months before Fon was diagnosed with cancer. That was enough. He assured her that he would be happy to support her at the finish. Even from 2013 to 2015, when a "Fon-tourage" at Imogene joined their friend who was undergoing cancer treatments, Billy was finish-line support.

This year, however, Billy got Fon to the start line as well. While walking the Big Brothers Big Sisters half marathon in Flagstaff with the Diehls and Montfort, Billy decided that someone had to wear Fon's bib at Imogene. She was registered to run, and had just passed away.

Who should do it was obvious too. In fact, he had blazed past them while winning the half that day. Back at Wheeler Park, Billy asked Chris Gomez to do the honors.

"We all got goosebumps when he was talking about it," Montfort said. "(Chris) said, 'I've got goosebumps now.'"

Gomez is an oncology nurse who had struck up a deep friendship with Fon when she was ill. He's also a spirited runner who attacks the course and seems to invite the pain such an approach brings.

Gomez put the exclamation point on an already emotional day when he raised Fon's bib for all to see as he rolled into Telluride with a second-place finish.

This weekend, the Flagstaff to Grand Canyon Stagecoach Ultra is taking place, a competition that honors our town's historical turn as the first major tourist route to the natural wonder in our backyard.

Much of the race cuts through Babbitt Ranches, where Billy is president. He and the Diehls will be helping at the Cedar Ranch aid station, and when Montfort arrives there at the conclusion of her 55K race there will be cheers and hugs.

Today at 4:00 p.m., the third annual BLE "5K-ish, Mega Party Run Walk or Stand" will be held at Buffalo Park. It honors Nate Avery, another beloved Flagstaffian who left the world too soon.

His BLE mantra has become a symbol of Flagstaff itself, and now the BLE–Fon stickers with the columbine are a complement to the BLE–Nate stickers with the paddleboard seen all over town in recent years.

At Imogene, Montfort wore BLE socks and a BLE sticker on her Nathan Hydration pack. "Nate's got my legs and Fon's got my back," she quipped.

BLE is now cherished by a Texas couple. Hundreds of Imogene runners have BLE in the photos they took by the sign at the top and then shared on social media.

How do you tell the story of a beautiful life?

Maybe, just maybe, through understanding three September running events, each with its own flavor and its own purpose but interconnected all the same.

Caleb Cordasco and his father, Billy, at the summit in 2017 (for their story, see page 182).

Fon and the Imogene New Year

BY CHRIS GOMEZ

THE FIRST I HAD EVER HEARD OF THE IMOGENE Pass Run was as a graduate student at Northern Arizona University. Though I had run on the track team as an undergrad at NAU from 2003 to 2005, I had not yet ventured to run any race on a trail, and all I could imagine was a treacherous, epic event that scaled jagged mountains and peaks.

An exercise physiology professor of mine, Richard Coast, mentioned it to me in passing in 2005, complete with details of the rigors of the course that caused him and many others to tumble down the mountain during the race. At the time, I never thought much about what he said. That year, I looked up results of the race and saw that former NAU athletes, many of legend, had run the event. Most notably, the Martin twins (Tim and Theo) had competed there, both coming up with runner-up finishes. I (a twin myself) thought maybe this was an event I could compete in and place well. However, never had I imagined the amount of training or fortitude needed to take on that challenge.

"One day in one of our many conversations, the topic of the Imogene Pass Run came up. From there, so many previously scattered, ambivalent, and unfinished thoughts and plans began to take focus."

As I continued my career as a graduate student and a post-collegiate, semi-professional athlete mainly focusing on track events, I never really gave the race a second thought. I continued on my way, eventually ending my serious running career with a knee injury in 2008. At the time, I had no interest in attempting to run on trails nor any plans to undertake serious athletic goals for a while.

I decided to go back to school and pursue a career as a Registered Nurse. Over the next two years, I completed my nursing degree at NAU. I finally started to indulge the idea of running on trails and began to dabble in a few trail races around Flagstaff. My first trail race was in 2008, the Soulstice Mountain Trail Run just off Schultz Pass Road, climbing Mount Elden on the Sunset Trail. I ran the "sprint" course, which was 6 1/2 miles. At the time, that was the longest and most difficult race I had ever completed on trails. (Fast-forward to the present—who would have known that not only would I continue to do Soulstice, but I would switch to the "long" course and run that 11-mile event for 10 years in a row and counting.)

The reason I mention this is that Soulstice was my first encounter with trail running and an introduction I would never forget. I heard countless stories from Soulstice veterans who had also undergone the difficult trek of Imogene.

It took longer than you might expect to get me to the starting line at Imogene after hearing those tales. I can't put my finger on why exactly it took me so long to sign up. The race seemed daunting, deserving of respect, so much so that I was simply scared and humbled by a mountain I had yet to climb.

•••

Best friends of mine—really, seriously, fast friends of mine—had made the decision to do the 2011 IPR. I had also apparently decided to do the run that year. I don't remember signing up for it, but I definitely did. A few friends and I caravanned to the race, making the six-hour trek to Telluride across the Four Corners region on a mostly cloudy day.

I never started the race.

I got to Telluride the day before, picked up my packet and bib, but decided not to do it. My calf muscle had been upset with me, and I was not confident I could run over a mountain. Ultimately, I decided my heart and soul were in Flagstaff. I realized I would much rather successfully complete a race at home than further injure my calf while attempting to run uphill for 10 miles. Interesting note: two of my fast friends, Jenny McCarthy and Mike Smith, ended up being the first overall male and female finishers in 2011 (see page 126) and left with some of the fastest times ever run on the course. All the while, I was merely a spectator, in awe of their terrific feats.

It took me four more years to officially run the race.

•••

Back in 2010, just prior to my first trip to the IPR, I received my RN license. After that, I was intermittently running trail and road races while working on the night shift. Due to the complexity and difficulty of working that schedule, running, and having a normal life with my partner, I decided to take a job in Sedona in a medical oncology office. It was still a rigorous schedule, however much more manageable.

Fon wrote me a note that said, "Go Chris Go, you can do it!"

There I worked directly with patients who had ongoing cancer diagnoses and helped steer them through difficult chemotherapy infusions. This job led me to the way of being and the beauty of Fon Cordasco. Diagnosed with colon cancer at age 44 in late 2012, Fon gave me a new understanding of what it meant to be alive and to truly live. She introduced me to a reality of existence I had never imagined. My life became much more meaningful and beautiful, and this was because of one person: Fon. She was a constant exhibition of gratitude and grace in what can be a very dark place. Beyond her treatments, she gave me so much insight into life, running, love, friends, and everything in between.

One day in one of our many conversations, the topic of the Imogene Pass Run came up. From there, so many previously scattered, ambivalent, and unfinished thoughts and plans began to take focus.

I can still hear her voice, so cheerful and full of happiness; she had a beautiful laugh that brightened any space she entered. I look back fondly on conversations we had in the infusion room, and so many thoughts and emotions flood my mind. One such talk led me to decide to run IPR. Running and living were deeply entwined for Fon. She told me in 2015 that this would be (at least) her 20th year doing the race. Seriously… 20 years! She likened Imogene to a reset, a new year for her: the "Imogene New Year." This thought resonated immediately and continued to slowly pinball in my mind over the years. Still does… the Imogene New Year. I did not completely understand what this meant, nor have I yet fully grasped the idea. But I do know that I will continue to foster and nurture it for years and years to come.

Fon is how I made it to my first Imogene starting line in 2015. Finally, I would officially complete the race. It's unbelievable to me that it had been almost 10 years since I first heard of Imogene. Ten years earlier, I was a different runner, a faster runner, a more calculated runner. The runner I was back then could have probably run the race much faster than I will ever again have the ability to achieve. But now, I was a different type of runner, one inspired by Fon. I am a more selfless runner, and I think a more selfless person, not defined solely as an athlete but rather someone who appreciates the fullness of life and the balance it can foster and provide.

I knew for certain already that year that all my future IPRs would have some memory, some quote, some piece of inspiration, derived from or dedicated to Fon and her, what word can I use to describe her… amazingness?

My first IPR was not my best, but it gave me the understanding of what it takes to be successful at a race of that magnitude. I mostly just did it to feel out what it would be like to undertake an event that still, to this day, is the longest, most difficult race I have ever run. I was reintroduced to multiple-year IPR champions like Timmy Parr. Participating that year gave me the opportunity to think more deeply about the Flagstaff contingent that had finished the race so successfully, from Fon's trips there starting in the 1990s to Mike and Jenny's wins in 2011 to hundreds more runners through the years.

Fon, in her signature grace and motivating way, convinced Natalie Metz, a close friend of mine and also a nurse, to run Imogene in 2015. They were together or within sight of

Carrying Fon's bib as I entered Telluride.

I was a different type of runner, one inspired by Fon. I am a more selfless runner, and I think a more selfless person, not defined solely as an athlete but rather someone who appreciates the fullness of life and the balance it can foster and provide.

each other most of the way during the race, encouraging, motivating, and supporting each other.

I'm not sure what exactly Fon told me after I dipped my toes into Imogene at the 2015 race, but I was disappointed that her proud prerace proclamations of knowing the fastest guy in Flagstaff were disproved. I was not the fastest person from Flagstaff that day (hat tip to runner-up Andrew Benford and sixth-place Kalib Wilkinson; I was one place and 5 1/2 minutes behind Kalib). But she didn't care. She was elated that I was a top 10 overall finisher and showered me with praise and encouragement. We immediately began talking about the next IPR and how fulfilling it would be to do it again and be there together.

She would have been 47 for her next Imogene Pass Run.

From left: Shiloh Mielke, me, and Seth Watkins had been teammates on the NAU cross country and track team. In 2018, we were top three for our age group (and fourth, third, and fifth overall).

•••

Fon passed away two months before the 2016 IPR. I found it hard to continue training for a race that I had only completed once before. However, soon enough, positive thoughts resurfaced. Fon was a person of "isms," and she had lots of them to help anyone through tough times.

I thought back to all the things she said that will always stay with me as encouraging reminders to go on. I continued training and running. I had not mastered the proper training for IPR in 2016 (and still haven't), but her incessant positivity got me through a lot of tough times on the trails.

Weeks before the 2016 race, Fon's husband, Billy Cordasco, asked me to do the most important and emotional thing I have ever done in a race. Fon was registered for this race, and she was supposed to be there that day. However, her time on earth ended much too early. Billy asked me to wear Fon's bib up and over the Pass for the last time. I'm not exactly an ultra-emotional person, but on that day it would be hard to hold back tears. How would I, a person who got to know Fon only in her later years, honorably be able to carry her over the Pass for the last time?

At that time, I didn't know. To this day, I still don't know if I did. But I carried out his wish as best as I could.

As I headed to the starting line that morning, the feeling was surreal. The usual suspects from Flagstaff were present in full force. Even more than normal, a multitude of hugs, greetings, and exchanges of luck were given. The collective mood was one of gratitude and love. I was just so happy to be there at the start and to be given such a beautiful and meaningful opportunity.

That day I wore two numbers—1019 for myself and 774 for Fon. I am not a focused religious person, but I am certainly spiritual. The events of the day affirmed my spirituality and lifted it. With the race underway, all thoughts in my head disappeared and one clear, focused, familiar voice helped me up the mountain. Ever positive and encouraging, Fon gave me the extra push I needed to crest the Pass efficiently and with little struggle.

I truly don't remember a lot of the race, but I clearly remember removing and unclipping Fon's bib from my race shirt. I held it in my hands for the last mile as I descended into Telluride. At the time I didn't know what compelled me to do so, but looking back I know it was an act of something else—something beyond or something above, but something intensely compelled me to carry Fon just one step in front of me. I have vivid and emotional memories of running down the finishing straightaway holding Fon's number above and beyond me for all to see.

I don't really know what the rest of downtown Telluride was experiencing as I finished. I cherish memories of getting to that finish line and sharing authentic happiness and gratitude with Billy. My attention was focused in that limited space. But as I look back, I sure imagine music playing and miles of smiles propagating the tunnel of spectators lining Oak Street because many of them had known Fon, and now everyone there knew that Fon had made it down the Pass that day and was at the finish line just loving life.

It was a new year.

I finished second overall. That remains my best finish and time, and by far it was my most memorable IPR. I know I will complete many more runs with likely faster finishes, and who knows… maybe one day I will win the event. But I will never gain as much as I did those first two years of the IPR. That's why my love letter from Flagstaff to Imogene is to Fon and for Fon. All those who knew Fon and read this will know what I mean.

Fon, thank you for crossing paths with me in this life, for encouraging me to run Imogene, and for giving me an eternal attitude of gratitude.

Thank you for shining so brightly. ☺

What started as a love letter
from the Flagstaff running
community became, in some way,
a love letter to the Flagstaff
running community.

afterword

THIS BOOK BEGAN WITH A SIMPLE IDEA—THAT there might be a bigger story behind the odd fact that our small mountain town regularly sends more participants to the Imogene Pass Run than any other town, including any town in Colorado.

As we began to ask Flagstaff runners how they experience Imogene and feel about her, we heard answers as numerous as the contributions to this book; we hope you, dear reader, see yourself in at least one tale here.

The way Flagstaff runners feel about Imogene is, to some extent, the way any athlete feels about a serious challenge accepted, endured, and ultimately, appreciated. Yet our town's relationship with Imogene is not generic but unique. Training for it means spending summers together on our magnificent home forest's toughest and most scenic trails. And when we go to Colorado each September, the people we see on the streets of Telluride and Ouray and along the trail that connects them are our neighbors and friends, family and running partners from back home.

It turns out that we go to Colorado to be together as a running community and to do something difficult and meaningful together. Imogene is a destination, a road trip, a long weekend to hang out with our friends. Imogene is an excuse. The real love is for our own.

In any true love affair, the beloved is appreciated for who they are AND because they bring out something special in us. The Flagstaff running community adores the Imogene Pass Run to the point of obsession because in meeting her challenge, we find out how strong we can be, as athletes and as people, alone and even more than that, in community. We love you, Imogene, and we love what our love for you says about us.

And so it came full circle; what started as a love letter *from* the Flagstaff running community became, in some way, a love letter *to* the Flagstaff running community, aka "the Running Nation." You're beautiful when you reach for the heights. See you next year in Colorado!

LSherman

Acknowledgments

We're grateful to everyone who shared their skills and their love for Imogene and the Flagstaff running community to make this book a reality, particularly...

The late Randy Wilson, esteemed managing editor of the *Arizona Daily Sun*, whose early support for the project was valuable beyond measure; and to Chris Etling and the *Arizona Daily Sun* for continuing Randy's early enthusiasm.

Mary Ross and Krista Nicole for their vision, artistry, and patience. They contributed to the DNA of the book with fresh ideas and skills that made it more beautiful than we ever dreamed.

Linda Sherman for cheerfully contributing not only her Imogene story, but also her photos and gorgeous watercolors.

Catherine Bell, Carrie Butler, Rory Faust, Nancy Schrag, and Claudine Taillac for proofreading the essays.

Annette Avery and Todd Schultz for advice on the art and business of creating books. Jen Saunders for her general advice and good wishes.

Wendy Kuek at Cedar House Coffee Shop and Lynda Apple at Single Speed Coffee Cafe and their respective staffs for welcoming and tasty "office" space.

Tom Dietrich, Jim Griffith, Brandon Kavanaugh, Kyle Taylor, and Diana White for advice on founding Soulstice Publishing. Imogene is the mother of Soulstice once again, and we appreciate the blessing our baby received from Paul Brinkmann, Bill Ring, and Neil Weintraub, the original Knights of the Soulstice Roundtable.

•••

FROM MYLES: Thanks to all the people in Flagstaff and western Colorado who have shown us how to imagine Imogene. Julie Hammonds, my successor as High Country Running coordinating editor, was a critical partner in making the book you are now holding a reality. While I ran a decent first leg, she was the anchor that ensured we (read: I) stayed on task and used a relatively efficient editorial process that resulted in the quality we both knew this book deserved. Our periodic brainstorming sessions were not only bright spots on those days, they created the energy and momentum that resulted in many of the wonderful editorial and visual ideas in these pages.

•••

FROM JULIE: Thanks to my family for your unflagging interest in the process of creating a book and your willingness to let me lock myself into my office at inconvenient hours. I'm also deeply grateful to Myles Schrag, whose column about this book idea in High Country Running inspired me to send a bold email offering my help as a professional editor. What I didn't know then was that Myles is a professional editor himself and actually has much more experience than I do. Why he didn't laugh and slide that email straight from inbox to trash remains a mystery. But to me, this book we've made together will always be a demonstration of the magic that can happen when you say "Yes, and" to the universe. And I'm ever so glad he invited me into the process of creating it.

Finally, we're grateful to our guardian angels, who never failed to drop a feather when we needed encouragement.

Flagstaff Imogene Circle

This select group of benefactors helped fund this community project, and our gratitude goes out to them.

Early support came from Nick Irvine at Dark Sky Brewing, Annette Avery at Bright Side Bookshop, and Bernadette Chavez at Mama Burger.

Neil Weintraub and the Northern Arizona Trail Runners Association, LLC

Susie Garretson

Rich Haag

Liz Brauer and Anne Leota Hart

Nat White

Paul Brinkmann

Alain Soutenet and Elisa Andreis

Paula Pluta and Jef Abramowitz

Catherine Bell

Jim Hammonds

CORDASCO FAMILY: **Hey, all of you Imogene Pass runners, "Touch the Sky."**

RYAN STEVENS AND BRUCE GRIFFEN: **From courtroom trials to running trails, from Imogene to Ironman, we're in it for the long haul with our Flagstaff community. Thanks for letting us be a part of it all.**

CAMILLE PAULIN: **In recognition of everyone who picks up a pen and endeavors to achieve success with the craft of writing, and in honor of my father, Joe Lincoln. He loved to fly, he wrote eloquently about flying, and his further writings inspired me to live in Flagstaff.**

About our Contributors

Note: After our contributors' names, there is a year in parentheses. This represents the person's Imogene Pass Run "graduation year"—the year he or she completed IPR for the first time.

Stewart **Aitchison** ('94) is a naturalist, writer, and photographer who has lived in Flagstaff since 1965.

Monica J. **Baker** ('01) has lived in Flagstaff for over 35 years. She loves the diversity of the trails, scenery, and wildlife one experiences while running here.

Dawn **Begley** ('96) has lived in Flagstaff since the winter of 1987. She would sing the "Tequila Song" while doing the downhill portion of the IPR to get excited about her waiting steak and margarita.

Andrew **Benford** ('15) is pursuing his occupational therapy doctorate through Northern Arizona University in Phoenix. While living in Flagstaff 2014–17, he was the head cross country and track coach at Coconino High School and ran professionally for Team Run Flagstaff Pro. Andrew finished runner-up at the 2015 IPR. His favorite high-elevation training run is the Peaks Loop (up Humphreys Trail, down Weatherford Trail, finishing on Kachina Trail).

Josh **Biggs** ('07) is a photographer who has lived in Flagstaff since 2004. He likes running up the Lost Burrito Trail to train for Imogene, because it's the only Flagstaff trail he can see from his kitchen window.

Liz **Brauer** ('09) is a "crazy cat lady" who has lived in Flagstaff since 1997. Her favorite high-elevation training run is on the Arizona Trail north of Aspen Corner.

Matt **Brydenthal** ('10) has been a Flagstaff local for over 20 years and owns the 928Rentals brand. After his wife ran Imogene in 2009, she said it was harder than childbirth. Matt wanted to know just how hard natural childbirth was, so he ran his first Imogene in 2010. He ran three more after that (and learned childbirth is very hard—especially the last two miles). To unite Flagstaff participants, Matt created the "Run Flagstaff Run" banner and started the Facebook page "Imogene Pass Run (Flagstaff Participants)."

Carrie **Butler** ('11) began her love affair with running Flagstaff's mountains in 1989, when she attended NAU. After graduating, she moved away before returning to Flagstaff to plant family roots and begin again. She can still be found, as jazzed as she was at 18, chasing the exhilaration she and other local runners find high on Flagstaff's trails.

Melody **Delmar** ('10) is an indigenous person to the Southwest as a member of the Navajo Nation. She lived in Flagstaff for most of her life (1992 to 2017). "The best thing about being a Flagstaff runner is the unforgettable beauty we have in the wealth of trails surrounding the Peaks."

Jerry **Diehl** ('06) is a Flagstaff native and a world-renowned phrynosomatologist (pretty sure he made that up) who has spent his career searching for the extremely rare Blue-eyed Horned Lizard (Horny Toad), fabled to live in the remote areas of Humphreys Peak. His favorite high-elevation training run is Grand Canyon, "as it operates in the negative. You're spending energy going down, but then have to turn around and power out."

Rory **Faust** is a journalism professor at NAU. He lived in Flagstaff from 1995 to 1999 and returned in 2008 as a sports reporter for the *Arizona Daily Sun*.

Susie **Garretson** ('95) is a past runner (but current hiker and explorer) who has lived in Flagstaff since 1978. "The best things about running in Flagstaff are the beautiful air, the weather, and the safe running opportunities on the endless forest trails and in Buffalo Park."

Chris **Gomez** ('15) is a Registered Nurse in Flagstaff. He moved here in 2003 to compete for NAU in cross country and track. "The best thing about being a Flagstaff runner is the awesome community of runners and the amazing, endless trails."

Rich **Haag** ('89) is a retired dentist who moved to Flagstaff in 1981. "The best thing about being a Flagstaff runner (by far) is the people you're out there running with."

Julie **Hammonds** ('18) kept a 32,000-word journal about her first IPR and managed to whittle it down to under 2,000 words for this essay. "The best thing about being a Flagstaff runner is the way this community inspires its members to live their Best Life Ever."

Anne Leota **Hart** ('09 crew) is a retired physical therapist who moved to Flagstaff in 1997. She's never run Imogene, but she has been part of a running crew three times.

Rachel (Taber) **Hart** ('15) describes her time in Flagstaff as "a great 29 years." Now that she lives in Wisconsin, she says, "I can truly answer what I enjoyed best about running at 7,000 feet: feeling superhuman at lower elevation."

Al **Hendricks** ('95) is a retired-from-full-time forester and grandfather of six who has lived in Flagstaff since 1983. His favorite high-elevation training run is the Kachina Trail. "The best thing about being a Flagstaff runner is the Flagstaff running community!"

Alicia **Hendricks** ('18) is a hairstylist who has lived in Flagstaff since June 2012. "My favorite thing about running in Flagstaff is seeing so many people out being active."

Sarah **Hendricks** ('96) is a kindergarten teacher who has lived in Flagstaff since 1980. "The best thing about being a Flagstaff runner is seeing the same faces and building friendships with people who feel as passionate about running as I do!"

Emily R. **Hoppe** ('13) is a professional flutist, college professor, and amateur runner. She moved to Flagstaff in 2006 and embarked on her running journey. She has completed one marathon and numerous half marathons and participated in the Flagstaff Summer Series. "The best thing about being a Flagstaff runner is getting smoked by famous runners at Buffalo Park."

Amy **Horn** moved to Flagstaff in 1993, but her interest in Imogene started in 2014, when her high-school-age son, Austin, ran it for the first time. When not capturing images of trail runners, her passion is photographing close-up and macro images of small details. She teaches photography at NAU and Arizona Highways PhotoScapes, and recently co-authored the book *The Art of Macro Photography*.

Nick **Irvine** ('12) is a former high school teacher and current brewery owner who has lived in Flagstaff off and on since 2003. The mantra that got him over Imogene Pass was "Smile."

Marsha **Jensen** ('13) started running at age 50 and has lived in Flagstaff since 1979.

Kristina Lee **Kaiser** ('13) has lived in Flagstaff and worked at W. L. Gore and Associates since 1998. What brings her the most joy are her two children, her animals, and time spent in nature. The mantra "You can do this, you are strong," along with thinking about her kids, got her up and over the Pass and continue to drive her.

Joanne **Keene** ('10) works at NAU and has lived in Flagstaff since 2004. Her favorite high-altitude training run is the War Dog Route: Weatherford Road to Fremont Saddle. "It's challenging and beautiful and gives me hours to catch up on life with my training partners."

Sara **Knight** ('16) is sadly not a Flagstaff local but did accidentally run up the Mount Elden Lookout Trail one time before making the drive back to Durango. She's started paying closer attention to elevation maps before going on unknown runs... and yet she still signs up for the Imogene Pass Run. Hmmmm.

Tony **Mangine** ('84 or '85) owns a retail kitchen store in Flagstaff and has lived here since about 1975. He has run for fun and fitness since junior high and says, "The running community in Flagstaff is incredible."

Dara Marks **Marino** ('10) is a former professional mountain-bike racer and triathlete who has lived in Flagstaff since 2000 and currently works on environmental and climate change issues. Her favorite Imogene training run is along Forces of Nature to Fat Mans Loop, up to the towers, down Elden Lookout Road, and back along Lower Oldham Trail.

Randy **Marlatt** ('01) is a retired builder/home inspector who has lived in Flagstaff since 1985. He's been an active Coconino County Search and Rescue volunteer since 2009. His favorite training area is the trails on Mount Elden.

Jenny **McCarthy** ('11) is a water planner who lived in Flagstaff between 2008 and 2013. "My favorite high-elevation training run was running up Humphreys, along Weatherford Trail to Kachina Trail, then down Humphreys."

Kate **McGee** ('17) is a mother-runner-teacher-coach who gets to combine her loves in the cool pines of the San Francisco Peaks. "The best thing about being a Flagstaff runner is... just step outside."

Christopher **McQuivey** ('11) is a bearded ultrarunner by nature, an eye doctor by trade, and a husband and father by love. He has lived in Flagstaff since 2010. His favorite training runs are always in his happy place, the Grand Canyon.

Mary **Mohr** ('14) is a retired librarian and freelance graphic designer who lived in Flagstaff from 1981 to 1989 and came back in 2005. Her favorite high-elevation training run is the Soulstice Mountain Trail Run courses. "They have wonderful views of the San Francisco Peaks and the terrain is varied, with uphill, downhill, rocks, and some nice, smooth stretches!"

Margaret **Montfort** ('05) ran her first Imogene in 2005 and fell in love with trail running in the mountains. Now she has passed that joy to her two daughters, Hannah and Tess. In 2019, she plans to cross the finish line with both of them.

Krista **Nicole** is a Flagstaff-based illustrator and graphic designer who loves drawing plants and people (and now, hearts, genies, and old vans). artbykristanicole.com

Michael **Olson** ('03) has been a Flagstaff-based probation officer since 1993, shortly after he graduated from NAU. He lives in Flagstaff with his wife, Natalie, and children Paige and Felix. His favorite Flagstaff trail is Oldham between Buffalo Park and Elden Lookout Road. Stevie Nicks' "Avalanche" carried him to the Imogene finish line. He has enjoyed being a part of Flagstaff running history and watching the superior talent of recent years fly by him.

Adam **Owens** ('18) is a geographer for a utility company based in Flagstaff who has lived here since 2015. His favorite training run for Imogene is the Weatherford Trail, a less busy trail that ascends into the San Francisco Peaks' Inner Basin.

Camille **Paulin** ('95) moved to Flagstaff in 1975 and lives here still. She is an avid hiker, photographer, and scuba diver. The song that got her over Imogene Pass is "Walking in Your Footsteps" by Sting.

Paula **Pluta** ('02) has lived in Flagstaff since 1997 and is still running, swimming, and biking here.

Patti **Quigley** ('14) lived in Flagstaff from 1989 to 2017, and is happy to have had running discover her. Her favorite high-elevation training run is the Elden Lookout Road. "The best thing about being a Flagstaff runner is the sense of community. It doesn't matter how fast or how slow one is, the running community is out there in person or on social media, cheering and providing positive feedback."

Cory (Sheeley) **Roberdeau** ('97) grew up in Flagstaff and has been here for 35 years, enjoying hiking the Grand Canyon, running trails, and breathing in the thin, clean air and all the beauty of northern Arizona. The song that gets her over Imogene Pass is "Come On Up to the House" by Tom Waits.

Mary **Ross** is a graphic designer with a love for all things creative, who finds inspiration living and working in Flagstaff, a wonderful mountain town she calls home. maryrosscreativedesign.com

Elise **Rumpf** ('18) has studied lava flows on four continents and at the bottom of the Atlantic Ocean. She's also an ultrarunner, rock climber, and beer lover. Having moved to Flagstaff in 2017, her favorite high-elevation training run is the Weatherford Trail. The views on the upper part of the trail are the best motivation for hauling it up that cobbled road!

Darlene **Ryan** ('06) is a retired cartographer who has lived in Flagstaff since 1974. "Praying the 'Hail Mary' at least 100 times got me over Imogene Pass."

Adair **Scantlebury** ('13) is a teacher who has lived in Flagstaff since 1986. "The best thing about being a Flagstaff runner is the community it builds and the support that develops."

Myles **Schrag** ('12) is a writer and editor who has lived in Flagstaff since 2010, when soft Old Caves Crater cinders revived his knees and got him running again. On many uphill climbs, IPR included, the refrain from Kate Bush's "Running Up That Hill" plays on an incessant loop in his brain, whether he believes the last three words or not: "Be running up that road, be running up that hill, with no problems."

Todd **Schultz** ('14) is a Flagstaff-based (since 2012) printing-business owner who enjoys trail ultra-running, coaching youth runners, and hanging out at home with his family. He's on the board of directors for Team Run Flagstaff. Todd treasures the opportunity Flagstaff affords to run with athletes of all levels from beginners to elites who all share a passion for the sport.

Linda **Sherman** ('01) is a retired teacher and artist who has lived in Flagstaff since 1962. Her favorite training run is the Weatherford Trail, where she enjoys meeting other runners training for Imogene. www.lindashermanart.com

Tess **Siemens** ('14) is a full-time student at NAU who was born in Flagstaff in 1998 and has spent most of her years living here. While she was struggling through her second IPR, a woman near the top told her to put her head down and focus on getting her "ass over the Pass." It helped her get up and over the mountain that day, and she hopes it will continue to give her much-needed oomph for many races to come.

Kermit **Smith** ('89) is a local life, health, and Medicare supplement insurance agent who attended NAU from 1963 to 1967 and has lived in Flagstaff continuously since 1979 (as well as from 1969 to 1971). "The best part about being a Flagstaff runner (when 'runner' was a more apropos description of me) is the elevation, which makes distance runs at any lower elevation significantly easier."

Chrissy **Speer** ('11) is a working mom to two very active daughters, a wife, skier, lover of the outdoors, cancer survivor, and "not-so-great" runner making a comeback after a big hiatus. She moved to Flagstaff in 1998 to go to NAU and is now back working for the university. Her favorite high-elevation training run is Weatherford Trail to Doyle Saddle.

Abe **Springer** ('03) has been a professor of hydrogeology at NAU for 25 years. He enjoys training with the Northern Arizona Trail Runners Association and Team Run Flagstaff to prepare for walking the final miles from Upper Camp Bird to Imogene Pass.

Ryan **Stevens** ('11) is an attorney who has lived in Flagstaff since 2008. "The best thing about being a Flagstaff runner is the community of fellow athletes who are motivated and caring."

Jim **Straight** ('18) is a financial advisor who has lived in Flagstaff since 2004. His favorite high-elevation training run is the Soulstice Mountain Trail Run short-course loop.

Steve **Sue** ('14) joined Team Run Flagstaff in 2010 and is a regular at TRF's Tuesday track workouts.

Claudine **Taillac** ('17) is a writer and librarian who moved to Flagstaff in 2004.

Nancy **Taylor** ('89) is a 51-year resident of Flagstaff. "Alligators All Around," by Maurice Sendak, got her up and over Imogene Pass.

Walt **Taylor** ('89) is a retired family physician who has enjoyed Flagstaff-area trails since 1968. "The best thing about being a Flagstaff runner is enjoying the trails with human and canine pals."

Beverly **Tew** ('15) is a former globe-trekker turned ob-gyn who has been adventurous in Flagstaff since 2012.

Emy **Tice** ('99) is an outdoor enthusiast who moved to Flagstaff in 1998 to attend NAU and never left. "The best thing about being a Flagstaff runner is the availability and accessibility of beautiful forest trails."

Sara **Wagner** ('08) is a Flagstaff-based writer, credentialed grant professional, and public health aficionado who has lived in Flagstaff since August 2006. "The best thing about being a Flagstaff runner is our wonderful community."

Neil **Weintraub** ('95) is an archaeologist for the Kaibab National Forest, cofounder and director of Northern Arizona Trail Runners Association, and race director for Flagstaff's beloved Soulstice Mountain Trail Run. "The best part of being a runner in Flagstaff is its all-inclusive running community, the benefit of training at high altitude, and the freedom of access to myriad trails in the surrounding Coconino National Forest."

John **Whipple** ('12) is a musician and writer currently residing in Salt Lake City, Utah. His travels have deposited him in Flagstaff on numerous occasions throughout his life. He trained for Imogene on Mount Elden. He had no mantra or song to help him over the Imogene Pass—he just kept breathing.

Nat **White** ('95) moved to Flagstaff in September 1969 to work as an astronomer at Lowell Observatory.

Staci **Whitman** ('17) is a physical therapist who works at Flagstaff Medical Center. She has lived in northern Arizona all her life, having grown up in Williams. She followed her family roots when she moved to Flagstaff in 1992 (her family has lived in town since the early 1900s, and her father was born and raised here). "The best things about running in Flagstaff are the excellent running community and the amazing trails."

Jason **Wolfe** ('10) first moved to Flagstaff to run cross country and track at NAU from 1997 to 2000. He moved back in 2007 with his wife to raise their four kids. "The best thing about being a Flagstaff runner is sharing some of the most beautiful trails in the world with a community of positive people who make Flagstaff feel like home."

Sheri **Young** ('18) has lived in Flagstaff for the past two years and in northern Arizona for the past eight. She found her tribe soon after moving to the area, when she joined the Flagstaff Trail Divas. Creating this poem in her head kept her moving and got her up and over Imogene Pass.

Cristy **Zeller** ('12) is the executive director of Haven Montessori School and has lived in Flagstaff since 1999. While her knees finally called it quits with running, you will still see her hiking the amazing trails of Flagstaff and cheering on local runners.

Names Index

In these essays, you'll find the names of family, friends, and crew alongside those of the running tribe in Flagstaff and beyond. It takes a village to get a person up and over Imogene Pass. Contributors' names, and the page(s) on which their story appears, are in bold.

Credits

Illustrations, Logos, and Watercolors

Watercolors © Linda Sherman: front/back covers and endpapers, x, xvi–1, 22-23, 50–51, 76, 80–81, 104–105, 124–125, 141, 146, 154–155, 170–171, 188, 194, 196–197

Illustrations © Krista Nicole: 7, 8, 12, 14, 15, 16, 17, 20, 30, 39, 53, 58, 62, 64, 67, 68, 69, 71, 72, 79, 89, 108, 114, 118, 122, 131, 135, 137, 140, 147, 148, 152, 157, 162, 168, 172, 178, 182, 183, 186; dingbats; and spot illustrations of leaves, flowers, feathers, pine cones, paw prints, and rocks throughout.

Soulstice Publishing logo and Imagine/Imogene logo by Mary Ross

NATRA logo courtesy of NATRA LLC: 48

BLE courtesy of BLE Flagstaff: v, 159, 187, 193, back cover

Imogene Pass Run Illustration © Sara Knight: 128–129

Photos

The photos in this book came from scores of generous people.
All photos are by or courtesy of the story's author unless otherwise stated here. L=Left, R=Right, A=Above

Front Matter

Sara Wagner: vii
© Larry Gassan, all rights reserved: viii
Linda Sherman: ix, xii
Jerry Diehl: xiv, xv

PART 1

Linda Sherman: 2–3, 8, 18
Sean Hickey: 9, 10
David Fain: 11A
Cory Roberdeau: 12, 13
Kirstie O'Donnell: 21

PART 2

Walt and Nancy Taylor: 26, 27, 28
Sara Wagner: 29, 42
Josh Biggs: 31
Linda Sherman: 32, 38
Nancy Taylor: 35 (shirts)
Julie Hammonds: 35R
Susie Garretson: 37
Carrie Butler: 41, 48–49
Rusty Lenners: 44–45
Amy Horn: 46

PART 3

US Geological Survey: 52, 53
Erin Strout: 55
Matt Brydenthal: 58
Carrie Butler: 59
Jerry Diehl: 63
Julie Hammonds: 70
Anne Leota Hart: 73
Alicia Hendricks: 75

PART 4

Stephen Ramsey, Denver, CO: 82L, 103
John Jett: 83L, 84
Elevation Imaging: 83R
Margaret Montfort: 88
Alicia Hendricks: 90
Linda Sherman: 95
Josh Biggs: 96, 97
Carrie Butler: 100
Rich Haag: 101, 102

PART 5

Sara Wagner: 106
Alicia Hendricks: 107R
Troy Marino: 108, 109
Natalie Jacobs: 110
Amy Horn: 113
Carrie Butler: 117
Linda Sherman: 121, 123

PART 6

Mike Smith: 126
Linda Sherman: 127, 143
Alicia Hendricks: 133
Thomas P. Colberg: 144R

PART 7

Linda Sherman: 159
Tanya Fields: 160R, 161
Rich Haag: 163
Carrie Butler: 164, 169
Charles D. Claude: 165

PART 8

Linda Sherman: 173L, 195
Jerry Diehl: 178, 179, 180, 186, 193
Julie Hammonds: 185
Margaret Montfort: 187, 192
Annie Phillips: 190, 191

Soulstice PUBLISHING
books with *soul* • Flagstaff, AZ

Soulstice Publishing took root between the ponderosa pines at the base of the San Francisco Peaks. Our mountain town of Flagstaff, Arizona, abounds with scientists, artists, athletes, and many other people who love to live in such an inspiring natural setting. Considering the dearth of oxygen at our 7,000-foot elevation, you might say life here leaves us breathless—which is what we strive for when you read a Soulstice book. We work with authors at every stage of the publishing process to shape their ideas into books with impact and purpose.

Learn more at soulsticepublishing.com.

Soulstice Publishing, LLC
PO Box 791
Flagstaff, AZ 86002
(928) 814-8943
connect@soulsticepublishing.com

About the Editors

Myles Schrag has been in book publishing for 20 years, has authored or edited six books, and has helped more than 200 other books reach publication as either an acquisitions editor, developmental editor, publisher, or manuscript broker. He holds a master's degree in kinesiology from the University of Illinois at Urbana-Champaign and loves to explore the high-altitude outdoor opportunities in northern Arizona with his two daughters.

Julie Hammonds is the editor of numerous books on natural history. Her favorite topics are science, nature, travel, the arts, history, and sports (especially running). She has a bachelor's degree in conservation and spent 12 years as managing editor for *Arizona Wildlife Views* magazine. In her spare time, she's the coordinating editor of the High Country Running column in the *Arizona Daily Sun*.

Flagstaff
+
Imogene